M

WITHDRAWN
FROM
UNIVERSITY
OF
GREENWICH
LIBRARY

MW
SAR
2006805

ENVIRONMENTAL DILEMMAS AND POLICY DESIGN

According to the logic of collective action, mere awareness of the causes of environmental degradation will not motivate rational agents to reduce pollution. Yet some government policies aim to enlist citizens in schemes of voluntary cooperation, drawing on an ethos of collective responsibility. Are such policies doomed to failure? This book provides a novel application of rational choice theory to a large-scale survey of environmental attitudes in the Netherlands. Its main findings are that rational citizens are motivated to cooperate towards a less polluted environment to a large extent, but that their willingness to assume responsibility depends on the social context of the collective action problem they face. This empirical study is an important volume in the development of a more consistent foundation for rational choice theory in policy analysis, which seeks to clarify major theoretical issues concerning the role of moral commitment, self-interest and reciprocity in environmental behaviour.

DR HUIB PELLIKAAN is a lecturer in the Department of Political Science at Leiden University. He is currently the managing editor of *Acta Politica*, the journal of the Dutch Association for the Science of Politics.

ROBERT VAN DER VEEN is a lecturer in Political Theory in the Department of Political Science at the University of Amsterdam. He is the author of *Between Exploitation and Communism* (1991), as well as the editor of *Basic Income on the Agenda* (with Loek Groot, 2000). He has contributed articles to many journals including *Economics and Philosophy*, the *British Journal of Political Science*, the *Journal of Political Philosophy* and *Acta Politica*.

WITHDRAWN FROM UNIVERSITY OF GREENWICH LIBRARY

THEORIES OF INSTITUTIONAL DESIGN

Series Editor
Robert E. Goodin
Research School of Social Sciences
Australian National University

Advisory Editors
Brian Barry, Russell Hardin, Carole Pateman, Barry Weingast,
Stephen Elkin, Claus Offe, Susan Rose-Ackerman

Social scientists have rediscovered institutions. They have been increasingly concerned with the myriad ways in which social and political institutions shape the patterns of individual interactions which produce social phenomena. They are equally concerned with the ways in which those institutions emerge from such interactions.

This series is devoted to the exploration of the more normative aspects of these issues. What makes one set of institutions better than another? How, if at all, might we move from the less desirable set of institutions to a more desirable set? Alongside the questions of what institutions we would design, if we were designing them afresh, are pragmatic questions of how we can best get from here to there: from our present institutions to new revitalised ones.

Theories of institutional design is insistently multidisciplinary and interdisciplinary, both in the institutions on which it focuses, and in the methodologies used to study them. There are interesting sociological questions to be asked about legal institutions, interesting legal questions to be asked about economic institutions, and interesting social, economic and legal questions to be asked about political institutions. By juxtaposing these approaches in print, this series aims to enrich normative discourse surrounding important issues of designing and redesigning, shaping and reshaping the social, political and economic institutions of contemporary society.

Other books in this series

Robert E. Goodin (editor), *The Theory of Institutional Design*
Brent Fisse and John Braithwaite, *Corporations, Crime, and Accountability*
Itai Sened, *The Political Institution of Private Property*
Bo Rothstein, *Just Institutions Matter*
Jon Elster, Claus Offe and Ulrich Preuss, *Institutional Design in Post-Communist Societies: Rebuilding the Ship at Sea*
Mark Bovens, *The Quest for Responsibility*
Adrienne Héritier, *Policy-Making and Diversity in Europe*
Geoffrey Brennan and Alan Hamlin, *Democratic Devices and Desires*
Eric M. Patashnik, *Putting Trust in the US Budget: Federal Trust Funds and the Politics of Commitment*
Benjamin Reilly, *Democracy in Divided Societies: Electoral Engineering for Conflict Management*
John S. Dryzek and Leslie Holmes, *Post-Communist Democratisation: Political Discourses Across Thirteen Countries*

1665585

ENVIRONMENTAL DILEMMAS AND POLICY DESIGN

HUIB PELLIKAAN
Leiden University

and

ROBERT J. VAN DER VEEN
University of Amsterdam

SHORT LOAN

UNIVERSITY OF GREENWICH LIBRARY

333
720
949
2
PEL

CAMBRIDGE
UNIVERSITY PRESS

PUBLISHED BY THE PRESS SYNDICATE OF THE UNIVERSITY OF CAMBRIDGE
The Pitt Building, Trumpington Street, Cambridge, United Kingdom

CAMBRIDGE UNIVERSITY PRESS
The Edinburgh Building, Cambridge CB2 2RU, UK
40 West 20th Street, New York NY 10011–4211, USA
477 Williamstown Road, Port Melbourne, VIC 3207, Australia
Ruiz de Alarcón 13, 28014 Madrid, Spain
Dock House, The Waterfront, Cape Town 8001, South Africa

http://www.cambridge.org

© Huib Pellikaan, Robert J. van der Veen 2002

This book is in copyright. Subject to statutory exception
and to the provisions of relevant collective licensing agreements,
no reproduction of any part may take place without
the written permission of Cambridge University Press.

First published 2002

Printed in the United Kingdom at the University Press, Cambridge

Typeface Times 10/12 pt.   *System* LATEX2e   [TB]

A catalogue record for this book is available from the British Library

Library of Congress Cataloguing in Publication data

Pellikaan, Huib.
Environmental Dilemmas and Policy Design / Huib Pellikaan and Robert J. van der Veen.
    p.   cm.
Includes bibliographical references and index.
ISBN 0 521 62156 9
1. Environmental policy – Netherlands.   2. Environmental protection – Netherlands.
3. Rational choice theory.   I. Veen, Robert J. van der.   II. Title.
GE190 .N45   2002
363.7′05′09492 – dc21

ISBN 0 521 62156 9 hardback
ISBN 0 521 62764 8 paperback

Contents

List of figures   *page* x
List of tables   xi
Preface   xiii

Part I   Background

1 Environmental pollution as a problem of collective action   3
  1.1 Can something be done?   3
  1.2 Environmental dilemmas and the logic of collective action   5
  1.3 Surveying environmental dilemmas from the actor's
     perspective: rational choice   10
  1.4 How motives speak to preferences   14
  1.5 Non-equivalent dilemmas and reported behaviour   17
  1.6 Policies of self-regulation in the Netherlands   18
  1.7 Moral commitment in environmental dilemmas:
     conditional or unconditional?   20
  1.8 Determinants of cooperation in environmental dilemmas
     and policy design   24

2 A Dutch approach: self-regulation as a policy concept   28
  2.1 Introduction   28
  2.2 Dutch environmental policy and the idea of self-regulation   29
  2.3 The social instruments   35
  2.4 An environmental ethos and the social dilemma   40
  2.5 Self-regulation: compliance-oriented or virtue-based?   42

3 The actor's perspective on collective action   47
  3.1 The subjectivity of the actor in rational choice theory   47

3.2 Problems of collective action 49
3.3 Social dilemmas 55
3.4 The actor's perspective 59

Part II The survey

4 Preference orderings and measurement 67
  4.1 Three potential social dilemmas 67
  4.2 Measuring preference orderings 71
  4.3 Three different environmental problems 78
  4.4 Avoiding response effects 82

5 Rational choice 84
  5.1 Conditions of rational choice 84
  5.2 The dominance rule of rational choice 87
  5.3 Choice of strategy 91
  5.4 The robustness of the dominance rule 95
  5.5 Conclusion 98

6 Consistency of motives and preferences 101
  6.1 A model of reasoned choice 101
  6.2 The motives of Valuation and Willingness 103
  6.3 The test of consistent preferences 108
  6.4 Consistent preferences in the three cases 116
  6.5 Does motive-preference consistency matter? 118
  6.6 Conclusion 121

7 The non-equivalence of the cases 124
  7.1 Hard and easy cases of the dilemma 124
  7.2 The model of the hardest case 125
  7.3 The scalability of the cases 131
  7.4 The non-equivalence of social dilemmas 133

8 Reported behaviour 136
  8.1 Determinants of behaviour 136
  8.2 The sociocultural model 138
  8.3 An alternative model 142
  8.4 From motives to behaviour 146

Part III Conclusions: theory and policy

9 Do people accept self-regulation policy? 151
  9.1 Introduction to part III 151
  9.2 Acceptance and agreement 153
  9.3 The acceptance of legal regulation and self-regulation 155
  9.4 Conclusion 160

10 Do people agree with the environmental ethos? 161
   10.1 Introduction 161
   10.2 The two stages of the environmental ethos 162
   10.3 Knaves, pawns or knights? 167
   10.4 The ethical interpretation of motives and preferences 169
   10.5 The agreement response 174
   10.6 Acceptance and agreement: overview 176

11 Moral commitment and rational cooperation 178
   11.1 Ranking preference orderings 178
   11.2 The meta-ranking approach 179
   11.3 Enlightened self-interest and moral commitment 183
   11.4 Consistent preferences in the meta-ranking 187
   11.5 An environmental meta-ranking 193

12 Reciprocity and cooperation in environmental dilemmas 197
   12.1 The puzzle of unconditional cooperation 197
   12.2 The reciprocity thesis 198
   12.3 Cost of cooperation and conditionalities in environmental dilemmas 205

13 Assessing self-regulation policies 210
   13.1 The context of environmental dilemmas 210
   13.2 Consistent ethical cooperation 211
   13.3 Background features of hard and easy cases 213
   13.4 Mapping problems and the salience of the environmental ethos 216
   13.5 Individual cost and collective gain 219
   13.6 Comparing motives in the polar cases 225
   13.7 The dimension of private significance 227
   13.8 Self-regulation policy: symbolic or real? 228
   13.9 A non-moralistic approach to environmental responsibility 230
   13.10 Self-regulation in proportion to facilitation 233

References 235
Index 239

Figures

3.1 Individual vs. The Others   *page* 53
3.2 The Prisoner's Dilemma game   54
3.3 The Potential Contributor's Dilemma   61
3.4 The Potential Contrubutor's Dilemma in the actor's perspective   62
4.1 The pay-off of the row player with ordering RPQS   75
4.2 Valid orderings   79
4.3 Identical orderings   81
5.1 RPQS: dominant Defect   88
5.2 QSPR: dominant Cooperate   89
5.3 QRPS: no maximizing rule   89
6.1 Model of practical reasoning   102
6.2 The Potential Contributor's Dilemma of Chemical Waste   109
6.3 Constraints and consistent sets of Valuation motives   112
6.4 Constraints and consistent sets of Willingness motives   113
6.5 Consistency between preference orderings and motives   114
7.1 The hardest case x and case y 127
7.2 The hardest case x and case z 128
7.3 Cognitive process and intensity structure   134
8.1 The extended sociocultural model   143
8.2 The actor's perspective model   147
10.1 Motives and preferences interpreted in terms of the ethos   173
11.1 The game form of the Prisoner's Dilemma   181
11.2 Sen's meta-ranking in the Prisoner's Dilemma   183
11.3 The reconstructed meta-ranking in the Prisoner's Dilemma   192
13.1 Preference orderings and motive structures of the environmental
     ethos   213

Tables

4.1	Ranking the four outcomes	*page* 74
4.2	Preference orderings	76
4.3	Valid orderings related with Age	80
5.1	Choice of strategy	92
5.2	Rational choice	93
5.3	Dominance rule and choice of strategy	97
6.1	Motives on the Valuation scale	105
6.2	Motives on the Willingness scale	106
6.3	Motive structures of Valuation and Willingness	107
6.4	Consistent preferences compared to the motive-preference response	116
6.5	Consistent preferences as control variable	120
7.1	Chemical Waste vs. Holiday Destination	129
7.2	Chemical Waste vs. Energy Saving	130
7.3	Holiday Destination vs. Energy Saving	130
7.4	Results of the hardest case analysis	131
7.5	Coefficients of scalability	132
8.1	Six cases of reported behaviour	139
8.2	Determinants of behaviour	141
8.3	A new determinant 'Choice'	145
9.1	Acceptance and rejection of three regulation types	158
10.1	Full and partial agreement with the ethos: motives	175
10.2	Full and partial agreement with the ethos: preferences	175
12.1	Expectation of the choices of the others	208
13.1	Cooperation and consistent ethical cooperation in the three cases	212

13.2 Consistent ethical cooperation, degree of ethical consistency,
      and share of ethical motives   214
13.3 Belief in the effectiveness of collective action   224
13.4 Motive response in Holiday Destination of respondents with
      ethical motives in Chemical Waste   225
13.5 Motive response in Holiday Destination of respondents with
      ethical motives in Chemical Waste, controlled for belief
      in effectiveness   226

Preface

This book has grown out of a research project commissioned by the Dutch Ministry of Environmental Affairs in 1994. The brief of the project was to form a survey database of citizens' responses to environmental collective action problems, in order to report on the effectiveness of 'self-regulation policy' in the environmental policy plans of the Netherlands. This type of policy, which exists to the present day, seeks to regulate behaviour in areas of everyday life such as waste collection, private car travel, or economizing on household energy, by obtaining voluntary compliance to environmental goals of reducing pollution, rather than securing compliance through legal compulsion or financial incentives.

Self-regulation policies depend on the challenging notion that government can persuade citizens to overcome *environmental dilemmas* of the kind that the standard logic of collective action for large groups of rational individuals predicts will arise inevitably. Voluntary cooperation to reduce pollution would thus be ruled out on that logic, unless citizens could be made to act irrationally.

To respond to this challenge, our research design aims to combine theoretical insights into motives and preferences underlying rational choice in environmental dilemmas with empirical methods of survey research, in a way appropriate to assessing the chances and limits of self-regulation policies. In the course of writing the book, and in discussion with numerous colleagues, we have been aware that the results generated within our theoretical perspective on rational choice need to be interpreted with some care. Hence readers will find a detailed programmatic overview, as well as a description of the policy setting, in the first two chapters.

From the start of the project, we have been fortunate to receive many critical responses and concrete suggestions for improving various aspects of the research. We are particularly indebted to Kees Aarts, our co-author of the original report (which appeared in Dutch in 1995), not least for his expert efforts in designing the questionnaire. (See Aarts, Pellikaan and Van der Veen, 1995. The original dataset is available from the authors, at <pellikaan@fsw. LeidenUniv.nl>.)

We are grateful to our Dutch colleagues who have taken the time to comment on various drafts and presentations of preliminary results and have suggested important clarifications: Jos de Beus, Cees van der Eijk, Henk van de Graaf, Loek Groot and Kees Schuyt (University of Amsterdam), Marius de Geus, Herman van Gunsteren, Galen Irwin, Jan de Keijser, and Hans Oversloot (University of Leiden) and Martin van Hees (University of Groningen).

For early and invariably helpful comments on several papers dealing with the theoretical analysis, we wish to thank Dean Lacy of Ohio State University, the members of the 1996 Political Theory Workshop at Nuffield College, Oxford, especially David Miller and Avner de-Shalit, the 1996 New York meeting of the September Group, in particular Sam Bowles, Jerry Cohen and Philippe Van Parijs, and those present at the seminar of the Center for Rationality and Interactive Decision Theory of Hebrew University, in March 1997, most notably Robert Aumann and Sergiu Hart. In the final stages, we obtained illuminating feedback (and close questioning) from colleagues at Warwick University: Susan Hurley, Andrew Reeve, Andrew Willams and Chris Woodard, as well as receiving incisive and encouraging comments from an anonymous referee.

Finally, we have benefited greatly from the patience and the excellent advice of Robert Goodin, the editor of this series, and from the support of John Haslam of Cambridge University Press. While it hardly needs to be mentioned in the face of these many and diverse responses over a long period of time, we alone must take responsibility for the final product.

Part I

Background

1

Environmental pollution as a problem of collective action

1.1 Can something be done?

The concern about environmental pollution in public policy and public opinion in the USA originates, according to former Vice President Al Gore, with the publication of Rachel Carson's *Silent Spring* (1962).[1] Its publication made everyone aware of the negative effect of pesticides (DDT) on agricultural production. The environmental movement in Europe got off the ground with *The Limits to Growth* (1972), the report of the Club of Rome. Concern with the natural environment is nothing new. It dates back to seventeenth-century air pollution in London and to Thomas Malthus's warnings in the eighteenth century about the negative effects of population growth.[2] However, there is an important difference between early and modern concerns. In the early days the public had no influence on the decisions of the political elite in handling environmental affairs. Nowadays, what politicians and policymakers propose or decide is closely followed by public opinion.

The publication of *Silent Spring* created a shock effect in the USA. As a result DDT was banned and laws protecting clean air, land and water were introduced. The notion of limits to growth of the Club of Rome created a political climate that made environmental politics and policy both possible and necessary. Since 1972, many other studies have been published on the ozone layer, global warming and the greenhouse effect, and the irreversible decline of biodiversity. But no report has yet been able to match the impact of *Silent Spring* or *The Limits to Growth*. The lack of effect of these later studies is not that most people disbelieve the scenarios. Aaron Wildavsky's exposure of the

---

[1] See Al Gore's Introduction in the new edition of *Silent Spring*.
[2] See Goodin, 1992: 1–18.

so-called weaknesses of the 'environmental crisis industry', in *But Is It True?* (1995), simply did not impress the public media.[3]

The real problem may be that people think 'It Is True', but also think that their individual contribution, or even that of their own government, to solving these global problems would be too insignificant to keep on bothering. In other words, the desire of people to act on facts about environmental pollution is not simply a matter of whether or not they believe that those facts are true. If the willingness of citizens depended solely on the reliablity of facts, environmental policy would no doubt be forced to respond more quickly to expert knowledge, such as the Intergovernmental Panel on Climate Change (IPCC). For example, in 1999, the IPCC released a report 'Aviation and the Global Atmosphere' that describes the impact of air travel on the atmosphere. The report compares estimates of changes in aircraft technology to the annual increase of flights, and warns that trends in aviation will lead to higher risks of global warming. Most passengers know that aircraft engines produce high emissions of gases, such as carbon dioxide, which contribute to the greenhouse effect and destroy the ozone layer.

That a continued expansion of air travel increases environmental risks of smog and associated health dangers is well established; that it leads to global warming and ultimately climate changes is contestable, up to a point. But as suggested, the real issue behind the failure to respond may be the collective action problem. Even if everyone in the world agreed about the facts on global warming, its probable consequences, and the most effective methods of counteracting it, rational actors, as Mancur Olson has it, 'will not act to advance their common or group objectives unless there is coercion to force them to do so'.[4] In global environmental issues like the ones described above, there are collective action problems at many levels. National governments cannot easily be forced to take action, in the absence of an international enforcement agency. At the national level, producers and consumers can be coerced to some extent by their governments, but only if there is robust political consensus to sustain coercive measures. Given the higher-level collective action problem, this consensus is not likely to be forthcoming. But even if it were, with effective legal regulation, tax incentives and the like in place, the licence to pollute would still remain at the micro-level of producer and consumer behaviour. Thus many collective action problems would exist even then, within a considerable space of private freedom. None of these is amenable to non-coercive solution. On the logic of collective action, then, there seems to be no hope whatsoever of solving even the most pressing global environmental problems. Yet somehow, one would be inclined to believe, the logic must be less compelling than it appears at first sight. For national environmental policies do exist,

---

3 See Wildavsky, 1995.   4 See Olson, 1971: 2.

citizens sometimes show a concern for the side effects of their own behaviour as consumers, and there is at least a framework for international cooperation offering the hope of slow progress. Especially at the global level where the prospect of doom looms largest, there is a need for a perspective that would affirm the rational capacity of human beings for stepping up efforts of environmental cooperation.

1.2 Environmental dilemmas and the logic of collective action

In this book, however, we are not in the business of suggesting, or even discussing policy solutions to truly global environmental problems. Our brief is far more limited. We want to look at how these problems appear at the micro-level of individual citizen behaviour, against the background of a reasonably vigorous and highly visible set of environmental policies in the Netherlands. Our reason for focusing on the Netherlands is not merely that being Dutch, it is the country we know best, nor that the country is a small one, heavily exposed to polluting emissions elsewhere, with a large population density, an open economy, and a high level of education; it is also that, no doubt partly due to these factors, from 1989 onwards, Dutch environmental policymakers have been systematically pressing firms and citizens to undertake voluntary action for the sake of precisely defined objectives of national environmental policy. The background of this is described in chapter 2. We shall be saying more about these matters of policy in section 1.5 below. Here it is important to state that a main aim of this book is to use a suitably refined framework of rational choice theory, in order to assess the viablity of environmental policies that try to inform, educate and persuade, rather than to regulate behaviour by legal restrictions and monetary incentives. The framework of rational choice theory will be loosely expounded in the course of this chapter. But the details of our approach are spelled out in chapter 3, which concludes the first of the three parts that comprise this book.

Our orientation to policy assessment fits into the perspective of empirical social science, and it will utilize some simple quantitative methods. We have not been conducting in-depth interviews; nor have we been engaging in participatory observation. We use a dataset based on a large-scale survey that was conducted in the spring of 1994. The core of the survey is described in the five chapters of part II. It involves studying the responses of the thousand people whom we interviewed, to questions that are designed to bring out their attitude towards voluntary collective action in a way that fully respects the format of rational choice theory. If there is anything novel in our research, it is our attempt to join together insights into rational behaviour in collective action situations with the empirical methods of survey research. To present this research design, and to invite a discussion of its merits, is the other main aim of the study.

The results of the survey will be applied specifically to the context of the policies we wish to assess. This is done in the five chapters of part III. Since what goes on in the field of environmental policies that tries to draw on the moral resources of citizens is rather complex, the application of the survey results is not straightforward. The concluding part of the book, therefore, will proceed at a leisurely pace, allowing the reader to check, step by step, how we deal with problems of interpretation. It will also try to clarify some major theoretical issues concerning the role of moral commitment, self-interest and reciprocity that arise along the way.

In this chapter, we present an overview of the main argument. We start by addressing the logic of collective action. By that logic, clearly, the attempts of Dutch policymakers to enlist the citizens in projects of voluntary collective action are just a waste of time. For as stated above, the logic holds that the (undoubtedly) large group of individual citizens in the Netherlands will need to be *coerced* into environmentally friendly behaviour. It will not be enough just to ask them politely to behave, nor even to appeal to their consciences. For since citizens on the whole are rational actors, the nature of most environmental decision problems prevents them from voluntarily contributing to any commonly recognized objective. The reason is a quite general one. It is that each individual realizes that cooperative action is costly, while incurring the cost does not have a noticeable impact on the attainment of the common objective. These features of the situation will move a rational actor to avoid the cost, whatever the other citizens may be doing. Thus, if most citizens are rational actors, their voluntary action will simply defeat their common objective. In order to achieve the objective, they will have to be forced to contribute. And they will also have a good reason to accept being forced, on reflection, because each of them will then be better off than he or she would be in the absence of coercive measures.

Our response to this challenge is as follows. While we are prepared to accept that most people are rational actors most of the time, it still remains of interest to ask in what environmental contexts individuals may fail to respond rationally, in so far as that can be observed at all. But even if everyone responded rationally all the time, the logic of collective action, we maintain, is too restrictive to be compelling as an account of rational action. In the present context, it is restrictive in two respects. On the one hand, it assumes too quickly that environmental problems of the kind that are commonly discussed as such, do indeed involve 'common objectives' to which voluntary action might then respond in the negative way predicted. On the other hand, given that an environmental problem does clearly involve a common objective, rational actors may have good grounds for doing their bit to to achieve it, even if they recognize perfectly well that their own actions, taken separately, do not noticeably alter the state of the environment.

If both of these caveats need to be made, then many decision structures on which Olson's reasoning focuses should be analysed in a less dogmatic way. As will be explained in chapter 3, one should conceive of these decision structures as *potential* collective action problems rather than *actual* ones, that is to say, situations in which a common objective is necessarily defeated by individual rational actions. Throughout the book, we shall often be referring to a potential collective action problem by using the shorthand expression of an 'environmental dilemma'. Our main claim is that empirical investigation will have to determine whether or not the logic of collective action holds good, hence whether environmental dilemmas are actualized or not.

To clarify this, let us look at the general structure of an environmental dilemma which citizens face, without assuming that there is a common objective in play. This structure is radically simplified, but it contains all the ingredients for making the point about potentiality versus actuality.

(1) In some area of action, citizens act in either of two ways: they pollute (*p*) or they do not pollute (*np*), and *np* is more costly than *p* for each citizen, in terms of time and resources.
(2) The impact of any single citizen's action (*p* or *np*) on the state of the environment is hardly noticeable.
(3) If almost all citizens *np*, the environment will be significantly less polluted (*NP*) and if almost all *p*, it will be significantly more polluted (*P*).
(4) Each citizen assumes that (almost all of) the others either *p* or *np*.

What is involved in the existence of a common environmental objective, given this structure? The question is often passed by quickly, but it needs to be addressed with care. For obviously, an environmental dilemma can only become actualized, if attaining *NP* through voluntary action is indeed the common objective. The structure itself does not determine whether or not this is the case. What one can reasonably say, perhaps, is that citizens will be likely to have the structure in their minds, if indeed there is a social presumption that *NP*, considered as a less polluted state of the environment, is a good thing. In extremely clear-cut cases of environmental pollution, there is more than such a presumption, however. For example: suppose it is known by all that *P* spells imminent, inescapable and large disaster. Then the question of the common objective is simply answered. The disaster must be avoided. Voluntary action to achieve *NP* is obviously held to be a good thing as well.

But the environmental dilemmas among citizens that we have in mind are not like this. If they were, it would be likely indeed that the citizens had already taken the further step of massively voting for government to enforce *NP*, just to be on the safe side of the logic of collective action, however inconclusive that logic may be in general. So we are looking at less clear-cut cases. For example, *P* may sensibly be held to *play a part* in bringing environmental disasters about, in the longer run. And such disasters may or may not occur, depending on what happens elsewhere in the larger domain of voluntary action, and on what is taken out of that domain, to be henceforth regulated legally. The collective goods involved in environmental dilemmas among citizens, such as toxic waste disposal, cutting down on energy consumption, cycling or walking to the neighbourhood supermarket instead of driving the car, buying organic products at higher prices and so on, are not typically decisive goods. If they come about, that makes a difference for the better, to be sure, but it does no more than contribute to a 'cleaner environment' in the end. Given this, it is not always certain that the social presumption that *NP* is a good thing will carry much weight, in any local case of the dilemma. In some areas of environmental degradation, failure to undertake voluntary action may be considered less of a big deal for other reasons as well. The joint outcome *P* may not spell disaster. Instead, *P* may be likely to contribute to loss of environmental qualities, for example wildlife, or more generally biodiversity. Such qualities are valued very differently by citizens.[5] Again, it is less certain that *NP* will be a common objective, in the relevant sense.

The social presumption that *NP* is a good thing may still be widespread, de-spite possible reasons for discounting its weightiness on the part of individual citizens. Nonetheless, the view that attaining *NP* through voluntary action is a good thing as well, might not be predominant. For *NP* to become a com-mon objective, there must be a widely shared agreement of another kind. The collective cost of achieving the less polluted state of the environment should be perceived as worth incurring. To explain, features (1) and (3) of the above decision structure imply that *NP* will come about only when (almost) all incur the cost of *np*. So whether *NP* is accepted as a common objective also depends on how individual citizens evaluate that cost. This should be distinguished from the familiar question about whether individual citizens will be disposed to pay the cost themselves *given* that there is a common objective. For, from feature (2), the attainment of *NP* does not depend on an individual's own action, even marginally. But attaining *NP* still presents costs to the many others, whose ac-tions are jointly decisive. Thus, even if certain individuals consider *NP* to be preferable to *P*, they may think that the accumulated cost of *np* (not necessarily including the cost to themselves) outweighs the prospective benefit to all of *NP* (including the benefit to themselves). They will then tend to disagree that *NP* is a common objective of collective action.

This issue is perhaps more important than is often recognized. For it shows that many citizens may be opposed to both voluntary collective action *and* to governmental regulation of their behaviour, even if they are aware of

---

[5] See Miller, 1999.

environmental issues, and even if they are not indifferent about the risks involved. In any such case of the environmental dilemma, action may be non-cooperative because most citizens hold that no one should reasonably be asked to perform the action *np*, because that is simply asking too much. Obviously, this is not a case where the environmental dilemma is being actualized. From the point of view of those facing the choice, there is no compelling reason not to continue polluting, since there is no common objective in the first place. It follows that citizens will object to coercive measures for reducing pollution in these environmental dilemmas, unless the cost of compliance is somehow lowered. The government may nevertheless hold coercive measures to be justified. But if it were possible to implement those measures, then the policymakers cannot say that government is stepping in to 'solve a collective action problem'. They can only say that government is taking responsibility for redressing a situation that the citizens should have properly viewed as a collective action problem, in the opinion of the policymakers. In a democratic regime, this is of course a much more risky line to take in defence of a coercive policy. All this suggests that one should not assume too quickly that mere awareness of environmental dilemmas automatically brings into existence a common objective of voluntary action on behalf of the environment. Therefore it is important to inquire what citizens actually think, with respect to the issue of the common objective, in each separate case of an environmental dilemma.

Compared to the unfortunate cases just sketched, the ones Olson has in mind are less problematic. If *NP* is accepted as a common objective in the sense we have just specified, then indeed the failure to attain it is suboptimal from the point of view of the citizens themselves. Coercive policies would then seem to be called for. Yet, in a free society coercive policies may often be infeasible, even if citizens might not strongly object to being coerced. Such are the cases on which we will be focusing below. These are also the cases in which one wants to know whether the logic of collective action really holds good.

Given the general structure set out above, this depends on the validity of a particular inference. This is the inference from its features (1) and (2), to the conclusion that rational actors will choose to pollute. But that inference, clearly, is not a valid one. To make it valid requires an additional premise: rational actors whose action is (1) costly in terms of time and resources, and (2) sure not to make a noticeable difference to the outcome of joint action, will best serve their interests by avoiding the cost, regardless of the actions of the others. This additional premise will close the inferential gap. But it is not obvious why it should be true, when there is a common objective in play. The truth of the additional premise generally depends on how rational actors compare the significance of the common objective to the significance of the resource cost of refraining from a polluting action, in terms of their perceived interests. The decision structure of the environmental dilemma does not logically fix these interests. So it seems that premises about individual interests must be brought in, so as to guarantee that the insignificance of the actions p or np, coupled to the cost of np, rationally mandates action p.

Much can be said about individual interests in the abstract, and we shall further look into this in chapter 3. Rather than dwelling on it here, one thing can be mentioned in advance. Even if one has no trouble with the additional premises that close the gap between the logic of collective action and the decision structure on which it is predicated, it is still important to try and find out what is actually going on. This is what we propose to do, by studying some environmental dilemmas in depth, by means of survey data.

1.3 Surveying environmental dilemmas from the actor's perspective: rational choice

Our research strategy is described in part II of the book. It is introduced in this section and the next two. We confront a representative sample of Dutch citizens with three cases of household behaviour that can be recognized as having the structure of an environmental dilemma: bringing toxic waste to a neighbourhood recycling point (*Chemical Waste*), economizing on energy at home (*Energy Saving*), and forgoing holiday travel to foreign destinations for the sake of reducing air pollution (*Holiday Destination*). Our reasons for selecting these three cases of the environmental dilemma will be elaborated in chapter 4. The respondents are asked to put themselves in the position of someone facing the dilemma, and our first aim is to let them state their preferences and choices, in order to study the issue of rational choice.

As noted in section 1.2, we consider the logic of collective action to be far too restricted an account of rational choice to be a sensible general predictor of people's behaviour. The way in which we shall study rational choices empirically will reflect this point of view in the strongest possible way. For we do not impose any restriction on preference orderings whatsoever. From the *perspective of the actor*, we say, following Arrow and Riker's 'thin-theory of rationality', all that rationality requires in respect of preferences over states of the world is that these states are ranked by a complete and transitive ordering. This means that our respondents will be candidates for the respectable status of rational choosers if they are able to rank all possible outcomes of an environmental dilemma consistently. They do *not* need to satisfy the assumptions of the logic of collective action in order to qualify as rational actors.

What they do need to satisfy, however, is a plausible rule of rational choice. As will be explained in chapter 5, we work with the least controversial of such rules, the 'dominance rule'. This rule simply says that if, among the available strategies of action, there is one that will make you better off than any other strategy, regardless of what the other players do (hence 'dominant strategy') then you ought to choose that strategy.

To explain the underlying rationale of a research design based on the actor's perspective, let us specify first how the decision structure that characterizes the environmental dilemma (see section 1.2) can be converted into a game form with four possible outcomes.[6] Represented in terms of strategy choices by the 'players', the four outcomes are labelled as P = (D,C), Q = (C,C), R = (D,D) and S = (C,D). The game form corresponding to the decision structure of the environmental dilemma has only one real decision-making agent, whom we call 'Individual'.

Individual is the person facing the environmental dilemma, whose possible actions, or 'strategies', are listed first within the brackets describing each of the four outcomes P, Q, R and S above. Given the fact, noted earlier, that the structure of the dilemma will usually involve at least the presumption that a less polluted state of the environment is preferable to a more polluted one, we shall follow the usual convention of labelling the non-polluting act *np* as the *cooperative strategy* (C) of the game form, and the polluting act *p* as the *non-cooperative or defect strategy* (D).

The second player in the game form is called 'The Others'. The second player is no real decision-making agent. According to feature (4) of the decision structure, 'The Others' simply represents the possible actions *np* or *p* of the many others, which Individual takes into consideration in his decision to act within the dilemma, on the assumption that (almost all) of them act in the same way. In the game form, then, Individual may form a preference ordering over the four outcomes, and he may rationally act upon these preferences, by choosing one of the two strategies, C or D. Each person included among 'The Others' can in turn assume the role of Individual, and become the decision-maker in an equivalent game form. In this way, the *n-person* structure of an environmental dilemma is broken up into as many individual game forms 'Individual vs The Others' as there are agents facing the dilemma.[7]

The survey questionnaire, of course, does not put the story in this extremely abstract way. As will be described in chapter 4, we ask each respondent to place himself/herself in the position of Individual, the decision-making agent who is faced with the environmental dilemma. We then ordinally measure the

---

[6] A 'game form' is a game-theoretical structure specifying how the strategies of the players jointly determine the possible outcomes, without specifying the utility pay-offs that the players attach to each of the outcomes.

[7] The outcome of the n-person game corresponding to an environmental dilemma will thus depend on the strategy choices of each of the n players in the 'Individual vs The Others' game form. If the players are rational, then strategy choices will depend on their preferences over the four outcomes. However, for our purposes, it is not being assumed in advance that the players are rational, as will be explained below.

preferences of the respondents over these four outcomes, as well as the strategies they intend to choose – to pollute (D) or to refrain from polluting (C). By comparing preference orderings with choices, one can test whether or not respondents satisfy the dominance rule of rational choice.

The point of all this may be easily gleaned from what we have been saying above about the need to investigate the logic of collective action. So let us cast that logic in the present game form, to see what would be required of a respondent to satisfy the conditions of Olson's rational agent. The logic of collective action presumes that the non-polluted state of the environment is seen as a common objective by each member of the large group of citizens. This may be taken to imply a preference for the universally cooperative outcome Q = (C,C) over the universally non-cooperative outcome R = (D,D). But at the same time, the logic of collective action insists that a rational individual will want to avoid the cost of cooperating even in the presence of this common objective. That implies a preference for outcome P = (D,C) over outcome Q = (C,C), and also a preference for outcome R = (D,D) over outcome S = (C,D). It is assumed that a rational agent with these three pairwise rankings (Q > R, Q > P, and R > S, where '>' means 'strictly preferred to') satisfies the property of transitivity in ranking the four outcomes overall. This implies that on the logic of collective action, the rational agent must form the preference ordering P > Q > R > S, or in shorthand 'PQRS'.[8]

As noted, the pairwise rankings P > Q and R > S express the assumption that the rational agent will want to avoid the cost of cooperating, whatever others do. Conversely, this means that the preference ordering PQRS necessarily gives the individual a dominant strategy to defect (i.e. choose D). That is to say: *if* an individual has this preference ordering, *then* he will always be better off, in terms of the two above pairwise rankings, by defecting than by cooperating, regardless of the collective behaviour of the others. Moreover, since an individual with ordering PQRS ranks Q > R, he will end up with his third preferred outcome R = (D,D), in case the others all defect. Since all the others are faced with the same dilemma, and each of them is a rational agent, each of them will act on the preference ordering PQRS, and defect. This produces the suboptimal outcome R predicted by the logic of collective action. So the common objective – defined as the attainment of Q = (C,C) – is defeated by the joint result of individual rational action.

Presenting the logic of collective action in this way is merely a formal restatement of the familiar reasoning. But it allows one to conclude that if that logic

---

[8] In the present context, the property of transitivity says that if an alternative x is strictly preferred to alternative y, and y is strictly preferred to z, then x must be strictly preferred to z. On transitivity, P > Q and Q > R implies P > R. Next, Q > R and R > S implies Q > S. Finally, P > Q and Q > S implies P > S. All six possible pairwise rankings of the four outcomes are now fixed. This yields the complete ordering P > Q > R > S.

holds for a respondent in the format of our questionnaire, then that respondent must necessarily report both the preference ordering PQRS and the strategy choice D. As will be seen in chapters 4 and 5, however, only a small minority of respondents in fact satisfy those two conditions, in each of the three cases of the environmental dilemma we have included in the survey.

To the contrary, on the test proposed, rational actors of a decidedly cooperative kind abound among our respondents in all three cases of the survey, though significantly more so in Chemical Waste and Energy Saving than in the case of Holiday Destination. Chapters 4 and 5 will show that most respondents are capable of specifying a complete preference ordering, and of making a definite strategy choice. Of all the possible preference orderings that might be reported (there are $4 \times 3 \times 2 \times 1 = 24$ of these), most are actually represented in the profiles of the three cases of the dilemma. But it will also be seen that the two most popular orderings in each case are the following: QSPR and QPSR.

On what has been laid out above, it is easy to see that these particular orderings are extremely environmentally friendly. Both have the universally cooperative outcome Q at the top, and both have the universally non-cooperative outcome R at the bottom of the ranking. This common property implies that both orderings impose a dominant strategy to cooperate on a rational actor. Why? Well, having a dominant strategy to cooperate here means that you will do worse by defecting, whatever the many others do, given the preferences you have. If you put Q at the top and R at the bottom of your ordering, it follows that you must have $Q > P$ and $S > R$. These are the two pairwise rankings that express a dominant strategy to cooperate, since if you decide to defect, you will end up with either of the two dispreferred outcomes $P = (D,C)$ and $R = (D,D)$. We will be going into this in more detail in chapter 5.

It may be of interest to learn straightaway that of the many respondents with either of the two orderings QSPR and QPSR, by far most indicate that they would want to cooperate in the dilemma. They report the dominant strategy C. Such respondents, who are most heavily represented in the cases of Chemical Waste and Energy Saving, thus choose in line with what one of the most solid rules of rational choice requires. Moreover, as one will see from chapters 4 and 5 as well, relatively many respondents in the case of Holiday Destination report preferences indicating that they do not regard voluntary action on behalf of the environment to be a common objective, and a large proportion of them chooses the corresponding rational strategy of non-cooperation. Preference orderings of this type, for example, would be RPSQ and RSPQ, the opposite numbers of the above mentioned environmentally friendly orderings.

What does all this show? So far, it shows that the logic of collective action is not among the most plausible theories for predicting what rational actors would want to do in situations of environmental collective action involving consumer behaviour. But of course, here we have run up against a sceptical objection, often voiced when we presented preliminary material from this book. The responses we recorded, that objection says, may well be biased in a 'socially desirable' direction. The overall predominance of cooperative responses might show that many are just reporting their *Sunday Preferences*, while in reality, they continue to pollute the environment at least six out of seven days in God's week, in accordance with the logic of collective action. The fact that many respondents show commendable consistency between Sunday Preferences and Sunday Choices only tells us, so the sceptic continues, that such respondents are rather sophisticated dissimulators, not easily caught out in a lie for the sake of environmental correctness. This in itself is of interest, the sceptic concedes. But in the end, one should not be carried away about what respondents report they would do in the hypothetical survey cases of the dilemma, unless this squares with what they report that they have actually been doing in the real world, and unless additionally, those reports are corroborated by the statistical *facts* about what the population at large has actually been doing, and how that has affected the environment.

We agree with the last of these strictures, and shall answer them in section 1.4 below. At this point, however, it is worth commenting briefly upon the first point. The objection that survey respondents have a tendency to give 'socially desirable' answers (especially in face-to-face interviews, such as ours) rests upon the notion that social pressure to conform to norms of environmentally good behaviour biases the responses in a cooperative direction. In any concrete instance of survey research, this is just as difficult to disprove as it is to prove, and there is an obvious burden of proof here on those who want to make much of the objection. But at least we can say that in our survey, the answers at the two independent measurement points of preference orderings and strategy choices in the three environmental dilemmas, show that the respondents have no difficulty in responding differently in different cases. Moreover, they often respond in ways indicating (notably in Holiday Destination) that they are perfectly comfortable to report 'environmentally incorrect' rankings of the dilemma's outcomes, consistently with reporting non-cooperative preferences. Of course it still may be true that there is an overall bias in the cooperative direction, despite the differences among cases we have recorded. If that bias is considerable, then this would have to show up by the failure of responses to the dilemmas to predict the response to properly matched questions about real world behaviour. As will be seen presently, we have no great worries on this score.

1.4 How motives speak to preferences

Meanwhile, our survey design calls for a further exploratory move, one which is relatively novel in empirical research. Recall that from the perspective of the actor, we have decided to accept any complete ordering of the four outcomes as a necessary condition of rational choice. This opens up a different charge of the following kind. It can be objected that many people may act rationally upon given preferences, but that those preferences, for all one knows, could be completely unrelated to their own assessment of the situation, if, that is, they assess the situation coherently at all. In other words, even though many of our respondents may score nicely on the test of rational choice, they may be defective in other respects of practical reasoning. And if this is so, then is there any good reason to think that such people will continue to act rationally on arbitrary preference rankings?

This is an issue that we have taken seriously. It is not only that empirical evidence of rational choice from observed preference orderings and choices will tend to be more reliable, if one can somehow show that the preferences are non-arbitrarily formed. It is also that once one embraces the actor's perspective, there arises a need to inquire into the grounding of people's preference rankings in environmental dilemmas. Remember that we have criticized the logic of collective action because it attributes a specific preference ordering (PQRS) to the rational agent, on the ground that such an agent has no good reason to cooperate towards a common objective, and a good reason to defect, irrespective of others' choices to cooperate or defect. If our critique is valid, then ideally at least, we should be able to give some alternative account of the possible motives that underlie the various different preference orderings that people may come up with. And the theoretical need for such an account arises also from our aim to assess people's responses to the environmental values and norms which were being promoted by the Dutch government at the time of the survey.[9]

While fully granting that survey techniques are not the best way of looking into people's minds, it is possible to collect additional information which enables one to check systematically whether the preferences that people report in the three environmental dilemmas make sense. In particular, we have asked the respondents two motivational questions about each of the dilemmas they face. These questions relate directly to the two points of inquiry identified earlier in section 1.2. The first concerns the issue of the 'common objective': do respondents think that cooperative action (not necessarily including their own) is a good thing, in each particular case? Answers to this question are assembled on a three-point 'motive dimension of Valuation'. The second point of inquiry is to what extent respondents are willing to help contribute to a less polluted state of affairs, in each of the environmental dilemmas. Answers to that question are assembled on a three-point 'motive dimension of Willingness'. Note

---

[9] Incidentally, this goes to show that the issue of biased response in a 'socially desirable' direction becomes far more complicated once one starts inquiring into the exact nature of a person's positive response to 'social pressures to comform'. If the agents exercising the pressure are citing a structure of reasons which can be picked up by the survey design (as we try to ensure), then it is not at all immediately obvious what the profile of the 'environmentally correct' response would have to be.

that the answers to both of these motivational survey questions are regarded as independent. For, in keeping with the actor's perspective, we would not want to rule out in advance that someone who does not consider, say, reducing pollution through toxic waste recycling to be a good thing might still, for whatever idiosyncratic reason, be willing to participate in a communal recycling scheme at some cost in time and effort to himself.

The point of collecting independent information on these two dimensions of motivation is that it might help to explain reported preferences. Motives may speak to preferences, to put it poetically. But what do they say? This is where we have to go out on a limb, and start thinking about consistency between motives and preferences. Our approach is tentative. But it works, to a surprisingly significant extent. There is at least one feature that we would like any test of consistency to reflect. This feature captures the exclusive motivation of the rational actor, according to the logic of collective action. In our consistency test, that actor should at least show up conclusively as someone who is (a) fully endorsing the desirability of collective action for the sake of the environment, and is (b) adamantly unwilling to contribute herself. This feature will impose a relation of consistency between, on the one hand, the respondent's observed positions of positive Valuation and negative Willingness on the two motivational dimensions and, on the other hand, the reported preference ordering PQRS. Likewise, and equally obviously, the environmentally friendly orderings QSPR and QPSR will have to be consistent with observed positions of positive Valuation and positive Willingness. Working along these lines, chapter 6 will propose a consistency test, in which each of the twenty-four possible preference orderings is assigned to just one of nine possible combinations of Valuation and Willingness on the respective three-point scales.

While the results of this consistency test will be extensively discussed in that chapter, here we can say at least this: motives and preferences of the cooperative kind are strongly related. Moreover, consistency between motives and preferences helpfully turns out to predict consistency between these preferences and their corresponding cooperative choice intentions, according to the test of the dominance rule of rational choice. Having consistent preferences thus helps to choose rationally. The empirical significance of these findings of course depends on the incidence of cooperative motives (positive Valuation and positive Willingness) in each case. As chapter 6 will show, such motives are quite predominant, although it must always be noted carefully that they occur most frequently by far in the two cases of Chemical Waste and Energy Saving, in which the environmental dilemma concerns voluntary action in the setting of daily household activity. When citizens are asked to forgo the pleasures of recreative travel so as to reduce pollution of the environment, as in the case of Holiday Destination, then they become less cooperatively minded. These facts show up at each stage of practical reasoning where the survey measures a response to the environmental dilemmas: at the level of motives, preferences and choice intentions.

1.5 Non-equivalent dilemmas and reported behaviour

In itself, this may not seem surprising. But note that on the logic of collective action, environmental dilemmas are supposed to be equivalent. They all convert into *actual* dilemmas. Whatever case one may want to study, the logic of collective action predicts that the environment will be messed up, because people will invariably find it in their best interest to pollute. So if it comes as no surprise that Holiday Destination appears to be a much harder case in which to cooperate than, say, Chemical Waste, then that shows that the logic of collective action is being discounted as a matter of course. For it is then recognized that environmental dilemmas, despite their common structure, are non-equivalent with respect to the likely behaviour they generate. Thus, it is well worth asking whether our findings about the *aggregate* differences in cooperative response in the three cases are also reflected at the level of the *individual respondent*. In particular, one will want to ask whether it is statistically likely that a respondent who wants to cooperate in the case of Holiday Destination (in terms of motive, preference or choice indicators) will also want to cooperate in Chemical Waste, or Energy Saving.

Propositions like this can be tested by means of Robert Mokken's scaling technique.[10] In chapter 7, we explain how. It will be shown that on most variables of the environmental dilemma, the cases of Holiday Destination, Energy Saving and Chemical Waste form a unidimensional scale. This means that for a respondent, statistically speaking, the obstacles to cooperation in the first of these cases are larger than they are in the second, and the obstacles to cooperation in the second case are larger than in the third. We are not able to give direct evidence that backs up our explanations of this main finding at the end of part III. But what we have to say is plausible enough, we hope, and it will be summarized presently.

At this point it is necessary, however, to take up the remaining sceptical points raised in section 1.3 above. How are responses to imagined environmental dilemmas related to reported behaviour? And does the behaviour reported in our survey faithfully reflect what actually goes on in the real world, with respect to the environmental effects of consumer behaviour? We want to be quite modest with respect to this last and generally debated question. There are two points to be noted. First of all, the reported behaviour on holiday choices, much the least cooperative of the three cases, is in line with Dutch studies, which clearly show that the volume of recreational trips by air, especially outside of Europe, has

---

[10] See Mokken, 1971.

grown considerably in the period 1988–97. It is also confirmed that, as far as recycling behaviour in general is concerned, consumers act quite cooperatively, and the case of toxic household waste that we have focused on is certainly no exception. But even though the evidence does not at all suggest a wide gap between reported and actual behaviour, secondly, that evidence is far too slim to draw any definite conclusions. This is mainly because in all three of our cases, the questions on reported behaviour are much too specific to be related directly to assessments of the environmental effects of Dutch consumption patterns, since the measurements involved in those assessments typically group together many different types of behaviour in large clusters, with respect to different pollution effects identified by environmental policy. Bearing that in mind, we are hardly in a position to back up the claim that what our respondents are saying they do is what they actually do, nor can we say anything useful about what difference this would make for measured emissions of carbon dioxide, units of acidification, and so on. These issues, obviously, are the object of a separate field of study, and our survey is not designed even to start addressing them.

What we are concerned to discuss, however, is the relationship between motives, preferences and choices in our three dilemmas on the one hand, and re- ported behaviour in the corresponding real-world settings on the other. Chapter 8 is devoted to this task. It will describe the questions we asked about past be- haviour in relation to the environment. More importantly, it will show that the explanation of reported behaviour in the three cases we studied, is considerably improved when the variable of strategy choice is added to a causal model which uses macro-sociological characteristics of respondents. As we shall argue, this goes to show that what people say they are doing with respect to the environment is highly sensitive to the area of behaviour, that is, to the case of the dilemma at hand. Reported behaviour is far less sensitive to age, education, political affil- iation, income level, or even people's scores on standard questions about their general awareness of, and concern about, the state of the environment. Thus we conclude that our research design, by looking at the way in which people's stance towards environmental action in specific contexts of behaviour hangs together consistently, does indeed have something to contribute to the general endeavour, in empirical social sciences, of explaining the behaviour reported in mass surveys.

1.6 Policies of self-regulation in the Netherlands

Part III of the book squarely places the survey results in the social context of the Netherlands. An important part of that context is that during the nineties, roughly speaking, environmental issues have been prominent in that country. Moreover, Dutch citizens have been, and still are, routinely addressed by the environmental policy sector to take account of the effects of their behaviour over a wide range of polluting emissions. The background of this has been explained in chapter 2 of part I. To summarize briefly, environmental policy plans in the Netherlands have had relatively ambitious goals up to the present. The official goal is that observed pollution should be decoupled, in absolute terms, from the growth of production and consumption in order to achieve a 'sustainable economy'. The point that concerns us here is that while changes in technology, restructuring of the agricultural sector, and industry regulation can achieve part of this overall goal, keeping consumption behaviour in check is held to be a quite important objective in service of it as well. Hence, Dutch consumers are targeted in environmental plans, and indeed in a pretty detailed way. People are not asked to consume less. Rather, and on this we shall focus specifically, they are being asked to consume in environmentally responsible ways.

To promote responsible behaviour, policymakers in the Netherlands employ various policy instruments of self-regulation, the *social instruments*. These consist of campaigns to increase environmental awareness, spreading relevant information, changing educational curricula, product certification, installing recycling facilities, and so on. What such policies of self-regulation have in common, formally expressed, is that they try to alter behaviour without limiting the feasible set of behavioural options open to people. Policies of self-regulation in the Netherlands are, to put it bluntly, instruments of moral reform. They aim to obtain voluntary compliance with objectives of reducing emissions, objectives which are specifically written into the national plans for the 'target group of consumers'. And their stated purpose is, as the local jargon has it, to achieve 'internalization of environmental values', and correspondingly, to achieve 'internalization of environmentally responsible conduct'. This means that the government, from the late eighties onwards, has formulated a fairly coherent environmental ethos, which is used to address consumers in their citizen roles to respond in the required ways, in their daily roles as consumers. Again, this is not to say that consumers are being asked to switch to lifestyles of self-denial. It does mean, however, that they are being asked to become aware of, and to cooperate in, environmental dilemmas of the kind that have been studied in the survey. Indeed, a major aim of this book is to assess the success of the social self-regulation approach.

In chapter 9, we focus on our three cases of the dilemma, this time to show the extents to which citizens actually accept policies of self-regulation. While this again depends on the cases at hand, we find a decidedly positive attitude towards the idea that the government should be engaged in holding citizens to account in the environmental matters of daily life. This is compared to the acceptance of legal regulation on the one hand, and to the acceptance of informal peer group pressure among citizens on the other. Governmental self-regulation policies turn out to be the most widely accepted, in all three cases.

Chapter 10 enters into a detailed analysis of the content of the general message underlying the official ethos of environmental responsibility. At the time of the survey, in 1994, that message had been quite widely disseminated in society. In large part, the results of our survey can therefore be interpreted in the light of this environmental ethos. What we propose, in this third part of the book, is to grade the motive and preference responses to environmental dilemmas in accordance with the extent to which they are consistent with the twin notions of 'internalization of environmental value' and 'internalization of environmentally responsible conduct'. In particular, we argue that the first of these notions aims at creating common objectives of voluntary collective action. As mentioned in section 1.4, this is measured on the motive dimension of 'Valuation'. The second part of the environmental ethos concerns the responsibility to act on common objectives, always noting that in an environmental dilemma, people are aware of the fact that their individual actions, taken separately, are causally insignificant. Indeed, as we shall see in chapter 10, the canonical statement of the environmental ethos, which was included in the first national environmental policy plan of 1989, enjoins citizens to 'recalculate' their behaviour, by bearing in mind the important joint consequences for the environment of these many insignificant individual acts.

The internalization of environmentally responsible conduct is measured by looking at the responses concerning common objectives, as well as the individual willingness to cooperate in working towards such objectives in the different cases. This involves putting together the responses on the two dimensions of Valuation and Willingness, and checking the combined motive response against the preference responses, given our test of consistency between motives and preferences. As is confirmed by scale analysis, responses in the easy cases of the dilemma (Chemical Waste and Energy Saving) are much in line with what the environmental ethos demands. As could be expected, Holiday Destination is the hard case again, and in this instance we find that a significant proportion of the motive response rejects the notion that environmental restrictions on recreative travel should be considered a common objective among citizens. Chapter 9 also shows, moreover, that this case of the dilemma is also the one registering a definite lack of acceptance with respect to any type of regulation: legal or social, by way of governmental campaigns or through peer pressure.

1.7 Moral commitment in environmental dilemmas: conditional or unconditional?

Our line that self-regulation policies are instruments of 'moral reform' should not be misunderstood. It is not as if black-frocked emissaries of the Environment Ministry are appearing on television every week with sententious messages of exhortation. Increasingly, the Ministry has also been trying to devolve policies of self-regulation to local government, firms, and voluntary associations, as the four-year environmental policy plans move further into what government calls the 'phase of implementation'. Moreover, the tone of official campaigns is often light-hearted and somewhat wistful, as in the slogan directed to car owners that 'the car can do without you once in a while'. How that slogan is taken up, it is recognized, will in part depend on what employers may arrange in the way of variable working times, and other facilitating measures that their businesses are legally obliged to be reporting on, within the framework of 'environmental impact assessments'. It is also recognized that good environmental behaviour of consumers chimes in with lifestyle choices. This brings marketing approaches into the arsenal of social instruments, and thus takes some of the moral weight off the shoulder of the individual *persona* of the citizen. But nonetheless, what all of this amounts to in the end is, we maintain, the systematic use of a social ethos of environmental responsibility.

Since we are trying to measure the impact of the environmental ethos within the general framework of rational choice theory, there is some need to clarify a theoretical issue involved in describing the rationality of moral commitment. In chapter 11, we take this up. The aim is to show that our consistency format of motives and preferences extends Amartya Sen's concept of a 'moral meta-ranking' of preference orderings. Sen has done much to argue that before individuals get down to making a rational choice, they are often confronted with an antecedent problem of fixing on the preference ordering that best captures their interests, all things considered. This antecedent problem requires taking into account all relevant aspects of the decision problem, as they perceive it. In particular, if moral considerations enter into an individual's understanding of the context of choice, within an interdependent decision problem, then moral commitment can be modelled as follows: the individual decides to adopt a preference ordering expressing some moral social code, while simultaneously repudiating the preference orderings that express narrow self-interest, or represent conceptions of limited group interest. The upshot is that while rational choice of a moral nature naturally involves acting so as best to satisfy the preferences dictated by a socially prominent morality under the circumstances, this choice is additionally characterized on the basis of the agent's reasons for refusing to act upon non-moral preferences of the kind that are dictated by a conception of personal interest. This is the thought underlying the notion that rational choice is to be analysed in terms of a moral 'meta-ranking' of preference orderings, in which an ordering corresponding to a code of morality is ranked first, and the narrowly self-interested ordering is ranked last.

Sen has most explicitly applied this idea to the game form of two-person 'Prisoner's Dilemmas'. As we shall be working out in some detail, however, the decision structure of the environmental dilemma, conceived as a collection of many 'Individual vs The Others' game forms (see section 1.3 above) is different in some crucial respects. To put the issue in the context of self-regulation policies, the notion of personal interest that the individual would need to reject, in order to consciously embrace the environmental ethos that the Dutch policy-makers want to promote, is a specific one. It is the one that rationally prescribes non-cooperative behaviour from the point of view that refuses to accept environmental improvements as a valid common objective. With this point understood, we construct an 'environmental meta-ranking' in the space of motives. This is a ranking of the possible positions on the two dimensions of Valuation and Willingness, and it captures the respondents' gradations of assent with the environmental ethos, as they have been previously identified in chapter 10. By applying the test of motive-preference consistency, the corresponding meta-ranking of preference orderings is then obtained. Our environmental meta-ranking is put to good use in the final chapter.

To understand the different responses of citizens to the environmental ethos, however, there arises a large issue which will be discussed in chapter 12. In this introductory chapter, that issue has been waiting patiently in the wings. It concerns the important contrast between conditional and unconditional cooperation in environmental dilemmas. To see what is involved here, just imagine that you have become convinced that toxic household waste should be collected separately, and then safely carted off to a recycling facility, rather than being absorbed in some noxious landfill, while messing up the environment along the way. You are thus well-disposed, let us assume, to cooperate in the local recycling scheme. But you still want to know what the others will be doing. If they are reasonably likely to cooperate, then surely, so will you. But if they massively defect on their responsibilities, then why should you cooperate? What's the use of doing so? In that case, reluctantly no doubt, you will go back to dumping your batteries in the garbage can and pouring your old paint down the kitchen sink. Obviously, that attitude is not inconsistent with the ethos of environmental responsibility. You wholeheartedly affirm the common objective, and what is more, you do not want others to shoulder the burden of cooperation by taking a free ride on their efforts yourself. What you are refusing is to end up as a sucker, quite understandably. Does the environmental ethos ask you to be suckered? Surely that would not only be asking too much, but the ethos would also seem to be requiring you, and for that matter everyone else, to make irrational sacrifices. So we face two theoretical problems here. The first one is this: in studying responses to environmental dilemmas, how do we discriminate between attitudes of conditional and unconditional cooperation in our research design?

To see just how, let us refer back to the survey results of part II. As noted in section 1.3, many different preference orderings have been reported in the three cases of the dilemma. Among those, there is the well-known Assurance Game-ordering (so coined by Sen, long ago). It faithfully represents the attitude of conditional compliance to the social ethos of responsibility, in the present

context. By the letter code we use, the Assurance Game-ord⌐
This ordering places the universally cooperative outcome Q
top, and the sucker outcome S = (C,D) at the bottom, puttir
non-cooperative outcome R = (D,D) in third place. It also
fusal to act as a free rider, since Q is preferred to P = (D,⌐⌐
of all this, the aspect of assurance is expressed by the fact that Individ⌐
best response is to defect when he is sure the others will defect (R > S), and
Individual's best response is to cooperate when the others are sure to cooperate (Q > P). Note that there are other possible preference orderings that
a conditional cooperator may adopt. The Assurance Game-ordering is simply
the most common of these. Note also that, compared to the preferences of
someone who follows the logic of collective action (ordering PQRS), the first
and second outcomes have been reversed (P and Q), while compared to the
decidedly environmentally friendly ordering QPSR, the two last outcomes
(S and R) have been reversed, in the Assurance Game-ordering. This is of
some interest, because it tells us that the conditionality of the Assurance
Game-attitude should make us locate this attitude in an intermediate position, in motive space, on the dimension of Willingness to cooperate. This
property is indeed satisfied by the motive-preference consistency test of
chapter 6.

So far, this goes to show that the contrast between conditional and unconditional cooperation is properly incorporated in the conceptual framework of
our survey design. But what do the respondents in the three dilemmas report,
concerning this contrast? Two main things emerge. First, and most importantly,
unconditionally cooperative motives and preferences predominate in all three
cases of the dilemma over conditionally cooperative ones. Secondly, the hardest
case, Holiday Destination, has a significantly smaller ratio of unconditional to
conditional cooperators, both in motive and preference space.

And here we encounter the second of our theoretical problems. The finding
that unconditionally cooperative responses predominate needs to be critically
examined, for the following reason. As we shall explain in chapter 12, there
is a strong consensus in recent literature on rational choice that in so far as
recurrent collective action problems get solved non-coercively, consistently
with rational behaviour, this will be by mechanisms that involve trust-building,
monitoring, sanctions on various kinds of observed non-cooperative action, and
investment in forming a reputation as a trustworthy person who will not stand
for being suckered. On this view, which is supported by ample evidence in
different fields of social inquiry, a morality of reciprocal cooperation tends to
get reinforced when these mechanisms operate successfully. On the same view,
a morality of unconditional cooperation would seem to be powerless against
predatory behaviour and free-ridership, and in consequence it would tend not to
be reinforced. But in our survey, in apparent contrast to the view, unconditional
morality seems to be quite common.

These arguments about reciprocity have been forcefully summarized in a detailed review by Elinor Ostrom. In examining them, we point out that our cases are located at the far end of a *size continuum* of social dilemma situations. And at this far end, it can not be expected that mechanisms of trust and reputation have any purchase to speak of. In environmental dilemmas of the kind we are looking at, the morality of reciprocal cooperation may even be an inefficient one to entertain, if a person is well-disposed to cooperate in the first place. The reason is simply that on the logic of the Assurance Game, one has to be continuously engaged in seeking assurance of others' good behaviour, in order to decide whether or not to cooperate. But it is not always easy to predict what others' behaviour will be, and moreover it is almost always impossible to retaliate selectively against the non-cooperators whose nasty behaviour one can sometimes observe. In many ways, the most efficient response would be just to cooperate as a matter of routine, and to switch to the stance of conditional non-cooperation (or perhaps outright rejection of the whole idea that there is a common objective to worry about) only when the others give conclusive evidence of behaving badly all the time *en masse*.

Of course, as we also suggest, this will be a sensible line to take only when it is more or less a matter of common knowledge that the individual cost of cooperating in the dilemma is not that high, and can on the whole be borne easily by most. If people expect others not to be able to bear this cost, then – still on the assumption that they themselves are well-disposed to cooperate – they will find it more reasonable to adopt the stance of the conditional, rather than the unconditional cooperator, in large-scale social dilemmas. Now that is exactly what we do find in the survey. For as mentioned above, the ratio of unconditional to conditional cooperators in the preference and motive response of the hardest case of Holiday Destination is much smaller than it is in the two easier cases of Energy Saving and Chemical Waste.

1.8 Determinants of cooperation in environmental dilemmas and policy design

This brings us to the concluding chapter of the book, where the main strands of the preceding chapters are woven together. As we argued above, the notion that Holiday Destination is the 'hardest case in which to cooperate' is one that can be made more precise by means of scale analysis. The object is to find out whether or not the three cases of the environmental dilemma figure as three 'items' on a unidimensional continuum, with respect to some observed variable that indicates a cooperative stance in the interlinked spaces of motive, preference or strategy choices. But intuitively, the very notion of the 'hardest case' also quite naturally suggests the presence of certain reasons militating against voluntary collective action on behalf of the environment. In reporting our hardest case findings above, we noted that few will consider it a big deal to learn that someone in the real world, who is aware of environmental issues, is more likely to cooperate in a recycling scheme, or economize on hot water, than to forgo the use of a private car to go to work in favour of public transport, or to refrain from participating in periodic mass migrations by air in the summer vacation. Common sense tells us that the last two of these environmental dilemmas are usually harder than the first two, given the considerable downside of acting cooperatively they so evidently involve.

The survey findings, as reported so far, make it easy for us to concede this triumph of common sense. But as noted before, the logic of collective action represents a powerful and conflicting common-sense point of view, according to which every single case of an environmental dilemma will prevent rational agents from cooperating, whatever the magnitude of the personal cost may be. In view of this, it seems best to keep on course in analysing the data we have collected, while always casting a sensitive eye on what various intuitions of common sense may suggest, when questions of interpretation arise. Moreover, in part III of the book, we are not merely trying to explain what is going on in the three cases. Our search for explanations is crucially guided by our aim of policy assessment. We want to be in a position to say something of interest about the viability of environmental policies of self-regulation.

Our final strategy in this chapter, therefore, is to look for the most reliable indicator of a cooperative stance which reflects the impact of the official ethos, since that ethos is being invoked by means of the 'social instruments', in Dutch environmental policy. Given the model of practical reasoning outlined above, the indicator we have in mind is a composite response of the following kind. A respondent whose attitude fully complies with the environmental ethos is someone who reports motives of positive Valuation and Willingness, and who rationally chooses to cooperate in the dilemma, from a preference ordering that is consistent with these motives. To put it less forbiddingly technical, this is a response that reflects someone's wish to act unhesitatingly on the thought that one ought to participate in collective action for the sake of a less polluted environment, whenever this is called for in a given area of behaviour. Hence we call this response 'consistent ethical cooperation'.

It turns out, first, that the three cases of the dilemma form a scale with respect to consistent ethical cooperation, and secondly, that the cases of Chemical Waste, Energy Saving and Holiday Destination compare (in percentages of consistent ethical cooperators in the total of respondents) as 60 : 50 : 10, respectively. This last figure gives a rough indication of just how difficult it is for respondents to comply fully with the dictates of the environmental ethos in each case, on the very exacting standard of compliance that we have chosen to use.[11]

As noted above, the survey provides no direct evidence of the factors that explain the non-equivalence of environmental dilemmas. One thing that does emerge from the policy setting is that cases differ with respect to how much the behaviour in question has become subject to the norms invoked in public discussion, and how intensively it is being focused on by policies of self-regulation. As will be explained in chapter 9, the case of Holiday Destination is a relatively unregulated one, whereas people have become used to the fact that their behaviour is publicly scrutinized for its environmental effects in the cases of Chemical Waste and Energy Saving. Thus it would be possible to argue, as some environmental analysts have done, that there is a 'normalizing' effect at work, which may make it easier for people to accept what environmental norms require of them in well-regulated cases. We think, however, that this can be only a very small part of the explanation of the differences we record in respect of consistent ethical cooperation. Indeed, the fact that behaviour in some cases has become 'normalized' by public intervention, while other cases have remained relatively free of such intervention, suggests that in the latter cases, people are just more resistant to the behavioural implications of paying attention to the *content* of public norms about the environment. For various reasons, people who respond to hard cases of the dilemma may think that the public norms, while generally acceptable, are simply inappropriate, because they regard their behaviour in these areas as a matter of private discretion. They may therefore hold that it is legitimate to keep a free hand in those areas, unrestricted by the dictates of the environmental ethos.

Our hypothesis is that cases of the dilemma, as they are perceived in the real world (rather than in the deliberately stylized reflection of the world within our survey interview), can be ranged on a 'dimension of private significance'. A given area of behaviour in the real world is of 'private' (as opposed to 'public') significance in three respects. For the area in question, the values and norms of the environmental ethos (1) have a low salience, and furthermore, they present

---

[11] Just how exacting that standard is may be appreciated by the following three considerations. First, it is by no means easy for respondents to pass both of the consistency tests that link motives to choices, via preferences. Secondly, we have focused upon rational choices from preferences (QSPR and QPSR) that are consistent with motives of positive Valuation and Willingness, rather than on rational choices from any other preference ordering that induces a dominant strategy to cooperate. Finally, we have not counted among the relevant cooperators those whose motives signal conditional willingness to cooperate, and whose preferences, accordingly, will not have a dominant cooperative strategy. This means that we exclude from our comparisons those reporting a cooperative choice who endorse the ethos conditionally (positive Valuation, and intermediate Willingness, hence the Assurance Game-ordering QPRS), who are therefore prepared to cooperate if others do, and who apparently believe that others will reciprocate. Taken together, these considerations show that the indicator of consistent ethical cooperation is a highly discriminating and conservative one, as far as measuring assent with the ethos is concerned.

(2) high individual costs of compliance, as well as (3) a low perceived gain of collective action.

We shall leave the details of our policy assessment for the reader to peruse, in the final sections of chapter 13. Our main conclusion is that self-regulation policies are effective at the public end of the dimension, and should be avoided at the private end, both because they are ineffective and because they run the risk of backfiring. We also have some suggestions for striking the appropriate balance for hard, but still tractable, cases located in the middle of the dimension. The arguments we advance depend for their plausibility on showing in some detail that the three environmental dilemmas which are studied in this book can be readily understood in terms of the dimension of private significance, and we adduce additional survey evidence to back this up, in a comparison of the polar cases of Chemical Waste and Holiday Destination. Our strategy will be to decompose the scores of each case of the dilemma on the variable of consistent ethical cooperation into two component parts: the share of ethical motives (positive Valuation and positive Willingness) and the degree of ethical consistency, which is the percentage of those with ethical motives who satisfy consistency on both of our tests. The aspect of salience in the dimension of private significance, we argue, is measured by the degree of ethical consistency, while the aspects of compliance cost and perceived gain of collective action are measured by the share of ethical motives.

The dimension of private significance is utilized in the final three sections of this concluding chapter, in which we comment on the strengths and weaknesses of the Dutch self-regulation approach.

2

A Dutch approach: self-regulation as a policy concept

2.1 Introduction

This chapter gives a detailed overview of environmental policy in the Netherlands. The reason for presenting the Dutch case is that it has gone far in attempting to obtain the commitment of individual citizens to an explicit notion of responsibility, in order to maximize compliance to ambitious environmental planning goals. First, from 1989 onwards, successive governments in the Netherlands have been concerned to develop a framework of indicative planning that integrates environmental considerations into the full range of public policies. We shall describe this framework in the next section. A key feature of the National Environmental Policy Plans, as they are called, is the notion of an *environmentally self-regulating* community. In such a community, the behaviour of corporate and individual actors is subject to state policies of moral persuasion. What is of particular interest here is that Dutch environmental planning utilizes a specific type of policy instruments, the *social instruments*. Their purpose, to be further discussed in section 2.3, is to induce the widespread voluntary cooperation of citizens and firms with a set of detailed environmental targets, which are specified in the national plans.

In the final two sections of this chapter, we show how these *policies of self-regulation*, as we shall label them here, are driven by a project of moral reform, as noted by Albert Weale.[1] This project was originally motivated by wide political consensus on the urgent need to adopt a stringent set of emission targets for preventing massive environmental degradation from occurring in the country, within the next generation. To use the terminology of the Brundtland Report, policymakers suddenly came to realize that far-reaching behavioural

---

[1] See Weale, 1992: ch. 6.

28

changes in production and consumption would be needed to achieve *sustainable growth*.[2] The moral reform project received its explicit policy expression in the *strategy of internalizing environmental responsibility*. This strategy, which is still in force today, commits the government to promote a specific environmental ethos. Its nature will be discussed below in some detail.

Thus, our main reason for focusing on the Dutch case of environmental policymaking is its attempt at bringing a public ethos to bear on personal behaviour with regard to the environment. Our method of survey research is well-suited to assess the possible impact of these policies of moral persuasion, as part III of this book will show. We do not want to claim that the integrated planning model of the Netherlands is easily exportable to other national policy cultures; but we think that the avowed purpose of the self-regulation approach to implicate citizens in a shared project of environmental protection is of sufficient general interest to be considered on its merits. Our final conclusions are given in chapter 13. We aim to provide a critical evaluation of the chances and limitations of this type of policy.

2.2 Dutch environmental policy and the idea of self-regulation

The concept of *self-regulation* is important in Dutch environmental policy. It figures largely in the architecture of the three national environmental plans which have been approved by Parliament since 1989.[3] Several referents of the term can be distinguished: ecological self-regulation (the capacity of a biophysical system to self-adjust), economic self-regulation (the spontaneous adjustment of utility or profit-maximizing agents in response to price signals), and social self-regulation (voluntary behavioural change as a result of social commitments which the agents come to share). What we have in mind here is the last referent.

To explain the policy concept of self-regulation, we start by outlining the general features of the environmental plans, by reference to the most recent one. The core element of these plans is a two-way typology of *problem-themes* and *target groups*. The problem-themes list a catalogue of emissions with important negative environmental effects, which are singled out for policy intervention. The target groups consist of the actors who are identified as controllable sources of the effects enumerated under the problem-themes. The problem-themes are developed in a complex interplay of scientific and policy thinking. On the scientific side, the plans follow a systems theory of the physical flows of substances in the natural environment. This analysis identifies the human interventions that endanger the regenerating capacities of ecosystems at several scale levels of spatial and administrative organization: the locality, the region, the fluvial

---

[2] See World Commission on Environment and Development, 1987.
[3] See NMP1, 1989; NMP2, 1993; and NMP3, 1998.

location, the continent, and finally the entire globe. In short, systems theory provides the scientific framework for a quantitative description of pollution effects at their sources, and for working out the feasible options to reduce these effects at each of the five scale levels.[4]

From their inception, the environmental plans were intended first to clean up the environmental degradation produced in the past, and then go on as quickly as possible to prevent further 'messes in the future from occurring'.[5] This emphasis on a forward-looking perspective of preventing environmental degradation generated a policy preference for source-oriented measures. The need for adopting a forward-looking perspective was vividly impressed on the government and public opinion by forecasts that environmental quality in the Netherlands was due to decline considerably in the next thirty years, even if it were possible to apply the full range of existing techniques for reducing emissions at the 'end of the pipe'. As a rousing example, it was estimated that only 20 per cent of the (already sparse) Dutch forests would escape damage by 2010, as a result of further acidification at the current rate of growth, given the ruling methods for controlling emissions.[6] To slow down the decline of environmental quality, major structural economic changes were needed, especially in the energy sector, agriculture, and transport.

The policy link between sources and effects in the environmental plans may be summarized as follows. First, the government formulates a set of qualitative policy goals, at each of the five scale levels. For example, at the local and regional levels, the goals of the 1998 environmental plan are to prevent pollution of soil and local airspace, reduce noise levels, promote cities with healthy living conditions, which must nevertheless be able to compete internationally, and to work towards a sustainable balance in living conditions between urban and rural regions. At the fluvial level, one of the goals is to restore the natural development of the big rivers and the lake (IJsselmeer); at the continental level, to strive for low health and ecological risks from air and particle pollution, and at the global level to prevent global warming and further deterioration of the ozone layer.[7]

Secondly, following the qualitative goals, an inventory of the 'desired levels of environmental quality' is drawn up, and translated into indicative planning objectives. Each objective gets expressed as a set of quantitative targets, for example reducing the growth of carbon-dioxide or nitrous gas emissions, or

---

[4] These elements of Dutch environmental planning were developed in a highly influential study 'Caring for Tomorrow', by the National Institute for Public Health and Environmental Protection, which was commissioned by the government shortly before the first national plan. See RIVM, 1988.
[5] As formulated by the Environment Minister Ed Nypels, who added: 'The mess we have caused in the last 30 or 40 years can not be cleaned up in just a few years'. *Trouw*, 14 December 1988.
[6] These forecasts were made in 'Caring for Tomorrow'. See RIVM, 1988. For an accurate comment on their political significance, see Weale, 1992: 134–8.
[7] See NMP3, 1998: 16.

lowering the number of people who are exposed to excessive noise. These targets are meant to be attained stepwise, within a time horizon stretching forward to 2010. The quantitative objectives and corresponding targets are then grouped into the problem-themes referred to above. Nine such themes are listed: climate change, acidification, eutrophification, diffusion, soil degradation, waste disposal, disturbance, dehydration, and squandering of resources.[8]

Thirdly, each of the targets appearing under the headings of the problem-themes is partitioned into definite task assignments. These are addressed to relevant groups of actors, in the form of specified shares in contributing to one or several of the targets. At present, no fewer than ten such target groups exist: consumers, agriculture, industry, refineries, public energy utilities, retailing, construction, transport, waste disposal firms, and actors in the water chain.[9] As this list shows, the target groups consist of administratively distinct collections of individual or (private or semi-governmental) corporate actors. Some target groups are singled out as sources of environmental degradation, by estimating the effects of their behaviour within the area of one or more of the given problem-themes. For example, some of the shares assigned to the consumers are: 10% of the target for climate change, a 14% share in waste disposal, 20% of the diffusion target for fine particles, and a 22% share in water eutrophification by phosphorous components (caused e.g. by the use of household detergents).[10] Other target groups, such as the actors in the water chain and waste disposal firms, are assigned shares on the basis of their functional capability to provide quality improvements in public amenities: clean drinking water, or safely getting rid of toxic wastes such as lead and cadmium.

Whatever the criterion for identifying a target group may be, though, the typology of problem-themes and target groups serves to bring home a message of collective responsibility, to be shared by governmental and non-governmental actors alike. Though governmental actors are not included in the target groups, they are linked together in a similar way, through mechanisms of interdepartmental collaboration and decentralization. The recent plans provide elaborate provisions for devolving authority and finance to provincial and municipal levels of administration. All this means that the behaviour of target groups can be approached in a multi-level regulation process. As will be apparent from the above examples, some of the qualitative goals are the result of trading off various environmental and economic concerns. However, as far as the environmental plans are concerned, the policy outlook on these trade-offs is guided by a steadfast belief in the ultimate compatibility of these two concerns. This is reflected in the substance as well as in the administrative set-up of the plans. With respect to substance, the 1989 plan strongly emphasized the basic tenet of the 1987 Brundtland Report, that environmental policy should not be defined

---

[8] See NMP3, 1998: 210.   [9] See NMP3, 1998: 96.   [10] See NMP3, 1998: 86.

ion to economic policy in its narrow sense. Rather, the two are to be ...a conception of 'sustainable growth', according to which careful plan-...ng of technological development and planned social changes in consumption patterns may enable economic growth to continue side by side with an accelerated reduction of environmental harm. The result would then be that the growth process is sustainable, in the sense that its continuation will not destroy the options of future generations to promote their living standards in ecologically sound circumstances.

In the 1989 plan, environmental protection was marked as the 'fourth pillar of government policy', alongside economic growth, reduction of the budget deficit, and the reduction of unemployment.[11] Thus the view of sustainable growth provides the guiding framework for judging the permissible trade-offs between ecological and economic concerns. It may be said that this framework is a rather tight one. To illustrate, the 1998 plan restates the overall goal as one of bringing about an 'absolute, rather than merely relative decoupling of economic growth and environmental pressures'. This is surely an ambitious goal. It means that any increase in the level of the gross domestic product (GDP) should be matched by a decrease in the selected levels of pollution, dangerous waste, and resource depletion. In other words, it is not enough to have 'relative decoupling', in which pollution levels increase, but only at a somewhat lesser rate than GDP. However, since the policy plans are indicative rather than binding, there is considerable room in practice for tolerating departures from the norm of absolute decoupling, in order to meet rival goals of, say, international competitiveness and full employment. To mention just two important departures noted in the third environmental plan (NMP3), absolute emission levels of carbon dioxide and nitrous oxides were not in fact reduced during the previous planning period (1993–7), while the smog levels expected as a result of the projected growth rate up to 2010 were seen to rise appreciably above the planned health norms. Likewise, though biodiversity in the Netherlands was said to deteriorate less rapidly than it did in the time of the first plan, the effects of acidification, dehydration, and eutrophification have prevented it from meeting the internationally agreed standard of protection.[12]

The government admitted that these failures can be attributed in part to unsustainable economic growth: rising volumes of consumption outstrip the beneficial effects of producing the goods in environmentally less harmful ways. While a realistic response to such failures might perhaps be to adopt a less stringent set of environmental constraints, successive governments have chosen instead, by and large, to retain the high ambition level of the first national policy plan. The official standpoint remains that the pursuit of sustainable growth is essential to an adequate long-term environmental policy, even though it must be recognized

[11] See NMP1, 1989: 74–5.   [12] See NMP3, 1998: 23–33.

that living up to that ambition is hard, because its success depends in part on factors that are difficult to control: international cooperation, and major structural changes within the Netherlands itself. Thus, in referring to the notion of absolute decoupling, NMP3 remarks:

> Ultimately, the achievement of environmental goals under continued growth is only possible if we adjust our patterns of consumption. However, this is difficult to achieve, and it requires a change in the behaviour and habits of citizens. To interfere with these, for instance by means of legal regulation, will often not be possible or desirable, since this touches upon the personal domain of life.   (NMP3 1998: 31)

In the last decade, then, the standard response of the government has been to reaffirm the ambitious mission of sustainable growth, while counting on the collective responsibility of the society as a whole for its help in redressing failures along the way. Of course, this type of response may be regarded cynically as one that covers the political incumbents for failing to meet part of their democratically assigned tasks. But alternatively – and not entirely inconsistent with the alleged cynical motive – it may reveal a genuine belief in the existence of a social consensus on the principle of sustainability, which can be appealed to in a genuine attempt to go beyond what can be realistically achieved within a given constellation of short-term trade-offs.

With respect to administrative form, the process of agreeing on the qualitative goals is designed to allow for trading off of economic and ecological values and interests. The formulation of the environmental plan as a whole, and the interdepartmental coordination of decision-making, is the responsibility of the Ministry of Public Health, Housing and the Environment (which harbours a large and powerful Directorate-General of Environmental Management). The recent plan is co-signed by no fewer than five ministries: Economic Affairs; Finance; Agriculture, Nature and Fisheries; Transport and Water Management; and Foreign Affairs. Each of the co-signing ministries has a set of specific responsibilities for carrying out certain strategic duties, which are identified in the plan's main lines. These are negotiated to fit in with each of these ministries' main responsibilities, taking account of the burdens imposed upon the more or less traditionally defined set of groupings or sectors whose interests are involved in carrying out the duties: farmers, fishermen, road transport, the tax authorities, diplomatic personnel, and so forth.

The involvement of the co-signing ministries ensures that they are well represented in the formulation of the plan's qualitative goals, which is the highest-level locus at which the philosophy of sustainable growth is brought into contact with the specifics of economic and social development. From there, the writing out of quantitative objectives and their time paths, the assignment of contributive shares for target groups, as well as the choice of policy instruments, becomes a process involving both the ministries and representatives of the target groups in civil society. Bearing in mind also the more recent decentralized structure of administrative responsibilities, this leads to a highly integrated form of elaborating the plan, which contains numerous moments for negotiating the environmental–economic trade-off. But once again, what is crucial in all this complexity is the operating assumption that government agencies, the main economic players in industry, agriculture, transport, and construction, the various 'social' organizations such as trade unions, or the Society of Nature Monuments, and last but not least, the great mass of consumers, are in principle well-disposed to support the ambitious nature of the environmental plan.

This sketch brings us back to the topic of self-regulation. As Albert Weale has observed in a perceptive overview of the early NMP-period, the plans embody a highly cooperative notion of policymaking.[13] Underlying this notion is the assumption on the part of policymakers that the actors involved in the environmental plan have the *capability for self-regulation*, given that they understand the significance of the environmental problems that have to be faced. Self-regulation, so conceived, refers to a disposition of *active compliance*. The assumption of a capability for self-regulation is most clearly at work in the policy model of target groups and problem areas which we mentioned above. On the one hand, the members of target groups appear as the agents who cause the problems, as the 'sources of pollution'. As such, they are regarded as objects of policy, whose compliance must be secured by applying traditional methods of administrative regulation and incentives. On the other hand, these same actors are presented as potential 'agents of change', capable of providing solutions for pollution problems, because they can be approached to take responsibility for the environment, and because they are endowed with learning capacity to reconcile urgent environmental requirements with their own legitimate interests. Actors can become responsible agents of change by including them in the policy framework. Hence, environmental policy must be of the cooperative kind.

The thesis of capability for self-regulation has prescriptive significance. When policymakers publicly ascribe a sense of environmental responsibility to actors in civil society, then they are in a position to hold those actors responsible for their environmental behaviour. This is most clearly revealed by a ringing expression, which summarizes one of the official starting points of the first national plan: the *internalization of environmental responsibility*. We shall be saying more about it when we discuss the social dilemma below. However, the language of Dutch environmental planning also uses the notion of self-regulation in a way that reveals some scepticism about the chances of obtaining active compliance in practice. This scepticism is evident in the ruling typology of governmental policy instruments: 'physical regulation' by coercively sanctioned means, 'financial regulation' by means of monetary incentives, and 'social regulation' or 'self-regulation' by public deployment of information and knowledge,

---

[13] See Weale, 1992: 140–1.

educational efforts, and straightforward persuasion. In distinguishing these types of policy measures, then, the moral notion of 'internalization' appears as a guideline for developing a separate category of 'social instruments', the main purpose of which is to bring about voluntary behavioural change that contributes to the environmental objectives of the plans. The social instruments are discussed in the next section. Here it is essential to note that the government, while counting on the sense of environmental responsibility of citizens and corporate actors to some extent, clearly recognizes the need to activate responsible behaviour.

Thus, the concept of self-regulation has two main connotations. On one hand, it refers to the basic assumption underlying cooperative environmental policy, according to which the actors who are affected by the national environmental plans are generally held to be capable of active compliance, that is to say, of doing the right kind of thing, without being forced, bribed or punished. On the other hand, self-regulation also connotes the efforts on the part of government in getting this capability for active compliance to work. This is done by bringing social instruments into the field of environmental policymaking. In this second use of the self-regulation concept, then, the government clearly does not take it for granted that the actors will in fact be capable of adapting their behaviour, even though they are capable of doing so in principle. Actors are recognized as having difficulties in internalizing responsibility for the environment, since – as the first national plan notes – 'there is always a tendency to shift one's personal or corporate responsibility onto others'. Policies of self-regulation are thus held to be *feasible*, given the capability for voluntary cooperation, and *necessary* in order to secure this cooperation in practice. Since policies of self-regulation are meant to change behaviour by tapping inner motives of responsibility for environmental goals, they can be thought to express an ambition on the part of the policymakers to undertake a project of moral reform. This project consists in changing the behaviour of corporate actors, of citizens, and of government agencies themselves, in accordance with the ethos of responsibility for environmental qualities. The significance of that official project will be discussed below. First, however, a closer look at the social instruments is appropriate.

2.3 The social instruments

In preparation of NMP2, the second of the national environmental plans, the government requested the Scientific Council for Government Policy to advise on the design of effective policy instruments for dealing with target groups.[14] Noting that the traditional arsenal of legislative measures had become very

---

[14] See WRR, 1992. The Scientific Council for Government Research (*Wetenschappelijke Raad voor het Regeringsbeleid*, henceforth referred to as 'the Council') is an autonomous advisory council whose members are nominated every five years by the government. The government is under a duty to respond to the council's reports in a parliamentary session.

costly in terms of obtaining compliance, and that it might not suffice to bring about the behavioural changes of corporate actors and citizens required by the first environmental plan's long-term goals, the government remarked: 'As far as instruments for obtaining behavioural changes are concerned, it will be helpful to make a distinction between "physical regulation, financial regulation and social regulation (self-regulation, inducing awareness)"' (WRR, 1992: 179). The report of the Council in response to this request was influential in creating a three-way typology of policy instruments. In pure form, these types are distinguished by three 'social interaction processes in which behaviour can be steered': command, transaction, and persuasion. 'Command' refers to the issuing of formal directives that legally prohibit or require certain behaviours, and 'transaction' refers to relations of contract, in which the voluntary behaviour of a target group is obtained by means of positive or negative incentives provided by governmental agencies. Both of these instrument types may be regarded as forms of *legal regulation*, since the changes in behaviour to be obtained by directives, or obtained by contract in response to officially applied incentives, are legally binding. By contrast, instruments in the category of *social regulation* attempt to induce behavioural changes in an interaction process of 'persuasion', hence without imposing any kind of legal requirement on the agents. The instruments of this type are the social instruments. So while the instruments of command and transaction aim to modify the parameters of the actors' feasible choice sets, the social instruments aim at inducing the actors to select environmentally friendly options within their feasible choice sets.

The Council's report paid special attention to situational factors affecting the applicability of various instruments. As far as the social instruments are concerned, the target groups of the environmental plans are, in principle, distinguished in two broad categories: corporate actors and citizens.[15] The corporate actors are regarded as more or less 'easily approachable' by policy efforts, due to their sectoral or functional organisation. This makes it possible to negotiate with the representatives of firms in industry or agriculture, whose members may be more or less bound to the results. Also, the environmental effects of the firms operating in an industrial or agricultural sector can often be monitored relatively well, within existing environmental legislation. In such circumstances, the social instruments take the form of voluntary non-contractual agreements, the so-called *covenants*, in which government agencies and representatives of corporate actors undertake to examine a specific part of an environmental problem area, taking the share of the target group concerned as starting point.

The purpose of covenants is to internalize the environmental management of corporate actors through mechanisms of trust. For example, firms engaged in production of plastic food wrapping may undertake to introduce new

---

[15] See NMP2, 1993: 11.

technologies for making the wrappings biodegradeable, or develop new marketing concepts for changing the appearance of consumer good packaging, each of which could be expected to reduce a given amount of waste within a stated time interval. Such voluntary undertakings could be made in conjunction with transaction instruments, such as an earmarked research subsidy, or, characteristic for the self-regulating approach, in return for government assurance that the industry will not become subject to legal regulation on sufficient evidence of progress in performance. If the tasks and responsibilities discussed within a covenant can be clearly defined and kept track of in orderly ways, then this kind of gentlemen's agreement can succeed in mobilizing information at ground level. It provides a platform for discovering what kind of informal controls on the industry's process of production give environmentally sound results and contribute to profitability, without the need for administrative regulation or the imposition of regulatory taxation. Thus, social instruments of 'persuasion by negotiation' may be able to achieve a high performance on the three criteria adopted by the Council's report on instrumentation: effectiveness in meeting targets, reduction of regulatory cost, and an increase in the social legitimacy of government intervention.[16]

The category of citizens has recently been included in the planning concept in a rather special way. On one hand, the third national plan explains that citizens figure as one of the three most important 'actors in environmental policy', together with government agencies and target groups, because they are thought to fulfil a crucial role in the social and cultural innovations which long-term environmental policy requires. This clearly reflects the cooperative planning concept discussed above. On the other hand, citizens are considered to form part of the large target group of consumers, which is subdivided in various areas of economic activity.[17] Consumers buy household products, use energy in the home, drive cars or ride bicycles, go on holiday, and so on. As consumers, the citizens appear as sources of the environmental problems identified by various quantitative planning objectives, as we have explained earlier. In this context, it is noted that citizens' behaviour is hard to control through their respective affiliations, and that they form widely dispersed units of pollution, the effects of which are very difficult to monitor at source. This is because compared to corporate actors, citizens possess wide freedom of action protected by their civil rights. For all these reasons, different groups of consumers are regarded as target groups, which are especially 'difficult to approach' by governmental policy measures. And in turn, this explains why the consumers have been elevated to the special status of a major 'actor in environmental policy', in their public role as citizens. This last point distinguishes the social instruments directed to consumers from those designed for corporate actors. While the

[16] See WRR, 1992: section 2.4.   [17] See NMP3, 1998: 87.

latter operate on 'persuasion by negotiation', the former employ 'persuasion by communication'.[18]

The 'communicative' social instruments for consumers include general information campaigns, agreements with the Ministry of Education to introduce environmental themes in primary and secondary curricula and in vocational training, and advertisements in the media under the direct responsibility of the Ministry of the Environment. Following the strategy of internalization, these general communications are meant to project a 'shared image on the state of the environment, causes, effects and new developments', which are held to be essential for establishing an awareness of the ubiquity of environmental aspects in daily decisions. They are to be backed up by specific information directed to show that – and especially how – it is possible to take account of the environment in the choices of ordinary life, in such a way that the general awareness can be translated into less polluting or wasteful patterns of behaviour.[19] Increasingly also, marketing techniques are used to focus on environmentally friendly lifestyles, especially directed at the young.[20]

However, the role of governmental agencies in policies of self-regulation is by no means limited to playing a part in civil society, as a participant on an equal footing with the target groups.[21] Some social instruments also involve legal constraints on corporate actors, for example in prescribing procedures for environmental impact assessment within the firm, or more stringently, by duties under private law to publicize adverse consequences of productive activities on the environment. The purpose of these so-called 'structurating instruments' is to organize the availability of relevant information and to ensure that it gets fed back periodically to all affected parties, in order to increase both social learning and mutual social control. According to the Council, the private law aspect of social instrumentation would be especially conducive for preventing the shirking of environmental responsibility: 'such a feedback not only offers a view on what "others" are in fact doing – important for counteracting the social dilemma – it also exposes actors to mechanisms of social control that could be more drastic than legal sanctions attached to direct regulation might be' (WRR, 1992: 96). In this same category, product certification is an important structurating instrument directed at the consumers. In a policy document devoted to this theme, the government announced that product certification should include provisions for designers, producers, and retailers, in order to reflect an 'integral chain approach, which is to say that account is taken of all environmental aspects of a product, in each phase of its lifecycle ("from cradle to – and including – the grave")'.[22] The information systems required by this

---

[18] Distinguishing between those target groups that are easy to approach and those that are not has become a key test for separating the category of social instruments into types corresponding to these principles. See, for example, VROM, 1993.
[19] See WRR, 1992: 95.   [20] See NMP3, 1998: 384–9.   [21] See figure 3.1, WRR, 1992: 48.
[22] See 'Nota Product en Milieu', 1993: 5.

rather ambitious goal are to be achieved by means of 'self-regulation within legal constraints'. Another more modest example of a structurating instrument is a set of special provisions for household energy accounting tied to a 'responsible consumption level', which is offered together with the monthly bill for gas, water, and electricity by provincial public utilities.

Finally, self-regulation policy recognizes a third type, the 'facilitating' social instruments. These are measures aimed at supporting policies of persuasion with physical provisions which make it easier to recognize and follow cooperative courses of action, while at the same time making it abundantly clear that such provisions are publicly being set up in order to motivate people to actually deliver the desired behaviour. In chapter 1, we have already noted the successful examples of facilitation in the municipal recycling provisions for separating various kinds of household waste, including local provisions for collecting toxic waste. A much less successful case of physical facilitation has been the creation of earmarked stretches of highway at peak periods, for privileged use of car-pooling arrangements. These were introduced in 1993, but abolished soon afterwards, when it turned out that they were hardly being used.

To make it even more complicated, the idea that government should engage in facilitating self-regulation has recently been employed in the following and quite different sense. The notion of 'facilitation' here indicates the government's aim to reduce top-down social regulation, in favour of a more diffuse pattern of intervention. In NMP3, for example, it is noted that environmental policy in the Netherlands 'has moved along from the design phase to the implementation phase'. Thus the Ministry of the Environment feels it must increasingly assume the role of social facilitator, by setting up procedures to ensure that social instruments are developed by other ministries (as in the case of education), local government (as in the case of urban planning), and last but not least, organizations of civil society, such as the Society of Nature Monuments, the Consumers Union, and local action groups of various kinds.[23] In the Scientific Council's report in preparation of NMP2, this *indirect* use of communicative instruments by 'environmentally active third parties' had already been strongly recommended as a way of spreading governmental responsibility for environmental persuasion in a broader circle of self-regulation. As this influential report explicitly notes: 'Here the government itself is not acting as a moral agent; it rather facilitates others to act in this role.'[24] An additional reason for following the indirect approach is that the scope for direct persuasion of citizens by government agencies may be limited by considerations of market competition. In our survey case of Holiday Destination, for example, the government has been far more inclined to subsidize so-called National Sustainability Debates, which include the theme of polluting recreational air travel, than to come out officially in favour of spending

---

[23] See NMP3, 1998: 89.   [24] See WRR, 1992: 99.

the vacation at home, and thus risking claims of unfair competition by domestic tour operators.

Finally, an often mentioned theme is the role of social regulation in establishing a reinforcing interplay in the 'environmental policy mix'. For example, in social regulation of consumer markets, the structurating instruments of product certification may be supplemented by price subsidies on certified products, or – a 1999 innovation of fiscal greening – by offering selective tax relief on certified 'green investments'. In NMP3, the use of price signals in support of social self-regulation is announced as an important 'new element of policy'. Conversely, however, the Council already recognized in its 1992 report that success in applying the communicative instruments may have the effect of changing the sensitivity of people's response to financial stimuli. For example, if people can be persuaded of the environmental soundness of reducing trips by private car, as the 1993 campaign slogan 'The car can do without you once in a while' had it, then they might also become more responsive to regulatory taxation. In this microeconomic perspective, the communicative instruments are counted upon to change people's preferences concerning the train–car trade-off, and thus raise the demand effect of an increase in tax on gasoline, or a reduction in train fares.[25]

All this shows that the concept of self-regulation has become firmly embedded in Dutch policy thinking. But as the sobering example of car-pooling may remind one, the role of social instruments in inducing desired shifts in demand should not be overestimated. For their success strongly depends on 'physical facilitation' measures which may require the government to lay out large infrastructural projects, such as finely grained commuter networks. Obviously, such heavy provisions cannot be regarded as mere appendages of social regulation policies. We shall return to these points in chapter 13.

In sum, the social instruments are primarily means for organizing persuasion. They serve to raise the environmental awareness of citizens and corporate actors, and induce these actors to regard the task of reducing pollution within the objectives of the national plan as a collective enterprise. The social instruments also aim to reduce the administrative burden of legal regulation, by mobilizing information at ground level and supplanting mechanisms of command and contract by mechanisms of social control.

2.4 An environmental ethos and the social dilemma

As we have noted, the concept of self-regulation in the Dutch approach to environmental planning rests on an explicit notion of environmental responsibility. It indicates the belief of policymakers that the social dilemmas of pollution can

---

[25] See WRR, 1992, figure 2.1.

be counteracted, at least in part, through moral persuasion backed by reliable facts. As described above, this belief manifests itself in three ways. First of all, the premise of a capability for self-regulation among actors leads to a decentralized and cooperative mode of formulating the details of the national plans, in an ongoing process of consultation and negotiation. This premise shows that policymakers believe in the possibility of engaging the actors of civil society in a common framework of problem-solving. Secondly, within this framework, social instruments are not only deployed to promote a shared image of environmental degradation as an issue of the highest urgency, but also to foster a sense among the population that problems of pollution are amenable to solution only if they are addressed at source, by introducing behavioural changes in conducting the daily business of life. This message basically casts the environmental issue in the mould of a set of collective action problems at the local, national, and global scale levels.

Thirdly, the strategy of internalizing responsibility, which underlies the whole self-regulation approach in the succession of national plans after 1989, is based on an environmental ethos. The content of this ethos is closely tailored to the moral solution of the social dilemma. To show just how straightforwardly the ethos is worded, we cite the relevant section of the first environmental plan.

> Those who take decisions on raw materials, production processes, products and handling of waste – as producers or consumers – also decide on emissions of pollutants, and hence decide indirectly on possible negative effects on environmental quality. The notion that environmental quality is ultimately determined by the collective behaviour of producers and consumers is not yet present in everyone's mind. Too often at present, the management of the environment is seen as the province of the government or the environmental policy sector . . . The strategy of internalization is to let this responsibility count in the different decisions. Public awareness about the consequences of behaviour for the environment has now grown to the point that everyone may be taken to know his responsibility regarding the environment, and may be expected to act accordingly . . . It is no longer merely a question of the responsibility that individual persons must bear relative to each other. The distance between sources and effects has become so large – both in space and time – that what is at issue now is the responsibility of individuals as members of one society for societies elsewhere in the world, and the responsibility as members of one generation for future generations. Individuals will have to give substance to this responsibility by doing everything reasonably within their capacities to prevent environmental degradation as the direct or indirect result of their activities. (NMP1, 1989: 86–87)

As we shall have occasion to explain in chapter 10, the ethos behind the strategy of internalization is a two-stage affair. It focuses first on providing reasons for convincing responsible citizens of the *positive value* that should be attached to environmental qualities such as clean soil, water and air, biodiversity, and a stable climate. Such qualities may be held to be important for intrinsic or instrumental reasons. But in keeping with the conception of sustainable growth, the environmental ethos predominantly stresses an instrumental outlook. As the passages above clearly show, the grounds for assuming responsibility are related to the well-being of present and future generations.

Secondly, and on these grounds, the ethos explicitly calls for responsibility in *individual action*. The government wishes citizens to take voluntary action within their own domains of personal choice, by adopting more environmentally friendly patterns of consumption instead of waiting for the 'environmental policy sector' to impose taxes or legal restrictions. This kind of appeal was aptly expressed by the slogan of the nationwide campaign undertaken between 1990 and 1993: *A better environment starts at your own doorstep.*

In short, the environmental ethos underlying the strategy of internalization strives to instil the following kind of maxim in citizens: 'The environment is valuable, therefore I ought to contribute to it in person.' It is important to note that this is a maxim of cooperative action in large-scale collective action problems. And indeed, a major purpose of the official campaign was to counteract the 'influence of the so-called "social dilemma", a situation in which the individual interest of interdependent people can run counter to their collective interest.'[26] It will be of major importance to find out to what extent Dutch citizens have been responsive to the injunctions of the environmental ethos. Our research design has been developed with that question in mind. After having laid out that design in part II, we shall return to the question in part III.

2.5 Self-regulation: compliance-oriented or virtue-based?

To conclude this chapter, we situate the self-regulation approach within normative political theory. In particular, we want to comment on the 'moral reform' aspect of environmental planning in the Netherlands. This issue has been discussed by Albert Weale, as mentioned in section 2.2. In *The New Politics of Pollution*, Weale devotes a chapter to the national environmental policy plans, called 'Turning Government Green'. There he stresses the novelty of the strategy of internalization as an integral part of the Dutch approach. Weale thinks that the incorporation of this strategy in the national environmental plans shows the wider significance of these plans for other industrialized countries: 'Not the least interesting feature of the NMP is its attempt to show how contemporary environmental policy calls for a virtue-based conception of citizenship rather than a conception which secures only a moral neutrality of the state in the face of competing ends of its citizens' (Weale, 1992: 151).

Though we do not entirely agree with this characterization, it certainly merits a closer discussion. Weale's thesis raises two related issues which can be

---

[26] See Veldkamp, 1994: 2.

treated separately: the issue of state neutrality and the issue of citizen virtues. With regard to the first of these issues, we think that the morality informing environmental policy in the Netherlands is largely compatible with the modern liberal doctrine of state neutrality. According to that doctrine, state action should maintain a neutral stance with respect to the worth of different ideas of the good life ('neutrality of aim'). It should therefore not engage in policies that can only be justified by reference to some perfectionist value ranking of ideas of the good life ('justificatory neutrality').

Now the question is whether the official motivation of environmental self-regulation policies satisfies these conditions. We believe it does. Our main evidence for this is that the value of preserving the integrity of environmental goods (prevention of pollution, biodiversity and the like) has been officially spelled out in the sustainable growth framework of the Brundtland Report. As we mentioned in the last section, the common good-character of environmental objectives is predominantly explained by their instrumental importance for improving the options for achieving well-being of present, and in particular, future generations. This stance seems to be perfectly in line with a neutral, i.e. non-perfectionist view, since it does not go beyond claiming that the environmental qualities identified in the plans are more than all-purpose means for achieving human well-being. For example, it is not being said (but neither is it denied) that an environmental good such as biodiversity has an intrinsic value, which would have to be preserved independently of its conduciveness to the pursuit of individuals' ideas of a good life. To show this resolute emphasis on the all-purpose character of the environment, we cite the official line on environmental management for which the Dutch government claims political responsibility. In NMP2, it is restated as follows:

> The principal goal of environmental management, as laid down in NMP1, is the preservation of the environment's carrying capacity in the service of a sustainable development. The carrying capacity of the environment will be degraded, if the adverse environmental effects can not be undone within one generation. Examples of such effects are serious obstacles to, and deterioration of, well-being: illness and death of human beings, extinction of plants and animals, the eradication of ecosystems, degradation of water supplies, soil fertility or the cultural heritage, and the impediment of spatial and economic development. Sustainable growth provides for the needs of the present generation, without thereby endangering the possibilities of future generations to satisfy their needs as well.   (NMP2, 1993: 28)

From this account, it seems to be clear that the government is not involved in a perfectionist ranking judgement regarding the comparative value of the competing ends of its citizens. It is simply appealing to their willingness to subordinate the pursuit of those ends, whatever they may be, to a set of environmental constraints which form a collective infrastructure for promoting aggregate human well-being over time. And it does so by explicit reference to considerations of intergenerational equity. In so far as a typically liberal conception of state neutrality forbids the justification of laws and policies by reference to a perfectionist hierarchy of human good, environmental policy in the Netherlands is certainly compatible with that conception, at least when judged from the standpoint of the official policy goals. We cannot therefore agree with Weale's suggestion on this point. Yet at the level of policy itself, the Dutch strategy of internalization is definitely at odds with another feature which is commonly associated with the complex notion of liberal state neutrality, to wit, a reticence on the part of government actively to influence the choices that citizens make within their free domains of action. As Weale points out:

> When the state affirms the importance of individual responsibility for the protection of the environment, it can be argued that it is doing more than simply seeking efficient and effective means to previously chosen ends; it is instead choosing ends, by selecting a particular interpretation of the network of rights and obligations that bind the state and the citizen in an identifiable political unit.   (Weale, 1992: 150)

We partly agree with Weale's view on this side of the neutrality issue. It is true that the ethos of internalizing environmental value, from which the appeal to individual responsibility for protecting the environment is derived, interprets the link between state policy and the citizens' private behaviour in a particular way. In the last section it was seen that the ethos morally enjoins the actors of civil society, both corporate actors and individual citizens, to regard a large variety of urgent environmental issues as ones which should be dealt with in frameworks of voluntary collective action. And as we also showed, the ethos does indeed intend to draw the actors of civil society together in an informal 'network of obligation', for it establishes an individual responsibility to cooperate in such frameworks, even though the actor's legal rights to defect in an environmental dilemma are left untouched.

Nevertheless, we hold that the reasons why the government thinks it proper to call for voluntary adaptation of individual behaviour do not amount to the formulation of 'new ends', as Weale suggests. Perhaps the ethos of internalization is best understood for what it officially claims to be: a policy strategy devoted to implicate the citizens in a web of responsibility for democratically agreed-on environmental goals, which government clearly cannot achieve on its own, if it is limited to using traditional methods of regulation under public and private law. As such, the policy conception of self-regulation is subsumable under a neutral type of state intervention, despite its avowed aim of changing the ways in which individuals behave in their private domains.

This brings us to the second issue raised by Weale's interesting comment: that of citizen virtues. According to Weale, the Dutch plans attempt 'to show how contemporary environmental policy calls for a virtue-based conception of citizenship', and more in particular, that such policy must have as its object not simply 'a good environment, but good citizens in relation to that environment.'[27] Again, there is something to be said for this last view, but only, so we would claim, as far as one takes it to be that the doctrine of self-regulation aims to create good citizens, *because* this is held to be a necessary condition for achieving a good environment. On our reading of the environmental plans, the doctrine of self-regulation is certainly not driven by the wish to create good citizens independently of a calculated assessment on the part of the policymakers, namely that the sheer size and the urgency of environmental problems simply make it impossible for the government to go it alone.

It certainly looks as if the doctrine of self-regulation invokes the ancient republican perspective of the virtuous citizen in the context of the environmental problem. But it should be clear from our description of target groups and planning objectives in section 2.2, that the policymakers are hoping to resuscitate the virtuous citizen for the purpose of persuading ordinary producers and consumers to satisfy their assigned targets, at the ground level of everyday economic behaviour. We conclude that the emphasis on the role of the citizen in the doctrine of self-regulation is compliance-oriented, rather than virtue-based. Citizen virtues are seen to be necessary for achieving policy goals which are recognized as being pitched infeasibly high otherwise.

It is worth repeating that the qualitative goals, and the quantitative objectives derived from these in the first environmental plan, were regarded as exceptionally stringent, following the dramatic official forecasts that were published shortly before the first environmental plan was approved. And as Weale also noted himself, the planners at the Ministry of the Environment recognized that without the cooperation of other government departments, of corporate economic interests, and without the participation of responsible citizens, these goals would not stand a realistic chance of being attained. More than a decade later, despite partial failures to meet the stringent targets in the meantime, it is also apparent that the high ambition level of environmental policy is still being maintained. This persistence of high ambitions in setting environmental policy objectives probably means that policymakers will continue to stress the active compliance of citizens in environmental policy.[28]

To summarize what we have argued so far, Weale has correctly noted the prominent aspect of moral reform in Dutch environmental planning. In our view, the attempt at moral reform is historically contingent. It is driven by a perceived urgency of society-wide changes to counter environmental degradation, which

---

[27] See Weale, 1992: 150.

[28] In its 1999 report to Parliament, the Ministry of the Environment announces that the government aims to reinforce the role of the citizen in environmental policy in the period 2000–3, and will include a section on sustainable consumption in the next national plan (NMP4) (*Milieuprogramma 2000–2003*, 1999: 38–41).

entered into politics some twelve years ago, and has shaped environmental policy ever since.

The content of the reform itself, that is to say, the moral principles from which successive governments have sought to obtain political support for the policy plans, is best described as a liberally neutral programme of incorporating environmental constraints on personal behaviour in a sustainable society. Finally, the central message of the self-regulation doctrine is that both the state and civil society are bound together in finding ways of raising the standard of life by acting within those constraints, over the next generation. The doctrine does not exemplify an autonomous desire on the part of the government to make citizens more virtuous in relation to the environment. Rather it seeks to harness environmental virtue, so as to obtain the desired degree of compliance. As we have shown, the premise of self-regulation is that actors of civil society who properly understand the urgency of the environmental issue are held to be capable of such virtue. On that premise, the state claims that it is entitled not only to expect passive compliance with its laws and formal regulations; it also asks each actor to comply actively, by behaving in accordance with an ethos of environmental responsibility that extends into personal life.[29]

[29] Within modern political theory, there is an interesting parallel with G. A. Cohen's egalitarian interpretation of Rawls's well-known liberal theory of justice. If the citizens of a well-ordered society are truly committed to the difference principle, then one may expect from them not only a commitment to respect the tax-benefit laws of the basic structure that serve to maximize the position of the least-advantaged. To some reasonable (but uncertainly defined) extent, the better-advantaged are under a moral obligation to live up to the spirit of the difference principle, by acting in favour of the least-advantaged within their free domains of action. For example, a brain surgeon could contribute to the position of the poor, by resisting the temptation to maximize the wage benefits of his or her scarce talent. This could be done by accepting a lower salary in a public hospital, and working as hard there as he or she would otherwise work in a private clinic at a much higher rate of pay. Thus, in Cohen's view, the 'site of distributive justice' is larger than the set of structural constraints on society's instititions needed for approximating fair shares. The domain of justice also extends to one's personal life, in the sense that it should count as more just to use one's equal liberty and economic opportunity in ways that contribute towards a fuller realization of what the difference principle wants to achieve, than it would be to use these rules of the game for maximizing private gain. This runs counter to Rawls's own view, on which upholding the difference principle only requires the observance of just laws, and compliance with just policies, but does not require making the kind of personal sacrifice exemplified by the brain surgeon case (Cohen, 1997). There is an interesting analogy between Cohen's demanding view on the scope of distributive justice and the view informing self-regulation policy, according to which preserving the integrity of the environment requires more than merely the loyal support of the right kind of regulations, taxes on polluting activity, or fair quota of permissions to pollute.

3

The actor's perspective on collective action

3.1 The subjectivity of the actor in rational choice theory

The Dutch policies of self-regulation discussed in the last chapter have been generally well received by the public, and we shall report our own findings on their acceptance in chapter 9. However, the question we wish to consider now is whether such policies can be expected to work at all, given what social science can tell us about rational behaviour in large groups. For this, we turn to theories of collective action.[1]

The prevention of environmental degradation is a classical example of a public or collective good. If everyone makes a contribution, pollution will decrease considerably. A cleaner environment is a collective good from which everyone benefits. The problem arises from the fact that these benefits are free, i.e., anyone can enjoy the benefits of a cleaner environment whether or not he or she has made a contribution. According to Mancur Olson, environmental behaviour is vulnerable to the logic of free-ridership. Olson's thesis on collective action has achieved the status of a scientific law in the community of environmental researchers. This 'law' states that rational individuals seek to maximize their personal welfare, and will not voluntarily contribute to advance their common good, when they are members of a large group. Olson's logic implies that the answer to the question 'can the policy of self-regulation really work?' must be: the policy of self-regulation will never work, because no one will make a contribution. In reality the policy of self-regulation seems to work very well in many specific cases, but in some cases it does not.

In this study, we want to show that rational individuals are not necessarily prevented from acting voluntarily to achieve environmental collective goods.

---

[1] See also section 1.2.

We do not disagree that very often large-scale environmental problems are problems of collective action of the kind to which Olson's thesis applies. Nor do we deny the usefulness of his approach. On the contrary, we will model several environmental cases as situations in which citizens face potential problems of collective action. Speaking formally, we call these problems Potential Contributor's Dilemmas, as will be explained below. More informally, as the title of this book has it, we discuss 'environmental dilemmas'. Our disagreement with Olson resides in the potential nature of these situations. For we dispute the theoretical assumptions underlying his conception of the actor's 'personal welfare' in these dilemmas. Briefly, our reasoning is as follows. If an individual firm or individual country is regarded as the 'actor' in a collective action setting, then most of Olson's conclusions would probably be right. A potential dilemma will turn into an actual one, and collective goods will not be realized short of coercion, because the interactions of firms in a market mechanism, or taking the realist approach, national governments in a system of international relations, lend survival advantage to narrow conceptions of self-interest. But if the actor is an individual, and in particular an individual in the role of consumer or citizen, then this conception of 'personal welfare' is less obvious.

The distinction between the firm and the individual as single actors corresponds with the standard microeconomic view of producers and consumers. The rational behaviour of firms is based upon the objective economic criteria of effectiveness and efficiency. If the firm's decisions do not satisfy these criteria, then it will soon be out of business. This means that the government must assume, at least prima facie, that firms will not voluntarily promote common goals of decreasing environmental pollution. The rational behaviour of consumers, on the other hand, is based upon subjective utility, which is maximized on the basis of given preferences. These preferences, however, need not be governed by the same criteria of effectiveness and effciency. If a person decides to spend most of his or her money on donations to Greenpeace or the World Wildlife Fund, because this is what best satisfies his or her preferences, then there is no ground to disqualify either the behaviour or the preferences as irrational. Of course the assumption of subjectivity does not imply that people are likely to give most of their money away to good causes. What it does suggest, however, is that the rational behaviour of individuals is more complicated than Olson's theory would suggest, in social settings that do not punish deviations from narrow self-interest.

Our empirical application of rational choice theory in environmental dilemmas starts out from the assumption of subjectivity, by measuring individual preferences. Proceeding from survey data, many people's responses to concrete environmental collective action problems will be seen to generate transitive preference orderings, motives and strategic intentions of choice, all of which can be analysed in terms of rational choice theory. Our approach allows that rational individuals either act as free-riders, or are willing to make voluntary contributions to environmental collective goods. They may want to contribute either conditionally, with an eye to the reciprocal behaviour of others, or unconditionally, in response to an ethos of environmental care or responsibility. Also, and quite importantly, we allow for the possibility that while individuals may regard environmental qualities as common goods, they may reject the notion that anyone should be under a duty to bear the cost it takes to produce these goods. As we shall explain below, our survey data reveal a rich diversity of subjective responses to environmental dilemmas, which can be captured in simple game-theoretic terms. In the next sections, we first discuss Olson's theory of collective action in some detail. As we said above, that theory is accepted as canonical, and thus it is of importance to explain just why we think it should be replaced by the subjective approach outlined above.

3.2 Problems of collective action

Standardly, the basic assumption of rational choice theory is that an individual actor aims to advance his self-interest. The question is whether a group of rational, self-interested individuals would cooperate to advance their common interest. If the interests of individuals are completely opposite, one can expect little or no cooperation between the individuals. If, on the other hand, the interests of individuals coincide and each individual achieves his maximum gain if the group or common interest would be realized, then one would expect mutual cooperation. Cooperation becomes less obvious if the group interest has the characteristics of a public good, i.e., if no individual can be excluded from the benefits of the group interest, whether or not he contributes to its achievement.

In his *The Logic of Collective Action* (first published in 1965) Olson shows that individuals in a large group will not make a voluntary contribution to a public good if they behave rationally. Rational individuals will act as free-riders, and they will not voluntarily act to further the common interest, whenever the benefits of the collective good are freely accessible to all. Problems of collective action can be solved by an authority that coerces individuals to bear the costs of realizing the group's objectives. As Olson argues, an alternative for coercion is to offer the individuals some separate incentives. Both solutions presuppose that the individuals are somehow organized into a group, instead of being just a number of isolated actors with the same objectives.

The idea that a group of rational, self-interested individuals will not cooperate to advance a common interest had, and still has, a great impact in rational choice literature. Its influence is not limited to the academic field. Environmental politics and policy are often shaped by the example of free-ridership that is captured by the expression 'not in my back yard' (NIMBY). The explanatory power of Olson's logic appears to be very disturbing, especially if one realizes how many real-life problems can be modelled as social dilemmas.

According to Olson, the situation where the self-interest of an individual actor coincides with the group interest is typified by firms in a competitive market. The individual interest and the group interest is being able to sell at a higher price. In a competitive market the price is uniform for all members of the large group of entrepreneurs. If the price can be made to rise above the competitive market price, then such a higher price constitutes a common good. A higher price is a common good because all firms will benefit from it, while no firm can be excluded.

To establish the higher price, however, total output of the industry must decline. To realize the common good, then, a sufficient number of individual firms should make a contribution by reducing their output. Rational entrepreneurs in a competitive market will never do that, simply because they cannot be excluded from selling at the uniform higher price, irrespective of whether they limit their firm's sales. Olson explains the implications of the economic theory of public goods for the social sciences. Public goods are defined by the properties of non-rivalness in consumption and non-excludability from consumption.[2]

If it is not possible to exclude consumers from consumption of a good, this good cannot be produced and sold in a market economy, or at least not in optimal quantities. In a perfectly competitive market it is not possible to realize an efficient use of resources in providing goods with the characteristics of non-rivalness and non-excludability. The market failure provides a rationale for the provision of these goods by the public sector. This acknowledgement of market failure is not based on ideological beliefs but on the economic principle of efficient allocation.

The notion that actors in a market cannot produce a public good, because it is not possible to exclude people from the good's benefit, is the basis of Olson's critique of the liberal theory of countervailing powers, as well as the Marxist theory of class struggle. Both of these theories assume that groups will act to further their common or group goals. The assumption 'that groups tend to act in support of their group interests is supposed to follow logically from this widely accepted premise of rational, self-interested behaviour'.[3] Olson shows that the premise of individual, rational, self-interested behaviour does not entail that groups will act in their self-interest.

Olson's distinction between the rational behaviour of a member of a small group and a member of a large group is based on the difference between the behaviour of a small number of profit-maximizing firms in an oligopolistic market, and a large number of such firms in a market of perfect competition. The firm's behaviour depends on the question of which of these two market structures the firm operates in. The output of a firm affects the price in a classical

---

[2] See Musgrave and Musgrave, 1984: 47–81.   [3] See Olson, 1971: 1.

oligopoly. In a market of perfect competition its output has no effect on the market price. This means that only in a situation of oligopoly can the firm choose between different actions to maximize its profits.[4]

The analysis of the rational behaviour of a firm in an oligopoly or a market of perfect competition clarifies the notion of group interest. In an oligopolistic market the small number of firms has as common interest the realization of a stable industry equilibrium with the monopoly price and monopoly outcome. They can jointly realize this common good by adjusting the firm's output. In a market of perfect competition, the large number of firms has the same common interest. However, in the absence of enforced output quota, they cannot realize this common interest, because adjusting the output of a single firm has no significant effect on market price, and a voluntary agreement to restrict output will not be viable. The common interest of firms is always the monopoly outcome, but it depends on the market structure whether reduction of output has any effect on the provision of the common good.

Rational behaviour thus depends on the effectiveness of the firm's behaviour. In a small group the firm can try to realize the common interest because its behaviour is effective. In a large group, the firm can never realize the common interest, because it is incapable of behaving effectively to influence price. Olson's logic of collective action is the logic of market behaviour of firms, and his distinction between small and large groups is based on the difference between an oligopoly and a market of perfect competition. For Olson, rational behaviour in general is thus defined by two criteria: effectiveness and efficiency: 'The only requirement is that the behavior of individuals in large groups or organizations of the kind considered should generally be rational, in the sense that their objectives, whether selfish or unselfish, should be pursued by means that are efficient and effective for achieving these objectives' (Olson, 1971: 64–5). Individual action in a small group can be effective. Effectiveness means that individual action is not insignificant or marginal. Action makes a difference to the realization of the common good. If someone's action is effective, then the next step is to see whether taking the action would be efficient or not. Only if the individual's gain exceeds the total cost of the collective good will his action be efficient, according to Olson.

Individual action in a large group will never be effective, because then the action has only a negligible effect on the outcome. If individual action is not

---

[4] If we assume a Cournot-like duopoly model, then the firm will change its quantity described by the reaction-curves. The outcome is a stable Cournot-Nash equilibrium, which is a Pareto-suboptimal outcome. If, on the other hand, we assume that the firm's behaviour is not based on the reaction-curve approach and firms recognize that their behaviour is interdependent, then they are capable of jointly maximizing profits, thereby establishing a Pareto-optimal outcome. The recognition of the beneficial effects of the change in the firm's output thus 'results in a stable industry equilibrium with the monopoly price and monopoly outcome' (Koutsoyiannis, 1985: 228).

effective, then the next step, to see whether or not it would be efficient, is simply irrelevant. In this way, Olson explains the motivations and intentions of any rational actor by the 'objective' criteria of effectiveness and efficiency. Olson's definition of rationality is useful for studying the behaviour of entrepreneurs. To stay in business an entrepreneur must pursue his self-interest. Entrepreneurial self-interest is an objective notion, and as long as the entrepreneur satisfies the neoclassical assumption of profit maximization, he behaves rationally.

Rational behaviour, for Olson, is defined by the criteria of effectiveness and efficiency. This means that for economic actors, such as entrepreneurs, we can tell what their self-interest is, without even asking them what they have to say about it themselves. Thus, if we are dealing with the economic choices of entrepreneurs, we can attribute specific goals and preferences to them, from a so-called observer's perspective. These goals and preferences are defined by analogy to profit maximization in market structures, as described in economics textbooks. The self-interest of the entrepreneur does not depend on the personal identity or the idiosyncratic values of a specific person. It is simply defined by what is in the best interest of the firm. However, Olson extends the specification of the goals and preferences of economic actors to cover individual rationality in general. It is thus being assumed that these goals and preferences can be ascribed to any rational person, even outside the domain of entrepreneurial choice. We shall describe this view on rationality as the 'perspective of the observer'. This perspective is the essence of the 'thick-theory of rationality' that specifies the goals and preferences an actor must have in order to qualify as rational.

Before commenting further on the validity of the observer's perspective, we shall first discuss Olson's view of rational behaviour, as it has been formalized by Russell Hardin in an n-person Prisoner's Dilemma game, in his *Collective Action* (1982). Hardin's formalization is a classic example of the thick-theory of rationality.[5] The criteria of effectiveness and efficiency are now interpreted as self-regarding motives that explain the preference ordering of the Prisoner's Dilemma game. Hardin remodels Olson's problem of collective action for a large group, in the terminology of a non-cooperative two-person game. Any individual member of the n-person group, can be picked as the row player, named Individual. The row player is assumed to play against the rest of the group, which consists of n − 1 persons. Together, these form the column player, named 'the Others'.[6] With these two players, each with two strategies, Cooperate or Defect, the game matrix of the n-person game is reduced to four cells. The pay-offs of the players are given by figure 3.1.

Before we present Hardin's calculation of the pay-offs of the players, it is important to clarify that the collective good in Hardin's game-theoretical

Column player: The Others

		Pay / Cooperate	Not pay / Defect
Row player: Individual	Pay / Cooperate	(1, 1) (C,C)	(−0.8, 0.2) (C,D)
	Not pay / Defect	(1.8, 0.8) (D,C)	(1, 1) (D,D)

Figure 3.1 Individual vs. The Others.

interpretation is defined only by the property of non-excludability from consumption. This means that the consumption of the group good is rival. Despite the rivalness in consumption, the good is still being regarded a (quasi) collective good. This does not contradict Olson's analysis of collective action, because his logic only requires the characteristic of non-excludability. The individual in a large group is faced with the choice whether or not to make a voluntary contribution to the realization of the collective good, which is assumed to require no initial start-up costs, only variable costs to be advanced by the players. The construction of the pay-offs in figure 3.1 follows Olson's view on rational behaviour. 'The payoff will be calculated by the prescription for rational behaviour: that is, the payoffs will be benefits less costs' (Hardin, 1982: 25). The calculation of the pay-offs is as follows. Suppose that all members of a group of ten people pay one dollar for the realization of the collective good, and the benefit to each member is worth two dollars. The advantage any individual i (Ai) will get from the collective good is the gain to the individual i (Vi = \$2) minus the costs (C = \$1). The pay-off for Individual is equal to the advantage of individual i (Ai = Vi − C = \$1), i.e., one unit in the upper left cell. The pay-off of the column player, the Others, is equal to the advantage per capita, likewise one unit. If Individual does not contribute but all other members do, then his pay-off in the lower left cell is 1.8 (Ai = Vi − C = 1.8 − 0) and the pay-off of the column player is 0.8 (1.8 − 1) per capita. In the upper right cell, Individual is the only one who makes a contribution and his pay-off is − 0.8 (0.2 − 1). The pay-off of the Others is 0.2 (0.2 − 0). Finally, in the lower right cell, no one contributes. Here the pay-offs of both players are zero. Each individual member of the group looks at the matrix of figure 3.1 from the perspective of the row player. Individual has a dominant strategy Defect: irrespective of what the column player does, Individual's pay-off is higher if he does not contribute to the common good. As Hardin points out, this conclusion corresponds with Olson's logic of collective action. 'The dynamic under which Individual performs is clearly the same as that for the Prisoner's Dilemma: the strategy of not paying dominates the strategy of paying' (Hardin, 1982: 26–7).

		Column player: The others	
		Pay / Cooperate	Not pay / Defect
Row player: Individual	Pay / Cooperate	(3, 3) (C,C)	(1, 4) (C,D)
	Not pay / Defect	(4, 1) (D,C)	(2, 2) (D,D)

Figure 3.2 The Prisoner's Dilemma game.

Inspection of the pay-offs of the column player suggests that 'the Others' also has a dominant strategy, namely to contribute to the common good. However, in the set-up of figure 3.1, the column player is not supposed to be a real player, acting as a collective. The pay-offs belonging to the two columns only indicate that the provision of the group good is beneficial for every single member of the group. However, each member of the group who is facing a problem of collective action is supposed to view the game from the vantage point of Individual, the row player. To underscore this, Hardin substitutes figure 3.1 with an other game matrix, figure 3.2, which is 'strategically equivalent' (Hardin, 1971: 474).

The term 'strategic equivalence' refers to the fact that the row player in both matrices has a dominant strategy Defect. The matrix in figure 3.2 illustrates the ordinal pay-offs of any two individuals randomly chosen from the large group, with the number 4 representing the highest, and the number 1 the lowest utility of a player. The two players do not constitute the group itself, because the logic of collective action for a small group is different from a large group. The purpose of this presentation of the n-person game is to show that the pay-offs of every individual in the group can be calculated the same way by the prescription for rational behaviour: benefits less costs. Figure 3.2 displays the preference ordering characteristic of the Prisoner's Dilemma.

For the row player, outcome (D,C) is preferred to (C,C), which is preferred to (D,D) and finally to (C,D). The preference of the column player is (C,D) above (C,C) above (D,D) above (D,C). Hardin's interpretation of Olson's logic of collective action is grounded on a number of assumptions that are important for our analysis. First, the assumption that every individual has the same pay-offs is based on the prescription for rationality 'benefits less costs'. This prescription is the *condition of efficiency as universal value*. Second, the assumption that the contribution of each member of a large group is marginal for the realization of the collective good, means that no one is significant for the provision of the group good. This assumption is the *condition of ineffectiveness* of individual behaviour.

The two conditions imply that all individuals in the group have the same preference ordering, and that all act the same way. These conditions allow Hardin to substitute the row player Individual with any other person that belongs to the Others. The possibility to substitute the row player by any of the n − 1 other persons is the *assumption of homogeneous actors*.

Hardin's modelling of Olson's theory of collective action in terms of the preference ordering of the Prisoner's Dilemma has been widely accepted. We do not deny the relevance of the Prisoner's Dilemma ordering for economic actors who are facing problems of collective action or common-pool resources. However, we argue that the observer's perspective is not a suitable one when dealing with ordinary citizens instead of profit-maximizing firms. The utility of citizens (or consumers) is not solely defined by benefits less costs. What defines utility for citizens or consumers is a subjective matter. This means that the goals and preferences of citizens cannot be specified only by the 'objective' criteria of effectiveness and efficiency.

3.3 Social dilemmas

Olson's observer's perspective on rational behaviour shows similarity with other theories, such as Garrett Hardin's 'tragedy of the commons'. His famous article in *Science* (1968) made the 'commons' a metaphor for all sorts of natural resources that are not privately owned property. The tragedy of the commons originates in the open pasture, where every shepherd in the neighbourhood could bring his sheep to graze. Hardin explains that rational herders will add more animals to the pasture than the optimal economic use of the commons allows. Tragedy lies in the fact that each rational herder will continue to add more animals, because the benefits collected from his own animals exceed the costs resulting from overgrazing. The relevance of the 'tragedy of the commons' is evident: the fish we eat, the water we drink, and the air we breathe, are all natural resources held in common. Hardin concludes that 'ruin is the destination toward which all men rush, each pursuing his own best interest in a society that believes in the freedom of the commons' (Hardin 1968: 1248).

The misuse of the commons becomes even more urgent and unmanageable when populations grow. The only solution to the tragedy of the commons then seems to consist in restricting the freedom of individuals. Recently, Garrett Hardin focused on the problem of overpopulation, in *Living Within Limits* (1993). The metaphor of the commons is now replaced by the concept of 'spaceship ecology'. However, the tenor of this more fashionable metaphor remains the same. For Hardin again proposes an authoritarian freedom-restricting regime to make life liveable for the present and the next generations. That regime is necessitated by the inevitable tendency of rational and procreatively free agents to continue breeding and consuming resources beyond the limits of the spaceship.

The implication of both models is troublesome. Olson argues that no common good will be realized in large groups without special incentives, and Hardin claims that existing common goods, the natural resources held in common, will be misused. Applied to environmental issues, these models lead to one conclusion: individual rational behaviour inevitably leads to environmental degradation.

In the mainstream rational choice literature the three models, Olson's logic of collective action, Hardin's tragedy of the commons, and the Prisoner's Dilemma game, as interpreted by Russell Hardin, have been amalgamated into one model, the so-called 'social dilemma'. It relays the solid conviction of the observer's perspective that large numbers of rational, self-interested individuals who are facing a social dilemma will never voluntarily cooperate to further their common interest. Invariably, in a social dilemma, individual rationality contradicts collective optimality.

Several solutions have been advanced in the literature to help achieve the Pareto-optimal outcome of mutual cooperation. These solutions can all be put into one of the following categories. The first category is the enforcement of mutual cooperation by a central authority. Since rational actors will not cooperate voluntarily, they must be forced to do so. Coercion is deemed necessary to protect us from ourselves. The second solution hopes to guarantee mutual cooperation by fostering the development of a cooperative disposition. To the extent that rational actors develop a Kantian morality, a strong commitment to others, or to social norms, they can and will cooperate with each other.[7] The third solution is built on the notion that self-interested choices in iterated social dilemmas might generate cooperative behaviour. In contrast with the one-shot game, in an iterated game the rational actor can voluntarily choose a conditionally cooperative strategy, such as Tit For Tat or the Grim-strategy.[8] The fourth solution stresses the voluntary management of natural resources by forming new institutions that are conducive to trust and reciprocity. These institutions are a form of (self-)organization by communities of citizens which help to avoid the adverse outcome of independent non-cooperative behaviour.[9]

None of these four types of solutions can provide a watertight guarantee that real-life social dilemmas will disappear. First, in a democratic society the power of the government to enforce the common good is limited. Some form and degree of regulation and enforcement by the state are accepted as necessary. However, many social dilemmas remain, on which there is no political consensus that can

---

[7] See, for example, Frank, 1988; Sen, 1974; Ullmann-Margalit, 1977; and Elster, 1989.
[8] See Axelrod, 1984; Taylor, 1976; and Taylor, 1987.
[9] See Taylor, 1982; Ostrom, 1990; Ostrom, Gardner and Walker, 1994.

justify forcing citizens into cooperative behaviour. The first solution is thus not a generally acceptable option in democratic societies.

Second, as to the acquisition of norms, most societies educate individuals towards cooperative dispositions in some way or another. A modern pluralist society does not, however, inculcate cooperative attitudes in all domains where social dilemmas can occur. And even if everyone has a cooperative disposition, not every individual will always choose to make a contribution to all the different collective goods that count. The second solution is therefore hardly adequate in general, even though, as we shall see in part III, it can certainly be made to go some way.

Third, cooperative behaviour based on iterated choice in problems of collective action cannot be guaranteed for a large group of actors in an n-person game. Without common knowledge of each other's behaviour, actors may still prefer unilateral defection to mutual cooperation. For a large society, again, the third solution does not guarantee cooperation.

Fourth, voluntary practices of reciprocity in forming new institutions of self-governance seem to solve the problem of collective action in some special cases. Nonetheless, these institutional arrangements often cannot be implemented, because the necessary conditions are not always satisfied, nor likely to emerge. So, the fourth answer does not give us the solution for real-life social dilemmas either.

This means that for a large, modern, pluralist democracy there is no guaranteed successful solution to the problems social dilemmas pose. Before we accept the pragmatic idea that environmental politics is some form of trial and error application of any one, or of some combination of the four solutions, we return to the underlying concepts of the models that compose the social dilemma.

All four solutions proceed from the assumptions that all problems of collective action can be modelled as in figure 3.2 and that each individual who is facing a social dilemma has a Prisoner's Dilemma ordering. This conclusion is based on two assumptions. First, each individual of the n-person group can perform the role of row player. In other words, the row player is some sort of representative agent. Second, the great variety of problems of collective action is treated as equivalent. The cost-benefit analysis may vary between the different problems of collective action, but the ranking of the four possible outcomes by rational individuals will – according to Hardin – always constitute a Prisoner's Dilemma preference ordering (PD-ordering). The combination of homogeneous actors and equivalent problems of collective action makes it possible to model all social dilemmas as an n-person Prisoner's Dilemma game. This is the crux of the thick-theory of rationality, and the associated observer's perspective. The differences that exist between real people do not matter because each person can be modelled as the row player. Also the differences between various problems of collective action do not matter because each problem is formalized as an n-person Social Dilemma.

The thick-theory of rationality, then, specifies the preferences of rational actors for a wide range of social contexts. This rationality is open to criticism from a formal point of view. The axioms of rational behaviour in game theory do not prescribe what sort of values and preferences an individual should have. Rationality is only defined by maximization of some sort and by the transitivity of the preference ordering. The content of the actor's preferences as such is not part of the formal definition of rationality. According to Kenneth Arrow, rationality only means that an actor formulates a transitive preference ordering. Arrow does not specify any particular preference or goal, nor does he assume that an actor must be motivated by the criteria of effectiveness and efficiency.

> It is assumed that each individual in the community has a definite ordering of all conceivable social states, in terms of their desirability to him. It is not assumed here that an individual's attitude toward different social states is determined exclusively by the community bundles which accrue to his lot under each. It is simply assumed that the individual orders all social states by whatever standards he deems relevant.
> (Arrow, 1963: 17)

Based on Arrow's axioms of rationality, William Riker defines the conditions of the so-called thin-theory of the rational choice model.

> The rational choice model consists of the following elements:
> 1. Actors are able to order their alternative goals, values, tastes, and strategies. This means that the relation of the preference and indifference among the alternatives is transitive so that, for a set of alternatives, A:$\{a_1, a_2, \ldots, a_m\}$, if a_i is preferred or indifferent to a_j and a_j is preferred or indifferent to a_k, then a_i is preferred or indifferent to a_k.
> 2. Actors choose from available alternatives so as to maximize their satisfaction.
> (Riker, 1990: 172).

For our study, the thin-theory of rationality is more fruitful than the thick-theory. Not every individual who is facing a real-life problem of collective action need be motivated by the kind of self-regarding motives that belong to economic actors. So when ordinary citizens are confronted with problems of environmental pollution that take the form of social dilemmas, there are no compelling reasons to assume that they should only be motivated by self-regarding motives.

For example, an ordinary citizen who is in possession of chemical household waste may consider what he will do with it. He can bring the chemical waste to a community recycling point, so that the chemical waste will not pollute the environment. Or alternatively, he can throw the chemical waste away with the rest of the household rubbish. The thick-theory of rationality has the following argument. The chemical household waste of each individual actor has only marginal effect on the environment. This means that throwing away the chemical waste with the rest of the household garbage has no discernible effect on pollution. Likewise, bringing the chemical waste to the recycling point has no discernible effect on restoring a clean environment. Because the action of one single individual is not effective, the rational action must be to throw away the chemical waste with the rest of the household rubbish.

Now the thin-theory of rationality does not disregard the possibility that individuals think in these terms, but from its perspective it is also possible that individuals follow a different line of reasoning. A citizen can be motivated by his love for a clean environment, or his concern for the future of his children. Many kinds of consideration may motivate the citizen to bring his chemical waste to the recycling point. If we accept Arrow's notion that every citizen has individual values, and that he can order all social states by whatever standards he deems relevant, then we also accept that the rationality of action is no longer defined by the criteria of effectiveness and efficiency. Our study supports the idea that a rational choice explanation has to incorporate the diversity and plurality of people and their motives.

3.4 The actor's perspective

Rational choice explanation based on the thick-theory necessarily disregards the diversity and plurality of people and their motives. In *Pathologies of Rational Choice Theory* (1994) Green and Shapiro claim that the pathologies of the approach are explained by the fact that 'much of the rational choice literature rests on unambiguously thick-rational assumptions'.[10] They argue that a lot would be gained by accepting the thin-theory. However, they also think that even though the rational choice literature that is based on thin-rationality does not suffer from the same pathologies, its usefulness for political science is limited, because scholars seldom use the thin-theory in empirical applications. For even though the thin-theory of rationality avoids questionable assumptions about human preferences and beliefs, according to Green and Shapiro it has a drawback: 'It will become plain, however, that what is gained by avoiding controversial assumptions about human nature can come at some considerable costs from the standpoint of measurement and empirical testing of rational choice hypotheses' (Green and Shapiro, 1994: 18). This drawback cannot be denied. Any empirical application of a theory that leaves open a wide range of behavioural grounds will involve considerable costs, compared to a theory that restricts the grounds of behaviour in advance. Yet rational choice scholars cannot simply ignore the 'hard-hitting critique' of Green and Shapiro.[11] The best way to counter their diagnosis of the pathologies of rational choice theory is to demonstrate the sanity of the approach, even if that involves a

---

[10] See Green and Shapiro, 1994: 19.
[11] See the discussion of rational choice theory in Friedman, 1995.

lot of hard work. We shall engage in some of this work by adopting the stance of the *actor's perspective*.[12] The actor's perspective requires one to accept Arrow's notion of individual values and Riker's corresponding notion of a thin-theory of rational choice. The actor's perspective is an empirical approach, which holds that the preferences of rational actors (in the minimal sense defined by Arrow and Riker) in social dilemmas are in principle diverse, because they may be expected to reflect the diverse individual values that actors bring to bear on the decision situations they face. And as we have argued above, when one is dealing with social dilemmas involving citizens and consumers, there are good reasons for adopting the thin-theory, hence for assuming a diversity of individual values as the default.

Thus in the survey of part II, we need to measure the preference orderings of respondents who face a Potential Contributor's Dilemma, in order to see whether these respondents qualify as rational. We must then present empirical tests of rational choice hypotheses. Moreover, we must attempt to explain the subjectivity of the actor's preference ordering by reference to the actor's underlying motives, on which we need to gather information independently of the preferences that we observe. In this way, we shall provide an empirical account of the reasons why individuals with diverse individual values have different preference orderings.

The difference between the thick- and the thin-theory can be explained by the problem of collective action depicted in figure 3.3. Individual, the row player, faces four different alternatives P, Q, R, and S. The letter P stands for the free-rider outcome for the row player; Q is the mutual cooperation outcome; R represents the mutual defection outcome; and finally, S is the sucker outcome for the row player. From the actor's perspective, Individual is no longer assumed to be motivated only by benefits less costs. In other words, efficiency is no longer assumed to be a universal value for every individual.[13]

Each player has individual values that underlie his personal preference ordering of the different social states represented by the four outcomes. If Individual prefers outcome S to outcome P, then we accept that he can have perfectly good reasons for this preference. Arrow's assumption that each individual can order the four alternatives or social states by *whatever standards he deems relevant* implies that every member of the group can formulate twenty-four possible strong orderings.

This means that the outcome matrix in figure 3.3, with the four social states P, Q, R and S, represents twenty-four different preference orderings or pay-off matrixes for each row player. The acceptance of individual values opens the possibility that an individual no longer thinks in terms of the effectiveness of his behaviour. If a person, for whatever reason, prefers to

---

[12] See Pellikaan, 1994: 229–329.
[13] The commonest true Prisoner's Dilemmas are Contributor's Dilemmas, see Parfit, 1987: 16.

The Others

	Cooperate	Defect
Individual Cooperate	Outcome **Q** Individual and The Others contribute. The collective good will be realized. No one is a free-rider.	Outcome **S** Individual makes a contribution, but The Others do not. No collective good is realized. Individual is sucker.
Defect	Outcome **P** Individual makes no contribution, but The Others do. The collective good will be realized. Individual has a free ride.	Outcome **R** Individual and The Others do not make a contribution. No collective good is realized. No free-riders.

Figure 3.3 The Potential Contributor's Dilemma.

make an insignificant contribution to the common good, i.e., if he acts on a preference which favours outcome S over outcome R, then the thin-theory cannot disqualify this preference as irrational. As we have seen above, Olson disqualifies behaviour that has no perceptible effect on the outcome as irrational behaviour. A single farmer in a perfect competitive market who limits his production in order infinitesimally to raise the market price is, according to Olson, a crank who tries to hold back a flood with a pail.[14] From this point of view it would be irrational to act on a preference favouring outcome S to outcome R.

With the acceptance of the diversity of individual values, and hence, with the denial of the condition of efficiency as universal value, we have abandoned Olson's prescription for rational behaviour in terms of benefits less costs. From the actor's perspective, any participant in a Potential Contributor's Dilemma may reveal any of the twenty-four possible strong orderings. If so, his preference ordering will meet Arrow's definition of rationality.[15] However, that definition does not in itself tell us whether the player will choose a rational course of action. A complete and transitive ordering is necessary for defining a rational choice in game theory, but it is not sufficient. Arrow's axioms only guarantee that the four social states P, Q, R, and S are strongly ranked one way or another. A rational choice between the strategies Cooperate and Defect involves further conditions, which relate the action to the satisfaction of one's preferences, whatever they are. As Riker has observed, the rational choice of an actor with given preferences must maximize his or her satisfaction. In chapter 4 we will discuss the rational choice for all twenty-four possible strong orderings. We will then establish empirical criteria for judging the rational

---

[14] See Olson, 1971: 64.
[15] Arrow defines a strong ordering as a ranking in which no ties (indifference) are possible. See Arrow, 1963: 13–14.

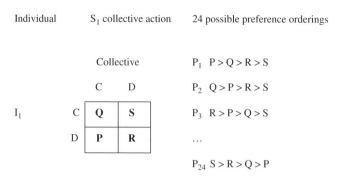

Figure 3.4 The Potential Contributor's Dilemma in the actor's perspective.

choice of actors with certain preference orderings, on the basis of the information that the survey questions generate. That information is unfortunately limited, and so it will be seen that we can only use the dominance rule of rational choice.

Once we allow that an individual can adopt any complete and transitive preference ordering, we must accept the subjectivity of the actor in rational choice theory in another way as well. Having rejected the notion of homogeneous rational individuals, whose preferences must conform to the dictates of the thick-theory, we must go one step further and reject the notion that a given actor would tend to act upon the same preferences in different social dilemmas. Thus we shall assume that social dilemmas, as structured by the game form of the Potential Contributor's Dilemma are in principle non-equivalent with respect to the way they will be played.

The reduction of all sorts of problems of collective action into the same social dilemma, where each individual has a Prisoner's Dilemma ordering, is not a fruitful way to analyse real-life situations. To advance the empirical study of political science, we think that rational choice theory should accept the subjectivity of the actor.

This idea is illustrated in figure 3.4. The core of this figure is the Potential Contributor's Dilemma, as illustrated by the outcome matrix of figure 3.3. Individual I_1, who is facing a specific problem of collective action S_1, can adopt a variety of orderings and not just one. This is the essence of the difference between the thick-theory and the thin-theory. The reductionist view of the thick-theory cannot explain the complexity of real-life problems, because it ignores the variety of individuals and the corresponding diversity of problems of collective action.

From the actor's perspective based on the thin-theory, it may be possible to explain why individual I_1 is not willing to make a voluntary contribution in a specific problem of collective action S_1 and behaves rationally, while another individual I_2, who is also facing S_1, is willing to cooperate and still behaves rationally. Furthermore, the actor's perspective may also be capable of explaining why a specific individual is willing to cooperate in S_1 but is not willing to cooperate in a different problem of collective action S_2. From the actor's perspective every individual encounters a specific problem of collective action as the row player, Individual. All the other individuals are represented by the column player. Only when every individual has a Prisoner's Dilemma preference ordering does the Potential Contributor's Dilemma become an actual Contributor's Dilemma. Whether or not this is in fact the case is no longer a theoretical conjecture but an important empirical question. The answer to that question can be given only by measuring the preference orderings.

Part II

The survey

4

Preference orderings and measurement

4.1 Three potential social dilemmas

As we have seen, social dilemmas can be analysed from two distinct points of view: the observer's perspective and the actor's perspective. The observer's perspective is the point of view most commonly taken in analyses of social dilemmas. Characteristically, this perspective attributes Prisoner's Dilemma preference orderings over outcomes to players. As a consequence, every Potential Contributor's Dilemma is regarded as an actual Contributor's Dilemma. In contrast, the actor's perspective aims at recovering the players' preferences over outcomes. According to this perspective, the researcher should limit his role to observing the actor's own assessment of a Potential Contributor's Dilemma. The central questions to be answered by empirical research are the following: how do Potential Contributor's Dilemmas play out? When do they transform into actual dilemmas with the suboptimal outcome of mutual defection? And under what conditions are actual dilemmas avoided?

To start answering these questions, the present chapter provides a design for survey research, in which the preferences of a large sample of respondents over the outcomes of Potential Contributor's Dilemmas are measured. In our survey, we recorded the orderings reported in three different Potential Contributor's Dilemmas. Based on the actor's perspective, we will attempt to explain the variety of preference orderings within each of the three environmental problems of collective action in the course of the book. Furthermore, as noted in chapter 3, the actor's perspective also enables us to address the non-equivalence of social dilemmas. We shall thus be devoting a lot of attention to explaining why some individuals are willing to cooperate in some of the three environmental dilemmas but not in others.

In our survey research we presented the Potential Contributor's Dilemma to the respondents in the form of stylized stories. The design of the questions which measure the preference orderings is presented in section 4.2 below. During the face-to-face interview, the respondents were asked to rank the four outcomes P, Q, R, and S illustrated in figure 3.4. Of course we did not confront respondents with the Potential Contributor's Dilemma in this highly abstract form. Instead, we asked respondents to react to three specific instances of a real-life environmental problem, each of which was cast in a recognizable form.

The first Potential Contributor's Dilemma offered to the respondents is the problem of toxic chemical household waste, which we refer to as 'Chemical Waste'. This environmental problem is well known to most people in the Netherlands. In the early 1980s, when problems of waste management and its consequences made headlines in the newspapers, many municipalities initiated policies aimed at separating toxic from non-toxic household waste in collecting garbage.

The legal basis for these municipal policies can be found in the Law on Chemical Waste Products of 1976. In governmental decisions on the scope of this law, it was explicitly said that most waste products resulting from transactions with private persons would be exempt from the general duty to report the depositing of chemical waste. However, the government also decided that the potential problem of chemical waste products in households should be addressed. Faced with the choice between either cleaning (former) dump sites and waste water from chemical waste products, or collecting those waste products separately, many municipalities opted for the latter alternative. The toxic products are stored in special depositories, which satisfy a number of safety conditions set by the provincial governments.

Toxic chemical household waste, including batteries and leftovers of paint and of aggressive cleaning products, is collected by a variety of methods. In some municipalities it is collected every few months or so by a special truck; in other municipalities there are fixed sites in each residential area where the waste can be dumped by private persons. Some industries have developed a deposit system for their own product, whereas other industries have cooperated in special provisions. For example, the battery-producing industry has placed bins for batteries near most supermarkets. Since the early 1980s, municipalities and the central government have initiated long-term communication policies aimed at convincing citizens of the desirability of separately dumping their toxic household waste. As we have noted in chapter 2, these policies are part of the Dutch approach to self-regulation.

No sanctions exist on non-cooperative behaviour. As long as the Law on Chemical Waste and related laws are not ostensibly violated, households in the Netherlands have a real choice between either dumping their toxic waste with the regular waste, or bringing it to a special collection point – which might assume several forms, as discussed above. The latter option always involves some extra cost to the individual who chooses it: time, attention, and effort.

Therefore, although the costs of cooperative (environment-friendly) behaviour are probably relatively small, and although governmental pressure to act cooperatively is considerable, even without formal sanctions, each household in the Netherlands faces a potential dilemma regarding toxic household waste. If everyone chose the non-cooperative alternative, and dumped the toxic waste with the rest of the rubbish, then it may be expected that the environment (in particular, the quality of soil and water) would further deteriorate. If everyone chose the cooperative alternative, and brought the toxic waste to a special collection point, then the state of the environment would improve. Finally, what any individual decides to do hardly makes a noticeable difference for the collective outcome – it almost exclusively affects his or her private calculus of costs and benefits.[1] If the actors involved choose their strategy exclusively by these private costs and benefits, the natural choice is to defect, and the potential dilemma turns into an actual dilemma. However, if the actors base their decision on other considerations as well, for example the quality of the environment, the natural choice is no longer to defect.

We have done some preliminary research on the problem of toxic chemical household waste in several pilot surveys.[2] The introduction to the environmental problem and the formulation of the questions are based on improved versions of these.

In order to study the diversity of social dilemmas, we presented the respondents two other Potential Contributor's Dilemmas. The second environmental case concerns household energy conservation. We refer to this case as 'Energy Saving'. The conservation of energy has been on the public agenda of Dutch politics since the first Report of the Club of Rome in 1971 and the first oil crisis of 1973. The Netherlands has considerable reservoirs of natural gas and oil, but has never assumed a position of independence on the world energy markets. The price for natural gas is linked to the world market price of oil. A mixture of environmental and economic considerations has resulted in a wide variety of energy conservation programmes from 1989 onwards. Consider the situation of home owners. The replacement of single glazing by double glazing was for a long time partly subsidized through measures of the government and public utilities. So was the insulation of walls and roofs, the installation of new types

---

[1] As discussed in chapter 2, it is no coincidence that the key slogan of the largest government-sponsored communication programme on environmental affairs reads: 'A better environment starts at your own doorstep'. From a game-theoretical perspective, success in getting people to act on this message takes the sting out of the Potential Contributor's Dilemma.

[2] See Pellikaan, 1991, 1994; Aarts and Pellikaan, 1993; Van der Veen and Pellikaan, 1994.

of energy-efficient boilers, and so on. Only lately have the subsidies on adapting private houses to energy-saving standards been cut.

At the same time, the consumer costs per unit of natural gas, electricity, and oil have risen steeply since the 1980s, thus providing another incentive for energy efficiency. Energy Saving is a classic source of Potential Contributor's Dilemmas.[3] But, as was the case with Chemical Waste, many of those potential dilemmas in reality meet with government policies. In Energy Saving, these policies of self-regulation are not just facilitating and persuasive. Quite understandably, they also provide financial incentives. In our presentation of Energy Saving as a potential dilemma, we try to avoid contamination of the problem by existing government subsidies and energy pricing policies. The choice problem is explicitly presented as a problem of economizing on the use of electricity and warm water, under the existing circumstances regarding the respondent's house and the prices of energy.

The third case presented to the respondents deals with the negative consequences of modern mass tourism for the environment. This case will be referred to as 'Holiday Destination'. It is a quite different one from the other two cases, especially since up to the present, there has been no government policy aimed at discouraging citizens to select distant holiday destinations, or at making it difficult or otherwise unattractive for them to travel to these destinations by the widely used and most polluting forms of transport, the automobile or aeroplane. The Potential Contributor's Dilemma in Holiday Destination thus focuses upon the choice every individual has when selecting a holiday destination.

On the one hand, people may choose a holiday destination far away from their homes, which, given the small area of the Netherlands, means travelling abroad. This supposedly offers a number of advantages, among others: better weather, a change of culture and food, physical liberation from the daily routine. However, the wording of the case at least suggests that the distance travelled from the Netherlands also often requires that people go by air, touring car or private car. Transportation, especially by air, contributes significantly to the pollution of the environment. In a small country like the Netherlands, air travel is not a normal thing for most people: except for business, most people travel by plane only to reach their holiday resort.

On the other hand, people may select a holiday destination near home, for example travelling by bike through the Netherlands, or camping on one of the islands near the Dutch coast. Comparatively speaking, this type of holiday destination is far more friendly to the environment, a fact that can be easily appreciated even though it is not always officially advertised. To be sure, a debate touching on the environmental issues posed by holidays started to

---

[3] See Elster 1989: 18ff.

develop in the early 1990s. The successful introduction of the 'Air Miles' programme in the Netherlands resulted in a number of critical newspaper articles about the growth of air travel. However, the spark soon died out. Meanwhile, air travel has become relatively cheaper over the past, exotic destinations are within the reach of many holiday travellers, and they are chosen increasingly.

In contrast to the other two cases, then, it is rather unlikely that people will instantly frame the problem of the choice of their holiday destination as an environmental problem, let alone as a potential environmental dilemma. Not only have there been few signals from the government to this effect, but apart from occasional exceptions in media coverage, the issue has on the whole been ignored so far in the larger public debate. At the same time, the choice of a holiday destination does have the characteristics of a Potential Contributor's Dilemma, as we have explained above. From our viewpoint, therefore, the situation is well worth studying, precisely because it is a less obvious one than the dilemmas of Chemical Waste and Energy Saving.

4.2 Measuring preference orderings

Our selection of the three environmental problems was in large part guided by the demands that three conditions should be satisfied: one cognitive, one affective, and one evaluative. The cognitive condition states that the respondent must be aware of the different outcomes, i.e., of the possible results of the interaction between his or her own action strategies and those of other members of the group or society. The affective condition means that respondents must clearly be capable of forming a liking or disliking of the different outcomes, when they are confronted with an environmental dilemma, so that it is reasonable to assume that they will not be completely indifferent to any two outcomes. Thirdly, the evaluative condition says that the respondents must be capable of attaching a certain value to each dilemma's outcome. This value might be a direct translation of their affective response, but of course it need not be. The attached value may also reflect other concerns, for example a reaction (positive or negative) to policies of self-regulation that appeal to the environmental responsibility of citizens.

The information about the underlying problem presented to the respondents about each dilemma should contain the following four elements of an environmental Potential Contributor's Dilemma:

Element 1. The consequences for environmental pollution of a collective choice must be stated. If all citizens dump chemical waste with normal household waste, the consequences for the pollution are negative. If, on the other hand, people collect the waste and dispose of it at a special site or facility, the consequences are positive.

Element 2. The effects of anyone's individual action on the collective outcome are negligible. This element is characteristic for social dilemmas involving many persons. Each person's contribution to the collective good is approximately equal, and, also equally marginal.

Element 3. Each case is implicitly presented as a two-person game. From each actor's individual viewpoint, all other actors can be represented as a collective, the Others, which may choose either to cooperate or to defect. The choices made by the other actors involved in the dilemma are unknown to each respondent. The respondent is thus invited to play the role of the row player, Individual, in the Potential Contributor's Dilemma of figure 3.4.

Element 4. Cooperative behaviour implies a personal sacrifice compared to non-cooperative behaviour. This personal sacrifice may take various forms. Money may be involved, or time, or effort, or different kinds of substitution costs. In some dilemmas, the personal sacrifice implied by cooperative behaviour may be relatively small, in others it may be large; the point is that there must be some sacrifice in all cases.

Following these guidelines, the Potential Contributor's Dilemma is translated into information transmitted in the survey interview. The precise formulation aims at making the respondents aware of the four possible outcomes, making clear that these outcomes are the result of collective choice processes, and pointing to the irrelevance of the individual contribution. The core information for the potential dilemma of Chemical Waste is given by the following questions. The interviewer first gives the following introductory statement.

I would like to ask you a few questions about chemical household waste such as batteries, leftovers of paint, and motor oil. If everybody in the Netherlands just throws this environmentally harmful waste away, environmental pollution will increase. If everybody brings the chemical waste to a special collection point, for example a chemical waste collector or a depository, environmental pollution will decrease. However, your own behavior hardly has an effect on environmental pollution. Every one of us, you just like any other person, faces the choice: either to throw this waste away with the rest of the household garbage, or to bring this waste to a special collection point.

The interviewer hands out four cards marked P, Q, R and S and says:

On these cards are four situations. I want to ask you to order these situations according to your preferences.

The four cards contain the following text:

P	You throw the waste away but other persons bring their waste to the collection point. This costs you no extra time and effort and environmental pollution will decrease

Q	You bring the waste to the collection point and so do the other persons. This costs you extra time and effort but environmental pollution will decrease

R	You throw the waste away and so do the other persons. This costs you no extra time and effort but environmental pollution will increase

S	You bring the waste to the collection point but the other persons throw their waste away. This costs you extra time and effort and environmental pollution will increase

The respondent lays down one card on the table and says that this outcome has his first preference. Then he lays down the second, the third, and the fourth card on the table. With a Potential Contributor's Dilemma consisting of four outcomes, the number of possible strong orderings over these outcomes is $(4 \times 3 \times 2 \times 1 =) 24$. By presenting the four possible outcomes by four different cards, each respondent is allowed to make a decision, by changing the order of the cards until the ranking of these four cards corresponds with his preference ordering within the time limit of the interview. If a person is not able to rank all four cards, because he does not understand the question or is not able to decide which outcome has a higher preference, then this person was not able to make a transitive preference profile and his answer is a 'missing case'.

Measuring preferences for only one case gives information about the diversity of individual values and preferences of the individuals. But it does not enable us to say anything yet about the diversity of problems of collective action. The other two cases of the Potential Contributor's Dilemma – Holiday Destination and Energy Saving – consist of a fully comparable set of questions. For these two cases the respondents were also asked to rank four show cards. The information of the cards describes the context of the cases in exactly the same way as is done in the case Chemical Waste. Persons were asked to rank the alternative outcomes of 'unilateral defection' (P), 'mutual cooperation' (Q), 'mutual defection' (R), and 'unilateral cooperation' (S) for all three cases. By this procedure we were able to measure the orderings of the respondents for all three environmental

Table 4.1 *Ranking the four outcomes*

		First	Second	Third	Fourth	Row total
Chemical Waste						
Free-rider	P	10	187	517	97	811
Mutual defection	R	17	30	93	671	811
Mutual cooperation	Q	749	37	12	13	811
Sucker	S	35	557	189	30	811
Column total		811	811	811	811	
Energy Saving		First	Second	Third	Fourth	Row total
Free-rider	P	41	192	483	97	813
Mutual defection	R	27	41	104	641	813
Mutual cooperation	Q	695	61	33	24	813
Sucker	S	50	519	193	51	813
Column total		813	813	813	813	
Holiday Destination		First	Second	Third	Fourth	Row total
Free-rider	P	139	268	267	85	759
Mutual defection	R	175	99	105	380	759
Mutual cooperation	Q	382	125	144	108	759
Sucker	S	63	267	243	186	759
Column total		759	759	759	759	

dilemmas. Table 4.1 shows the results of the ranking of the four cards for all three cases.

Table 4.1 presents the number of respondents who successfully ranked all the four cards for each case. Most respondents (N = 993) were able to choose a card as their first preference. Only a few respondents had some difficulties with the ranking of the second card. The ranking of all four cards was too difficult for 182 persons in Chemical Waste.

In the case Energy Saving, the construction of a full ordering was too difficult for 180 respondents; and for 234 in Holiday Destination. The number of respondents unable to formulate their ordering for any of the three cases was 116. This is largely the result of the age of the respondent. The elderly, in particular, had problems with the ranking of the four cards. Table 4.1 lists the ranking of the four outcomes of the respondents with strong orderings, i.e., with complete and transitive preference orderings. The figures show that the environmental problem of toxic chemical household waste is evaluated very differently from the one on the negative consequences of modern mass tourism. On the other hand, the results of the ranking in Chemical Waste look very similar to those of Energy Saving. In these two cases only a few respondents prefer the free-ridership outcome (P) to the other three outcomes: respectively

Figure 4.1 The pay-off of the row player with ordering RPQS.

10 and 41. Also, the mutual defection outcome (R) is chosen only by a few as first preference. The mutual cooperation outcome (Q) is by far the most popular outcome. For most respondents, the sucker outcome (S) is their second selection.

In Holiday Destination, 139 respondents ranked the free-rider outcome (P) as first preference. Even more respondents choose the mutual defection outcome (R) as their favourite. Mutual cooperation is, compared with the other two cases, not very popular. Nevertheless, 382 respondents ranked Q as first preference.

For our purposes, of course, the information regarding the distribution of outcomes in terms of the first-best, second-best, third-best, and worst preference is not decisive. It does already show, however, that the respondents do not remotely satisfy the assumption of the thick-theory of rational choice in social dilemmas. For the free-rider outcome P is not at all predominantly at the top of the table for respondents, as would have to be the case if most of them were to display the Prisoner's Dilemma-ordering PQRS, which corresponds to what the thick-theory assumes.

As we have seen above, most of the respondents were able to manipulate the showcards so as to form a strong ordering under the direction of the interviewer in the available time. The procedure that we have followed was described above. It is one which ensures transitivity, if the rankings are complete, as is the case when the respondent manages to indicate the first, second and third preferred showcards representing outcomes of the dilemma. A more rigorous procedure would have been one in which respondents were asked to rank the six possible pairs of the four outcomes. We decided against this, in view of the confusion it would have generated.

Table 4.2 presents the full orderings for the three cases. The notation in the first column of the table – from PQRS to SRQP – corresponds with the notation of figure 3.4. For example, if an individual ranks the four cards P, Q, R, and S as follows: first R (mutual defection), second P (free-rider), third Q (mutual cooperation), and fourth S (sucker), then his preference ordering is R > P > Q > S, or RPQS in short. The preference ordering RPQS fixes the pay-off matrix of Individual, who is facing the Potential Contributor's Dilemma as the row player. The preference ordering RQPS is illustrated in the matrix of figure 4.1.

As explained by Element 3 of our interview design, we measured the preferences of Individual, the row player in the Potential Contributor's Dilemma, whose position in the game form the respondent is implicitly asked to assume.

Table 4.2 *Preference orderings*

Ordering	Chemical Waste		Energy Saving		Holiday Destination	
	N	%	N	%	N	%
PQRS	2	0.3	4	0.5	27	3.6
PQSR	3	0.4	13	1.6	31	4.1
PRQS	4	0.5	13	1.6	49	6.5
PRSQ	0	0.0	6	0.6	19	2.5
PSQR	1	0.1	3	0.4	4	0.5
PSRQ	0	0.0	2	0.2	9	1.2
RPQS	0	0.0	8	1.0	72	9.5
RPSQ	7	0.9	11	1.4	60	7.9
RQPS	2	0.2	2	0.2	12	1.6
RQSP	5	0.6	2	0.2	11	1.4
RSPQ	2	0.2	3	0.4	13	1.7
RSQP	1	0.1	1	0.1	7	0.9
QPRS	16	2.0	19	2.3	20	2.6
QPSR	159	19.6	146	18.0	105	13.8
QRPS	6	0.7	5	0.6	6	0.8
QRSP	15	1.8	15	1.8	17	2.2
QSPR	491	60.5	443	54.5	201	26.5
QSRP	62	7.6	67	8.2	33	4.3
SPQR	2	0.2	7	0.9	7	0.9
SPRQ	3	0.4	1	0.1	4	0.5
SQPR	15	1.8	29	3.6	32	4.2
SQRP	10	1.2	11	1.4	12	1.6
SRPQ	1	0.1	1	0.1	3	0.4
SRQP	4	0.5	1	0.1	5	0.7
Valid orderings	811	100%	813	100%	759	100%
Missing cases	182		180		234	

Thus the pay-off matrix in figure 4.1 only shows the ordinal utility of the row player Individual. Each of the remaining twenty-three preference orderings in table 4.2 then corresponds to a different pay-off matrix. As discussed in chapter 3, the measurement of preference orderings is the core of the actor's perspective. Most importantly at the present stage of our report, it enables us to verify to what extent the respondents in the survey display Prisoner's Dilemma orderings, which the observer's perspective ascribes to any rational individual.

The first column of table 4.2 gives the twenty-four possible strong orderings: PQRS to SRQP. Under the heading of each case of the dilemma, the first column gives the frequencies of respondents for each of the possible orderings, while the second column gives the percentage of the ordering in the total of valid preference orderings. These totals are listed at the bottom of table 4.2, together with the missing cases. As we explained above, the missing cases consist of responses that represent incomplete rankings.

The results in table 4.2 seem to confirm the relevance of the actor's perspective. Individuals who are facing a specific problem of collective action have reported a wide variety of orderings – 21 different orderings in the case of Chemical Waste, and all of the 24 possible orderings in the two other cases. Only two respondents ranked the four cards so as to express a Prisoner's Dilemma ordering PQRS in Chemical Waste. In Energy Saving, only four respondents report a PD-ordering. And, while Holiday Destination shows the highest number (27) of PD-orderings, this is still under 4 per cent of the 759 valid orderings reported in this case.

The pattern of the first two cases in table 4.2 is very similar. Apparently most individuals consider Energy Saving and Chemical Waste to be related environmental problems. However, the table cannot clarify the question whether or not most individuals have identical orderings in both of these cases. We will deal with that question in the next section.

Despite the differences between Chemical Waste and Energy Saving on the one hand, and Holiday Destination on the other, it is remarkable that in all three cases the orderings QSPR and QPSR are embraced by a majority of respondents in Chemical Waste and Energy Saving, and by over a quarter in Holiday Destination, as can be seen from table 4.2. A moment's reflection will show, at least intuitively, that these two orderings display a decidedly cooperative attitude to the dilemma, since both of them put the universally cooperative outcome Q at the top, and the universally non-cooperative outcome R at the bottom of the ordering.

Based on this fact, as well as on the observed diversity of orderings in table 4.2, we can reject the assumption of homogeneous actors of the thick-theory of rationality. The diversity of preference orderings in all three cases alone is sufficient to show that this assumption does not hold. But the most frequently reported highly cooperative orderings QPSR and QSPR also show that most respondents do not subscribe to Olson's criteria of effectiveness and efficiency: these orderings indicate that they would want to cooperate, even if others defected, as will be formally discussed in the next chapter, when we turn to the issue of rational choice from observed preferences.

The fact that only a few individuals report the non-cooperative PD-ordering assumed by the free-riding rational agent of the thick-theory is highly problematic for that theory, prima facie. Of course, at this stage it would be possible to claim that most of the respondents with 'deviant' orderings might simply be irrational agents, whose strategy choices are completely unrelated to their rankings of the four outcomes. However, in the next chapter it will be seen that many respondents with non-PD orderings do in fact indicate a strategy choice that is in line with what the dominance rule of rational choice prescribes, while those with PD-orderings do not do better. And that does present a problem for the thick-theory which is more difficult to ignore.

As we have been keen to note, the actor's perspective is in principle capable of providing explanations for the diversity of orderings across individuals that emerge from table 4.2, as well as across cases of the dilemma. Before turning to such explanations in part III, however, the last source of diversity must be studied, since as we remarked above, it cannot be directly read off from that table. The next section is devoted to this task.

4.3 Three different environmental problems

Each environmental problem generates a great variety of preference orderings, but table 4.2 also suggests that the first two cases, Chemical Waste and Energy Saving display a similar pattern. This suggested similarity could be misleading. In this section we perform two investigations of overlap between cases. First, we record the frequencies with which respondents have reported a valid ordering (any one of the twenty-four possible kinds) once, two times, or three times, and how these occurrences are distributed among the cases of the dilemma. And secondly, we show the number of identical orderings of the twenty-four possible kinds that are shared by the three cases.

The number of valid orderings in each of the three cases is an indication of whether or not the cognitive condition is satisfied in these cases. This means that if a particular case has a relatively high number of missing cases, then apparently the respondents must have had some difficulty in ranking their alternatives. Table 4.2 shows that the numbers of valid orderings in Chemical Waste (811) and Energy Saving (813) are very much alike, and the case Holiday Destination (759) has a lower number of valid orderings. If we compare these figures of missing cases in table 4.2 – between 18 per cent and 24 per cent – with the rest of the answers in the survey – missing cases below 5 per cent – we must conclude that the measuring of the preferences is by far the most demanding in the questionnaire. Furthermore, the respondents have had more trouble in stating their preferences in the case Holiday Destination than in the other two cases. To verify our intuition that the cognitive requirements in these two cases differ from Holiday Destination, we must look at the overlap between the three cases.

Looking at the overlap of valid orderings is one very elementary way of analysing the extent to which the cases are perceived as similar by the respondents. Figure 4.2 gives a Venn-diagram, each circle of which represents one of the three environmental dilemmas. The diagram shows (1) how many valid orderings were reported in each case, and (2) how many respondents with valid orderings the cases have in common. To explain this diagram, consider the

Chemical Waste N = 811   Holiday Destination N = 759

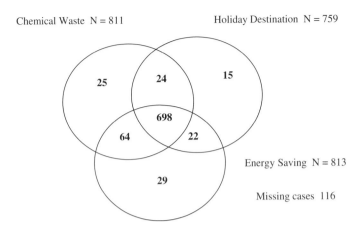

Energy Saving N = 813

Missing cases 116

Figure 4.2 Valid orderings.

left-hand circle, which encloses the 811 valid orderings reported in the case of
Chemical Waste. Of these 811, 698 respondents also reported orderings in the
two other cases. Next, respectively 64 and 24 of these 811 respondents only
reported orderings in Energy Saving and Holiday Destination, while 25 only
reported an ordering in Chemical Waste itself.

The composition of the complement of the left-hand circle, which is the 182
missing cases of Chemical Waste (those who did not report a valid ordering
in that case of the dilemma), can also be traced. First, 116 of these 182 respondents did not report a valid ordering in any of the cases at all, indicated
in figure 4.2 in the area outside of the three circles. Secondly, 22 of the 182
respondents managed to report valid orderings in both of the two other cases,
while respectively 15 and 29 of them reported only one valid ordering, in Energy
Saving and Holiday Destination. In the same way one can calculate the distribution of respondent overlap with respect to valid orderings for Energy Saving
and Holiday Destination.

Figure 4.2 shows that the overlap between Chemical Waste and Energy
Saving is higher than the overlap between one of these cases and Holiday
Destination. This Venn-diagram also illustrates that if a respondent has stated
only one ordering it is more likely that he has formulated a ordering for
Chemical Waste (or Energy Saving) than for Holiday Destination. Although
we see some differences between the three cases, figure 4.2 also illustrates that
the measurement of the orderings demands high cognitive capabilities of the
respondents. The only factor that is related with the number of valid orderings
seems to be the variable 'Age'. In table 4.3, variable Age is divided into six
age categories: 18 to 25, 26 to 35, and so on, until the last category of age 66
and older. Age is the independent variable that causes the right answers for the

Table 4.3 *Valid orderings related with Age*

| Valid Ordering | Age | | | | | | | |
	(%) 18–25	(%) 26–35	(%) 36–45	(%) 46–55	(%) 56–65	(%) 66–99	total	N =
zero valid	6	5	12	16	18	23	12	116
one valid	1	5	6	11	9	15	7	69
two valid	9	9	11	10	16	16	11	110
three valid	84	82	71	63	57	46	70	698
	100	100	100	100	100	100	100	
N =	148	258	214	158	123	92		993

dependent variable 'Persons with Valid Ordering'. The dependent variable is an index of the number of times someone has given a valid ordering.

Table 4.3 shows that there is a relationship between Age and the number of times someone was able to make a complete and transitive ordering.[4] Young people are more likely to answer all three cases with valid orderings than the elderly.[5] This means that our method of measuring orderings is perhaps to difficult for elderly people.

The Venn-diagram of figure 4.2 has no bearing on the overlap of identical orderings reported by the respondents. This is the second type of overlap between cases that we want to investigate below, for the reason explained in chapter 3. There, we remarked that the actor's perspective is sensitive to the possibility that a specific individual may cooperate in one specific problem of collective action without any reserve, but may nevertheless defect in another problem of collective action, or may cooperate only if he thinks others will do so as well, despite the fact that all of those problems can be modelled by the same game form, here the one of the Potential Contributor's Dilemma.

In so far as people's actions are guided by their preference orderings, this implies that any single respondent in our survey may or may not adopt a different preference ordering in the three cases of the dilemma. From the actor's perspective, this is something that one would want to check carefully for the whole sample, and the result would then need to be investigated systematically, following a further inquiry into the rational choices of the respondents. By contrast, from the observer's perspective of the thick-theory of rational choice, there is nothing much to be explained, since it is assumed in advance that rational actors will display the same PD-ordering in all cases of the dilemma. If they do

---

[4] The relationship is statistically significant: Somers' D value is $-.17$ and the T-value is -8.66.
[5] The bivariate relationship between Age and Valid Orderings has been controlled by the level of education. This control or third variable Education has 'no effect'. See 'The Logic of Multivariate Contingency Analysis', in Knoke and Bohrnstedt, 1994: 233–61.

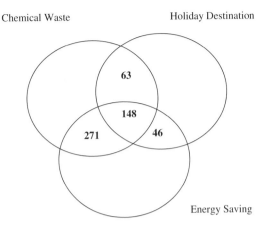

Chemical Waste   Holiday Destination

Energy Saving

Figure 4.3 Identical orderings.

not, then that means that those displaying deviant orderings in a particular case of the dilemma just fail to be rational in that case. But we have argued that the thick-theory is wrong in assuming that rational individuals are homogeneous, and thus we now want to show that the implication of this is also wrong: not all problems of collective action are equivalent with respect to the preferences that rational actors may have. As mentioned above, the rational choices of the respondents will be investigated in the next chapter.

Meanwhile, figure 4.3 again presents a Venn-diagram, in which each circle represents one of the three social dilemmas. In contrast to figure 4.2, where the circles contain the number of respondents with valid orderings, the circles of figure 4.3 contain the number of identical valid orderings.

There are 148 respondents with identical orderings in all three cases, or 15 per cent of all 993 respondents. As can be expected from the results in table 4.2, most of these come from those who reported the popular preferences QPSR or QSPR. This rather small percentage shows that the three cases of the dilemma were certainly not perceived as equivalent. Figure 4.3 also shows that Chemical Waste and Energy Saving are perceived to be more similar to each other than they are to Holiday Destination, in terms of orderings shared in common. Chemical Waste and Energy Saving have a relatively high number of the same orderings. In addition to the 148 three-case occurrences, these two cases have an overlap of 271 identical orderings. Thus, more than 50 per cent of the valid orderings in Chemical Waste and Energy Saving are identical.

Disposing of toxic household waste and economizing on energy are in many ways comparable environmental problems, but the Venn-diagram of figure 4.3 indicates that these cases are somewhat less similar than table 4.2 suggests. From tables 4.1 and 4.2 it was already clear that Holiday Destination is a different case altogether. The Venn-diagram of figure 4.3 confirms this. The overlap of the cases Chemical Waste and Holiday Destination is relatively small, only 63 identical orderings. The overlap of the cases Energy Saving and Holiday Destination is even smaller, namely 46 identical orderings.

The display of common orderings in figure 4.3 is only one way of showing the non-equivalence of the three environmental dilemmas. In chapter 7, we shall examine the extent to which our cases can be seen to differ in respect of the likelihood that an individual respondent would adopt a cooperative stance, in terms of either preferences, strategy choices, or motives. It will be seen that Holiday Destination is surely the hardest case in that respect.

4.4 Avoiding response effects

The wording of a survey question may have important consequences for the answers that are given in response. A question might give unintended cues in one direction or another, and it has often been shown that these cues do have effects on the answers obtained. In our survey, we have presented the three different instances of Potential Contributor's Dilemmas in an identical fashion. Although this does not preclude the presence of question wording effects, at least it results in comparable effects over the three cases. Response effects, or effects of the order in which the questions are put, occur when answers that are assumed to be independent from previous questions, in reality are affected by them. In our survey, response effects may occur at several levels. Within each of the cases to be investigated, the sequence of questions pertaining to that case may lead to a narrowing of the respondent's perceived range of answers. Respondents may then adopt a routine mode of answering, after having responded to one or two of the three dilemmas.

We have tried to counteract these response effect tendencies in two ways. First, within each case, we have separated the questions pertaining to the dilemma from the others by asking it in a different place of the questionnaire. By doing so, we aimed to limit the response effect per case. Secondly, the first of the three cases was presented to the respondents early in the interview, whereas the other two followed only after a set of unrelated questions had been asked. Moreover, the order of presentation of the three cases was randomized for each interview. The measurement results of the three Potential Contributor's Dilemmas indicate that the respondents did not adopt a routine mode of answering. The large diversity of reported preference orderings makes it very unlikely that the questions frame the answers. Apart from these rather common problems of survey research in the social sciences, particular problems of measuring preferences in Potential Contributor's Dilemmas arise. The most important of these are the following three. Potential Contributor's Dilemmas always involve situations in which individual interests may conflict with collective interests.

According to the actor's perspective, this conflict is not something which is given in advance; nevertheless, most potential dilemmas will be recognized as such by many respondents. Certain types of behaviour will generally be regarded as less desirable from a social viewpoint than other types. The face-to-face interview is a social event in which two persons, the interviewer and the respondent, interact. Because of the difference in social desirability of various preferences in social dilemmas, respondents who recognize this may be inclined to give one type of answer rather than another, although the given answers do not represent their true feelings. Thus, social pressure effects may result in invalid measurements.

Remedies for this problem are hard to find. The meaning of what is socially desirable and what is not can hardly be changed during an interview. Moreover, the very nature of Potential Contributor's Dilemmas requires that not all outcomes are regarded as equally desirable from the point of view of society. In our survey, we have tried to present the potential dilemmas so that the normative and evaluative connotations of the presentation, and the subsequent questions, are as small as possible. Also, we decided to emphasize a particular element present in Potential Contributor's Dilemmas, namely the insignificance of each respondent's personal contribution to the public good. This element is essential for understanding the dilemma, and by stressing it, it also serves to counteract a possible bias towards 'cooperative' answers.

We think that we have taken due precautions to avoid these familiar problems. In any case, if our questions are still biased in the sense that they invite respondents to give cooperative answers, it becomes hard to explain why we have found so many 'non-cooperative' answers in the case of Holiday Destination. The difference in the number of non-cooperative preference orderings between Chemical Waste and Energy Saving on the one hand and Holiday Destination on the other hand, is a strong indication that people are able and – more importantly – willing to express their individual values and preferences. In conclusion, we think that the results of our survey reported so far amply confirm the notion of the actor's perspective that each individual may adopt different orderings for various social dilemmas. On the other hand, the actor's perspective also accepts that each individual may have good grounds to express identical orderings across different social dilemmas. The crux of this perspective is that we have to measure the preference orderings, and not simply assume that people who are facing problems of collective action have identical preferences.

In the next chapter we move to the issue of rational choice. We present answers to survey questions on the strategy choices of respondents in the three cases. Next, we propose a consistency test for judging whether or not the respondents made a rational choice, given the preference orderings they reported.

5

Rational choice

5.1 Conditions of rational choice

Our empirical application of rational choice theory in the Potential Contributor's Dilemma includes the concept of a strong preference ordering and the dominance rule. Following Arrow and Riker, we assume that a rational individual is able to make a complete and transitive ranking of the outcomes. The content of the preference ordering is rooted in individual values, i.e., the actor orders the outcomes by whatever standards he deems relevant. This assumption of the subjectivity of the actor in rational choice theory implies that the content of the preference ordering can only be specified by the actor himself.

Though the content of an ordering has a free format, it must satisfy the conditions of transitivity and completeness.[1] If the preferences satisfy these conditions, we regard any ordering as the materialization of this actor's own interest, as he or she sees it. From this perspective one cannot disqualify an ordering like QSPR as irrational and claim that only the Prisoner's Dilemma ordering PQRS is the hallmark of a rational actor. The content of a preference ordering should not be considered part of the definition of rationality. This is the lesson of the thin-theory of rationality, which refuses to specify any particular goal. 'Everybody is presumed to be self-interested, choosing what provides the most satisfaction, but the content of the self-interest is not specified' (Riker, 1990: 173). As explained earlier, the crucial difference between the observer's perspective and the actor's perspective on social dilemmas is that the former ascribes the Prisoner's Dilemma ordering, while the latter accepts any of the twenty-four possible strong orderings. Both perspectives assume that a

[1] See Arrow, 1963: 13.

rational actor maximizes satisfaction of his preferences in the formal sense of the thin-theory. The thick-theory is thus a special case of the thin-theory.

To establish whether or not individuals make a rational choice, we must make use of some game-theoretical rules. In the next section we elaborate which of these rules are appropriate for our empirical application of rational choice theory, given the information that the questions of the survey generate. Next, in section 5.3, we show the strategy choices that respondents have made in each of the three environmental dilemmas, and present the results concerning the rational choices of respondents. In section 5.4, before concluding the chapter, we examine how the different cases of the dilemma compare in terms of rational choice, by means of a statistical analysis.

Meanwhile, it will be helpful to set out our approach to the crucial issue of rational choice in the remainder of this section. In the survey we measured the preference ordering of the respondent by the ranking of the four show cards. The next question the respondent has to answer, in each particular case, is what he will actually choose to do. For instance, in Chemical Waste, the respondent may indicate that he would bring the toxic waste to the collection point, or that he would throw it away with the rest of the household waste. The former action is interpreted as the cooperative strategy (Cooperate) in this case, while the latter is interpreted as the non-cooperative strategy (Defect). Given the information on the respondent's preference ordering and strategy choice, we can then verify whether or not this choice satisfies the appropriate rule, i.e., whether or not he or she makes a rational choice consistently with his or her observed preferences.

This approach may be explained by contrasting it to the well-known theory of revealed preference in economics. For our purposes, knowledge of the preference ordering is a necessary condition for confirming or rejecting rational choice. It is not enough to know what choice someone has made. The idea that a choice reveals a preference is only valid if one is dealing with a choice set of alternative states from which the actor can choose any element, and stipulates in advance that the actor is rational in the sense of being disposed to choose the best element of the choice set. If we present two feasible alternatives, for example coffee (x) and tea (y) and the actor chooses coffee, we can then safely infer from this choice that coffee is preferred to tea. In other words, his choice has revealed the preference $x > y$. If there are more than two alternatives in the choice set, say, lemonade as well, then the actor's choice of coffee only reveals that this alternative is the best one in the set.

However, in dealing with the environmental problems that we are discussing here, the knowledge of a specific choice does not give sufficient information, for the following reasons. First, because the decision situation is an interdependent game form, the actor cannot control the outcome he might wish to attain by his choice of action. In the Potential Contributor's Dilemma, as represented by figure 3.4, the strategy Cooperate gives access to outcomes Q and S, depending on the behaviour of the Others, and the strategy Defect gives access to the outcomes P and R, again depending on what the Others do. Hence, the preferences revealed by each of these strategies, if the actor is assumed to be rational, do not even tell us what the actor's most preferred outcome is. But secondly, as we have noted in sections 4.2 and 4.3, in seeking to refute the thick-theory, the survey responses must be scrutinized empirically, without prejudging the issue of whether an actor is actually making a rational choice. Thus we cannot just assume that a respondent's choice of strategy is a rational one. Hence the revealed preference approach is unsuitable right from the start. This means that knowledge of the preference ordering is a necessary condition to establish if someone is making a rational choice or not in the game-theoretical setting of the Potential Contributor's Dilemma.

Even from the observer's perspective, one cannot say that a strategy choice would reveal the preferences of the actor. The choice is used to confirm or reject the rationality of the actor's behaviour, while assuming in advance that actors, if they are rational, will have to rank the outcomes as PQRS, in accordance with the Prisoner's Dilemma-ordering. The choice obviously does not reveal anything about that preference ordering, nor about any other ordering.

It is worth spelling out this point, because it illustrates clearly in what respects the observer's perspective based on the thick-theory differs from the actor's perspective, which proceeds from the thin-theory. Let us suppose that an actor in an environmental dilemma chooses to cooperate. Then the thick-theory must dismiss this choice as an irrational one, irrespective of this actor's actual preference ordering. There are two possibilities here, both of which are compatible with the actor's choice to cooperate. One is that the actor's ordering is observed to be PQRS. Then, even though he qualifies as rational in the sense of having a complete ordering of the kind that rational actors must have, on the thick-theory, the conclusion is that the actor fails to choose rationally. For as we have seen, with ordering PQRS, an actor will always end up worse in terms of these preferences if he cooperates, hence the rational choice is to defect. (That is why the thick-theory holds that any Potential Contributor's Dilemma is an actual dilemma, one which produces the suboptimal outcome R as a result of rational defection by all.)

The other possibility is that the cooperating actor is observed to have a different ordering – say QPSR – contrary to what the thick-theory requires of rational actors. Then that fact alone disqualifies his choice as being a rational one, on the thick-theory. No further information can disturb this conclusion.

We have no quarrel with the reasoning leading to the first of these conclusions. But of course we do dispute the second conclusion, since in contrast to the observer's perspective, the actor's perspective accepts any complete and transitive ordering as a valid basis of rational action in a Potential Contributor's

Dilemma. So we would apply the reasoning of the first conclusion here, and check whether a cooperating actor with ordering QPSR could possibly do better, in terms of these preferences, by defecting. The answer is no. If the actor were to defect, he would end up with either his second-best outcome P (if the Others cooperate) or his worst outcome R (if the Others defect), while by cooperating he ensures either his best outcome Q (if the Others cooperate) or his third-best outcome S (if the Others defect). So with these particular preferences, the rational strategy is to cooperate, because it ensures a better outcome whatever the Others may do. It is in fact the strategy which is recommended by the dominance rule of rational choice, as will be further discussed below.

Having made clear our position, then, the question to be addressed next is this: what can be said in general about the rationality of the strategy choices of respondents, given that they may adopt any of the twenty-four possible preference orderings?

5.2 The dominance rule of rational choice

Rational choice in game theory is usually defined in terms of an equilibrium. The concept of a Nash-equilibrium plays an important role in defining strategically stable or self-enforcing games. If no single player can obtain a higher utility by unilaterally changing his strategy, while the other player(s) stick to their strategy, then the players have reached a Nash-equilibrium. The Nash-equilibrium, or any other concept of self-enforcing stable outcome, is of no use for our empirical application of rational choice theory.[2] We only measured the pay-offs of the row player Individual, and in order to establish an equilibrium the pay-offs of the other player(s) must also be known. Without knowledge of the pay-offs of the column player, the Others, the row player Individual is simply playing a game against nature.[3]

The concept of a 'game against nature' has a specific meaning in game theory. The essential elements of a game against nature are a specific player and a non-player Nature. The player makes a decision and his goal is to maximize his utility by the choice among available actions.[4] In the present context, Nature stands for the Others, since this column player does not make a decision, as we explained in section 3.2. Nature takes random actions in the game with probabilities that may or may not be known, but which need to be specified, in order to apply a general rule of rational choice. This is the rule of choosing the strategy that maximizes expected utility.[5] Failing any information about the probabilities that the respondents assign to the strategies of the Others, we

---

[2] See Kreps, 1989: 167–77.
[3] The strategies of 'nature' are determined by change. See Morrow, 1994: 55–8.
[4] See von Neumann and Morgenstern, 1971: 9.   [5] See Rasmusen, 1991: 22.

Nature

Cooperate   Defect

		Cooperate	Defect
Individual	Cooperate	2	1
	Defect	3	4

Figure 5.1 RPQS: dominant Defect.

may here assume that they are unknown, and that the column player's strategies Cooperate and Defect are equally likely to occur.

This specification of the probabilities of Cooperate ($p = 1/2$) and Defect ($1 - p = 1/2$) is simply based on the view that we have no reasons to assign any other probabilities to the two actions. In other words, we assume that since the row player Individual has no idea what actions Nature will choose, he might as well proceed from equiprobability, in picking the strategy with the highest expected utility.

This generates some problems for establishing the rational choice for Individual on the basis of the expected utility of choosing a strategy. The most pressing of those problems is the fact that preference orderings of respondents are measured ordinally, which means that the informational basis for calculating the expected utility of the strategies Defect and Cooperate is lacking.

However, this general definition of rational choice will surely present no problems, as long as our row player has a preference ordering with a dominant strategy. We have already mentioned in the previous section that an actor with preference ordering QPSR has a dominant strategy to cooperate, and that the rational actor of the thick-theory, with the Prisoner's Dilemma-ordering PQRS, has a dominant strategy to defect. Ordering RPQS in figure 4.1 is another example of a preference ordering that will present no problems for the row player. For reasons of convenience the pay-off matrix of ordering RPQS is illustrated again in figure 5.1.

The goal of row player Individual is to maximize utility, given his or her preferences. In order to maximize utility Individual has to find the best response to every action that Nature might take. If Nature picks strategy Cooperate, then Individual maximizes utility by choosing strategy Defect. And if Nature picks strategy Defect, then Individual also maximizes utility by choosing strategy Defect. In other words, strategy Defect is a dominant strategy because it is Individual's best response to any strategy Nature might pick.[6] This reasoning about what Nature will 'pick', is purely hypothetical because Nature is a non-player who does not really make choices. But the importance of the reasoning for

---

[6] See Myerson, 1991: 57.

Nature

Cooperate   Defect

		Cooperate	Defect
Individual	Cooperate	4	3
	Defect	2	1

Figure 5.2 QSPR: dominant Cooperate.

Nature

Cooperate   Defect

		Cooperate	Defect
Individual	Cooperate	4	1
	Defect	2	3

Figure 5.3 QRPS: no maximizing rule.

our purposes is that it establishes a rule of rational choice in the absence of complete knowledge. Without knowledge of the pay-offs of the Others, and without
subjective probabilities that could be attached to the actions of Nature on a
Bayesian rule, rather than using the equiprobablility assumption, we can be sure
that Individual maximizes utility only by choosing the dominant strategy Defect.

Besides RPQS, there are five other orderings which also have a dominant
strategy Defect: RPSQ, RSPQ, PRQS, PRSQ, and the PD-ordering PQRS. The
mirror image of the orderings with dominant Defect are the orderings with
dominant Cooperate. Figure 5.2 illustrates the preference ordering QSPR. This
is the most popular ordering among our respondents, as is recorded in table 4.2.

The pay-off matrix indicates that strategy Cooperate is the best response of
Individual to any actions Nature would undertake if Individual's ordering is
QSPR. There are six orderings with a dominant strategy Cooperate: QSPR,
QSRP, QPSR, SQRP, SQPR, and SRQP.

So far, we have a definition of rational choice for twelve of the twenty-four
possible orderings. Actors with the remaining twelve orderings have no best
response, regardless of what Nature's actions may be. Figure 5.3 illustrates a
game against Nature, when Individual has ordering QRPS. This pay-off matrix is
an example of the problem that arises when Individual no longer has a dominant
strategy available. Only if Nature picks strategy Cooperate will the best response
of Individual be to choose Cooperate. And only if Nature picks strategy Defect
will the best response of Individual be to Defect. This means that the row
player has no dominant strategy in this game against Nature, since unlike a
dominant strategy, his best response is here conditional on what Nature does.

In the context of the survey, respondents have been asked to identify with the position of Individual, the row player. However, we have no information on how likely a respondent with ordering QRPS thinks it to be that the Others will cooperate or defect. Failing such information, the respondent's own subjective view on the best response in this game of nature cannot be determined, and it thus is impossible to assess the rationality of his strategy choice.

There is one other way of trying to resolve this problem. This is to assume that a rational individual always chooses the strategy that avoids his worst possible outcome (here: S). Then, the rule of rational choice would be to choose the maximin strategy, which in the case of figure 5.3 would thus be to defect. The maximin strategy is the strategy which avoids the smallest of the four ordinal pay-offs.[7] In a game of Nature, the maximin rule does not have the self-evident status of the dominance rule. For example, Rapoport argues that the assumption of avoiding the worst possible outcome is only valid when one is dealing with a pessimistic actor.[8]

The pessimist asks: what is the worst that can happen? And the pessimist then chooses his maximin strategy. However, a decidedly optimistic actor would ask: what is the best that can happen? He will then go for the strategy which contains the highest of the four pay-offs. According to Rapoport, game theory offers no compelling reasons to adopt the reasoning of either pessimists or optimists, and thus to accept the maximin rule would be just arbitrary, failing solid information on the pessimistic dispositions of the actors. Since no such information is available from the survey, it must be concluded that we can not come up with a convincing rule of rational choice for respondents with any of the twelve preference orderings without dominant strategies.

Thus the consistency test of rational choice we shall adopt is necessarily incomplete. It uses the dominance rule of rational choice, which says that a rational actor chooses the dominant strategy, in case such a strategy is available. The consistency test requires that the reported strategy in the Potential Contributor's Dilemma is the dominant strategy of the reported preference ordering. The consistency test encloses six orderings with dominant strategy Cooperate (QPSR, QSPR, QSRP, SQPR, SQRP, and SRQP), and six orderings with dominant strategy Defect (PQRS, PRQS, PRSQ, RPQS, RPSQ, and RSPQ). The necessary and sufficient conditions for an ordering to have the strategy dominant Cooperate (Defect) are given by the pairwise rankings $Q > P$ and $S > R$ ($P > Q$ and $R > S$). As mentioned, the other twelve orderings have no dominant strategy attached to them. These orderings satisfy the following pairwise rankings: *either* $Q > P$ and $R > S$, corresponding to the orderings: QPRS, QRSP, QRPS, SRPQ, SPQR, and SPRQ, *or* $P > Q$ and $S > R$, corresponding to the orderings PQSR, PSQR, PSRQ, RQSP, RQPS, and RSQP. These twelve orderings are not enclosed by the consistency test.

---

[7] See Rapoport and Guyer, 1966: 205.   [8] See Rapoport, 1964: 33.

In sum, we have noted that it is impossible to make use of game-theoretical solution concepts in the games against Nature constituted by our environmental dilemmas. Nor is it possible to run expected utility calculations in these games. Moreover, the maximin rule cannot be accepted as a convincing rule of rational choice. We thus have to fall back on the the the dominance rule of rational choice, and this seriously reduces the number of responses that qualify for our consistency test. But in all honesty, that procedure will have to be accepted as the result of the informational limitations that were discussed above.

5.3 Choice of strategy

In the last section we presented a consistency test for the respondent's preference ordering and his or her strategy choice. A respondent satisfies this test if, and only if, he or she makes a rational choice. If the preference ordering reported has a dominant strategy, either Cooperate or Defect, then he or she must actually report that strategy in order to satisfy the test. In this section, we analyse how many respondents make a rational choice in the three environmental dilemmas. The question of the survey is presented for the case Chemical Waste. The question measures the respondent's intended behaviour in the setting of the Potential Contributor's Dilemma.

Interviewer: 'What would you do yourself with chemical household waste? Do you throw the waste away with the regular rubbish or do you bring it to the collection point?'

The answer to this question is interpreted as the respondent's choice of strategy. If he answers that he would throw away the chemical waste with the rest of the rubbish, this constitutes a choice for the strategy Defect. If the respondent answers that he would take his chemical waste to the collection point, this constitutes a choice for the strategy Cooperate. The same procedure is followed in the other two cases. Table 5.1 lists the answers of the respondents for all three cases in terms of Cooperate or Defect. The response category 'no choice' consists of answers showing that the respondent was unwilling or unable to specify a choice one way or the other. Most respondents were able to make a choice between Cooperate and Defect. But whereas in Chemical Waste and Energy Saving only 30 respondents fail to make a choice either way (1 per cent of the respective totals), Holiday Destination has no fewer than 140 respondents who were unable to choose, which is 13 per cent of the total response of this case. This case shows a very different picture from Chemical Waste or Energy Saving in the distribution of the strategy response as well. In Holiday Destination, 50 per cent of the respondents defect, against under 10 per cent in the other cases, while 37 per cent cooperate, against 90 per cent or more in the other cases.

Table 5.1 *Choice of strategy*

	Chemical Waste		Energy Saving		Holiday Destination	
	N	%	N	%	N	%
Choice:						
Defect	57	6	90	9	496	50
Cooperate	921	93	888	90	357	37
No choice	15	1	15	1	140	13
Total	993	100	993	100	993	100

The results of table 5.1 thus indicate that the respondents are prepared to make a personal sacrifice for handling chemical household waste, and for the conservation of household energy. However, most of them will not make such a sacrifice when their holidays are at stake. The results of table 5.1 are not very different from the preference response patterns which were recorded in tables 4.1 and 4.2. The resemblance suggests a positive outcome for the consistency test of rational choice. This will now be examined.

The question on the strategy choice in the Potential Contributor's Dilemma was answered by all 993 respondents in every case, irrespective of whether they reported a valid ordering. However, the consistency test imposes certain conditions on the response which need not be met by all respondents. These conditions are the ones that make it possible to check whether or not the response satisfies the dominance rule of rational choice. The respondent must report (1) a valid ordering with a dominant strategy and (2) either the strategy Cooperate or the strategy Defect.

There are several ways in which respondents can fail the consistency test. They may either fail to choose the dominant strategy that belongs to their reported ordering, or they may fail to satisfy conditions (1), (2) or both. These different ways of failing the test have a different significance. Failure to satisfy the dominance rule means that even though a respondent is rational in Arrow's minimal sense – he or she has reported a valid ordering – this choice is an irrational one. Failure to satisfy condition (1) may mean either of two things. First, the respondent is able to rank the four outcomes, but the ordering does not come with a dominant strategy. We do not have sufficient information to decide whether or not such a respondent has made a rational choice, in case he or she has reported a strategy. Secondly, the respondent may not be able to rank the four outcomes. In this case, the respondent fails to qualify as rational in Arrow's minimal sense, irrespective of whether he or she has reported a strategy. This category will not appear in our summary of the results of the consistency test below. Finally of course, failure to satisfy condition (2) simply means that no choice has been made one way or the other. In the remainder of this chapter we shall be looking at the results of the consistency test, keeping these various

Table 5.2 *Rational choice*

Preference Orderings	Dominant Strategy	Chemical Waste			Energy Saving			Holiday Destination		
		Defect	Coop	no	Defect	Coop	no	Defect	Coop	no
PQRS	Defect	2*	0	0	0	4	0	23*	2	2
PQSR	None	0	3	0	2	9	2	22	6	3
PRQS	Defect	4*	0	0	4*	7	2	42*	4	3
PRSQ	Defect	—	—	—	2*	4	0	15*	4	0
PSQR	None	1	0	0	1	2	0	4	0	0
PSRQ	None	—	—	—	0	2	0	7	2	0
RPQS	Defect	—	—	—	2*	6	0	67*	1	4
RPSQ	Defect	7*	0	0	5*	6	0	54*	3	3
RQPS	None	0	2	0	1	1	0	10	1	1
RQSP	None	0	5	0	1	1	0	10	0	1
RSPQ	Defect	1*	1	0	1*	2	0	9*	4	0
RSQP	None	0	1	0	0	1	0	3	1	3
QPRS	None	0	16	0	1	18	0	10	7	3
QPSR	Cooperate	5	153*	1	7	138*	1	38	50*	17
QRPS	None	0	6	0	0	5	0	3	2	1
QRSP	None	1	14	0	1	13	1	9	5	3
QSPR	**Cooperate**	**18**	**468***	**5**	**35**	**407***	**1**	**46**	**127***	**28**
QSRP	Cooperate	3	59*	0	4	63*	0	5	27*	1
SPQR	None	1	1	0	1	6	0	3	3	1
SPRQ	None	0	3	0	0	1	0	1	1	2
SQPR	Cooperate	1	13*	1	1	26*	2	13	15*	4
SQRP	Cooperate	1	8*	1	2	9*	0	2	10*	0
SRPQ	None	0	1	0	0	1	0	1	1	1
SRQP	Cooperate	0	4*	0	0	1*	0	1	3*	1
Column total		45	758	8	71	733	9	398	279	82
total valid orderings		811			813			759		
total rational choice		719* (89%)			658* (81%)			442* (58%)		

kinds of failure in mind. Table 5.2 summarizes the results of the consistency test of rational choice.

The twenty-four possible preference orderings are presented in the first column. The second column lists the dominant strategy that corresponds with each ordering, or the absence of a dominant strategy. The next three columns record the three possible answers to the strategy choice question for the various preference orderings, in each of the three cases.

The last row of table 5.2 shows how many individuals made a rational choice, in total and as a percentage of the valid orderings reported in each case. The information in the table may be illustrated by discussing the choices of the respondents with the most frequently reported ordering QSPR (printed bold-face). The dominant strategy that belongs to ordering QSPR is Cooperate. In Chemical Waste, 18 respondents with ordering QSPR choose not to bring the chemical household waste to the collecting point. In terms of game theory, they have chosen strategy Defect, contrary to their dominant strategy. Hence these 18 respondents have not made a rational choice.

Also, the 5 respondents who did not report a choice are labelled as not having made a rational choice. Finally, the 468 respondents with ordering QSPR who are willing to bring their chemical household waste to the collecting point report a cooperative strategy, in line with the dominance rule of rational choice we have adopted in our consistency test. Having made a rational choice, they thus satisfy the consistency test. To indicate this, these responses are marked with an asterisk '*'.

The respondents with ordering QSPR in Energy Saving are not necessarily the same people as the ones reporting that ordering in Chemical Waste. In Energy Saving, 35 respondents with QSPR report strategy Defect, and only one has 'no choice'. These respondents did not make a rational choice. 407 respondents are willing to save energy for a cleaner environment, i.e., they choose to cooperate. They satisfy the consistency test, hence they are considered as actors that made a rational choice.

In the last columns of table 5.2 we find the respondents with ordering QSPR in Holiday Destination. The 46 respondents with ordering QSPR who decide to travel far abroad have chosen to defect, hence they do not satisfy the dominance rule, which says that they should cooperate. These 46 are not rational choosers. Also, the 28 respondents in the category 'no choice' are not rational. Only 127 respondents choose to cooperate in this case, and they are marked with '*' to signify their rational choice. The responses for the other twenty-three orderings in table 5.2 can be read in the same way, taking account of the fact that responses from orderings without dominant strategies are lumped in the category 'no rational choice'.

Next, let us characterize the cases in terms of rational choices. In total, Chemical Waste has 811 valid orderings. 719 of these respondents made a rational choice (89 per cent). Energy Saving has 813 valid orderings and 658 respondents are marked as rational (81 per cent). The pattern of these cases is very similar. The high score of rational choice is largely due to the fact that most respondents with ordering QPSR or QSPR make a rational choice. The number of respondents who made a rational choice by defecting is almost negligible, below 2 per cent in each of these cases.

In the last columns of table 5.2, in the case Holiday Destination, we find a relatively high number of respondents with dominant Defect orderings. In contrast to the other two cases, very many respondents were not prepared to make a personal sacrifice concerning their holidays. Of the 759 respondents with a valid ordering, 442 made a rational choice (58 per cent). Compared to the high percentages for Chemical Waste and Energy Saving just mentioned, this is a much lower figure. Part of that is due to the fact that the orderings QPSR and QSPR, which score highly on consistency, are less frequently reported in Holiday Destination. But it should also be noted that this case has a somewhat higher percentage of orderings (16 per cent) without dominant strategies than Chemical Waste (7 per cent) and Energy Saving (9 per cent), as can be calculated from table 5.2. This depresses the consistency percentage of Holiday Destination, given the fact that its total of valid orderings is also lower than that of the other cases.

Staying with Holiday Destination for the moment, it is also instructive to look at the dominant Defect responses. A relatively large proportion of the 442 respondents made a rational choice by choosing to defect: 210, or 48 per cent. The combination of a large number of respondents with dominant Defect preferences and corresponding choices might suggest that in this case, the rational choice is often to be a free-rider. Yet, as one can see from table 5.2, no fewer than 121 of the 210 respondents who rationally defect do so from the orderings RPQS (67), RPSQ (54), and RSQP (9). These are not orderings that show a tendency to free ride on others' efforts to spend the holiday close at home. For the respondents who report them have the universally non-cooperative outcome R as their first preference. Clearly, such persons do not seem to believe that the cooperation of the others for the sake of the environment is the collective good on which they would wish to take a free ride, by playing dominant Defect.

We shall further discuss this kind of response in part III, when we examine the significance of the preference and motive results for the question of how effective the Dutch policies of self-regulation are. Those policies, as we discussed in section 2.4, wish to convince citizens that they should act responsibly in their daily lives, in order to help achieve environmental collective goods, for instance the reduction of greenhouse gases that are caused by mass recreative air travel. The preference responses that were just identified in the case of Holiday Destination may well indicate a refusal to live up to such environmental responsibility.

On the whole, the three cases perform rather well on the consistency test of table 5.2. Our method of assigning the qualification 'rational choice' seems to work out quite satisfactorily. But the characterization of the cases in terms of rational choices needs to be examined more closely than we have done above. This is the task of the next section.

5.4 The robustness of the dominance rule

The consistency test appears to be satisfied often, both in cases where most of the individuals are willing to cooperate, and in cases where the majority wilfully defects. This means that many respondents with dominant Cooperate orderings satisfy the conditions of rational choice, as well as the respondents with dominant Defect orderings. As mentioned above, in Chemical Waste 89 per cent of the respondents made a rational choice. In Energy Saving and Holiday Destination the respective percentages are 81 per cent and 58 per cent. We now want to examine what these percentages may mean.

The twenty-four preference orderings are presented in table 5.2 as just as many categories of a nominal variable. This makes it difficult to tell which of the three cases stands up best in the consistency test. Based upon the percentages of rational choice, it seems that Chemical Waste (89 per cent) has passed the test with flying colours, and Energy Saving (81 per cent) follows as a close second. Holiday Destination (58 per cent) falls behind the other two by far. However, the success of Chemical Waste and Energy Saving is highly dependent on two orderings. As we showed in section 5.3, these are the orderings QPSR and QSPR. The consistency percentage of Holiday Destination is far less dependent on these two orderings, and moreover it does very well with non-cooperative orderings. In this respect, Holiday Destination appears to be a more solid case than the other two.

We now analyse the robustness of the dominance rule in the three cases. This will allow more refined conclusions on performance than the overall consistency percentages permit. All orderings with the same dominant strategy are placed in two separate categories, Defect and Cooperate. We ignore the twelve orderings without a dominant strategy. The orderings in Defect and Cooperate are now matched with the two choice categories Defect and Cooperate. Respondents who made 'no choice' are again ignored. We now have constructed two dichotomous variables, one for orderings, which will be called Dominance Rule, and one for strategy choices, which is called Choice. The two are confronted in table 5.3.

The three cross-tabulations represent each of the three environmental cases. For the analysis of the robustness of the consistency test, Dominance Rule is taken to operate as the independent variable, and Choice as the dependent variable. The operational hypothesis for testing the relationship is formulated as follows: 'Individuals with preference orderings that have dominant strategy Defect will have a higher probability of choosing the strategy Defect than individuals with orderings that have a dominant strategy Cooperate.'

The hypothesis states that the variable Dominance Rule has an antecedent or causal role, and the variable Choice has a consequent or affected role in the relationship. The statistical inquiry of table 5.3 does not reject the operational hypothesis in the three cases. In other words, the proposition that individuals with maximizing rule Defect choose the non-cooperative option, and that individuals with maximizing rule Cooperate choose to make a contribution, is not disproved. Again, all three cases satisfactorily meet the consistency test. However, a comparison of the overall consistency percentages in table 5.2 and the statistical results in table 5.3 offers a different evaluation of their performances.

Table 5.3 *Dominance rule and choice of strategy*

Chemical Waste	Choice		
Dominance Rule	Defect	Cooperate	row total
Defect	14 (93%)	1 (7%)	15 (100%)
Cooperate	28 (4%)	705 (96%)	733 (100%)
column total	42 (6%)	706 (94%)	748 (100%)

Somers' D with Choice dependent .89 (T-value 3.84)
  Rational Choice: 719 (14 + 705)

Energy Saving	Choice		
Dominance Rule	Defect	Cooperate	row total
Defect	14 (32%)	29 (68%)	43 (100%)
Cooperate	49 (7%)	644 (93%)	693 (100%)
column total	63 (9%)	673 (91%)	736 (100%)

Somers' D with Choice dependent .25 (T-value 3.17)
  Rational Choice: 658 (14 + 644)

Holiday Destination	Choice		
Dominance Rule	Defect	Cooperate	row total
Defect	210 (92%)	18 (8%)	228 (100%)
Cooperate	105 (31%)	232 (69%)	337 (100%)
column total	315 (56%)	250 (44%)	565 (100%)

Somers' D with Choice dependent .61 (T-value 18.75)
  Rational Choice: 442 (210 + 232)

In Chemical Waste and Holiday Destination, the strength of the relationship among the two dichotomous variables is very strong: their respective coefficients of Somers' D asymmetric are .89 and .61. By contrast, the magnitude of the relationship between variables in the case Energy Saving is relatively weak: .25. In Energy Saving only 14 of the 43 individuals with dominant Defect have chosen the strategy Defect: 32 per cent.

In the case Chemical Waste 14 of the 15 respondents with dominant Defect actually choose Defect: 94 per cent. Holiday Destination has the highest number of respondents with dominant Defect (228), and 210 of the 228 have chosen the strategy Defect: 92 per cent. Since only a small number of respondents with maximizing rule Defect has chosen Defect in Energy Saving, the difference between the column percentages in table 5.3 is relatively small: 25 per cent (32% − 7%) and (68% − 93%). The difference of the column percentages in Holiday Destination is relatively large: 61 per cent (92% − 31%) and (8% − 69%). Also, in Chemical Waste the difference is very large: 89 per cent (93% − 4%) and (7% − 96%).

These figures indicate that the case Holiday Destination performs better than Energy Saving, although their respective percentages of rational choice in table 5.2 suggest otherwise. Table 5.3 confirms the results of table 5.2 for Chemical Waste. This case has the highest number of rational choices, and it also has the strongest measure of association.

5.5 Conclusion

The results of tables 5.2 and 5.3 contradict the assumption of the observer's perspective that rational actors in a large group will not voluntarily cooperate. From this perspective, all individuals who make a personal sacrifice for a cleaner environment must be irrational. Now, the findings of our survey might be questioned, by supposing that the respondents' answers are biased in the direction of a politically correct attitude to environmental problems. However, if this were true, it is hard to explain why the respondents express non-cooperative orderings and strategies in Holiday Destination, while the same respondents report cooperative orderings and strategies in the other two cases.

We see no a priori reasons to assume that respondents will disguise their 'true preferences' or strategy choices. Also, the question to what extent some preferences and choices might be more politically correct in one case than another is debatable. In contrast to most other countries, the environmental pollution of air traffic has become a political issue in the Netherlands, even though it is not an issue that is debated all the time. From a green perspective, it would probably be worse to confess that one travels by air to some exotic holiday destination, than to admit throwing away one's chemical household waste. So, if individuals are willing and able to express non-cooperative preferences and choices in Holiday Destination, while expressing cooperative preferences and cooperative choices in the other two cases, then it seems best to discount speculations on political correctness and take their answers seriously.

We have to emphasize the importance of the notion that the pursuit of maximizing utility does not prejudge the issue of what preferences an individual must have. An ordinary citizen facing environmental problems of collective action is like a consumer. The preferences of a consumer are by definition subjective, and the microeconomic definition of rationality of a consumer does not fix his preferences. The rationality of a consumer is defined by a consistency test, given his utility function.

By contrast, the observer's perspective treats the citizen as if he were an entrepreneur who thinks in terms of the criteria efficiency and effectiveness in order to survive. The entrepreneur is an economic actor whose rational behaviour is defined by marginal costs and benefits. If the entrepreneur chooses to incur costs in voluntarily contributing to a common goal, although he would gain without making such a contribution, then his behaviour is not rational. For example, the owner of a firm that produces chemical waste as a by-product will not cooperate to protect the environment unless he is forced to do so. Consider the owner of a small garage that runs a business in a highly competitive market, without environmental regulations. To avoid pollution of the environment, by taking care of waste, such as motor oil and other chemicals, involves considerable costs. If the garage-owner is the only one who does not throw away his chemical waste in the sewer, then he will be incurring extra costs without getting extra benefits in return. In the absence of regulation, none of our garage-owner's colleagues would be punished for their non-cooperative action. Thus, even though the garage-owner might personally regret dumping his own chemical waste in the sewer, it is the rational thing for him to do as an entrepreneur. If he chose to accept the extra costs for handling the chemical waste in order to improve the common good, he would eventually go broke. Only if all garages are forced by the local government to take care of their chemical waste will the problem be resolved.

Many rational choice theorists believe that any individual facing a problem of collective action will behave like our garage-owner. They conclude that the government must intervene to ensure that individuals make a contribution. In reality, most citizens in the Netherlands cooperate by voluntarily bringing their household chemical waste to the collecting point. It would be very peculiar if this were not the case. After all, most of the respondents stipulate their cooperative choices, when asked what to do with their chemical waste. Our point is that in most circumstances, the citizens can afford to make environmentally friendly choices, while the garage-owner cannot afford such a cooperative behaviour. For him, the strategy choice is part of his business decision-making. For a citizen, by contrast, the choice is not an entrepreneurial but a personal decision. He does not lose his competitive edge to another citizen if he decides to bring his batteries to the collecting point while no one else does. A garage-owner, however, can not justify incurring extra costs without receiving extra benefits.[9]

From an analytical point of view, the situation of the citizen and the garage-owner can be modelled as an n-person problem of collective action. Both actors are facing the outcome matrix of the Potential Contributor's Dilemma, and both must form a preference ordering and choose a strategy. In this respect the potential social dilemma is equivalent for the two kinds of actors. But as we have argued, this does not provide solid ground for assuming that the citizen and the garage-owner must have identical values and preferences.

It is plausible to assume that an entrepreneur will act according to the criteria of effectiveness and efficiency. Economic actors, such as fishermen who are facing common-pool resources, can sensibly be treated this way. But, the respondents of our survey are not entrepreneurs. They are ordinary citizens who

---

[9] For a large company the decision to cooperate can be influenced by, for example, green activists. Media exposure of protests changes the cost–benefit decision.

can formulate any preference they want. If one wishes to give a rational choice explanation of their behaviour, one has to regard citizens as consumers with subjective individual values and not as profit-maximizing entrepreneurs.

Rational choice theory has to assume that individuals are able and willing to express their subjective preferences based upon a variety of individual values. The implication is that one can no longer assume the existence of actual social dilemmas, but only of Potential Contributor's Dilemmas. Only by measuring the preferences of the individuals will it be possible to know whether or not there is a real-life actual dilemma.

The actor's perspective provides the theoretical framework to analyse the heterogeneity of individuals. It considers a diversity of preferences in a variety of environmental problems. So far, the findings of our survey confirm the usefulness of our approach. The results have important implications for political institutions that are dealing with the protection of the environment and other potential social dilemmas.

We discuss these implications in part III below. In the next chapter, we look at the motives behind the preference orderings. Explaining the relationship between preference orderings and choices is only one aspect of the actor's perspective. Another important aspect concerns the relationship between individual values and preferences.

In theory, each individual can have a variety of beliefs and values that lie at the root of his preference ordering. With the acceptance of the notion that an individual can order the outcomes of the Potential Contributor's Dilemma by whatever standards he deems relevant, we also accepted the prospect of dealing with idiosyncratic relationships. This means that from the actor's perspective, each individual can have a unique reason for his preferences. However, by measuring values in a survey research we have to assume some common ground to explain the relationship between preferences and individual values.

Another problem will arise when different people have different reasons for the same ordering. In contrast to the consistency test of rational choice, one cannot fall back on game-theoretical rules here. Our adoption of the dominance rule in the consistency test of rational choice is more or less a standard method of game theory. But game theory does not provide us with a counterpart method to deal with the link between individual values and preferences.

In the next chapter we present an empirical method that associates individual values with preference orderings. Our explanation of this relationship is an experimental model. There are different ways to implement the model and we have presented several try-outs.[10] The importance of the explanation of the relationship between individual values and orderings lies in the fact that it provides the thin-theory of rationality with a substantive empirical foundation.

---

[10] See Pellikaan 1994; Aarts, Pellikaan and van der Veen, 1995; van der Veen and Pellikaan, 1994.

6

Consistency of motives and preferences

6.1 A model of reasoned choice

The preference orderings of the respondents measured in chapter 4 reflect considerable diversity in the mix of motivations, beliefs, and social norms to which Arrow's shorthand term of 'individual values' refers. This diversity needs to be captured in manageable form, in order to explain the variety of preferences in environmental dilemmas.

In this chapter, we represent the individual values of the respondents in the survey by their responses on two general dimensions of motivation. The first dimension measures the evaluation of environmental collective action in the cases of Chemical Waste, Energy Saving, and Holiday Destination. We ask whether the respondent thinks that collective action for reducing environmental pollution is *desirable*. The responses on this dimension are regarded as motives of 'Valuation'. The second dimension measures the respondent's *own willingness* to take part in collective action. Here we ask whether the respondent is prepared to cooperate in the case at hand, at some cost to himself. Responses on this dimension are regarded as motives of 'Willingness'. Thus the individual values of respondents are described as a point in a two-dimensional space of motives. Each of the twenty-four possible preference orderings can be characterized as the consistent counterpart of a point in the motive space.

The next two sections explain the details of this procedure. But first we clarify the model of practical reasoning which links together the information on motives, preferences, and choice intentions. Briefly, it is assumed that successful practical reasoning involves choosing rationally from preferences which reflect the person's motives in the situation. The model is schematized in figure 6.1.

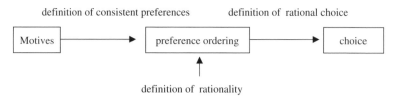

Figure 6.1 Model of practical reasoning.

The key element of the model is the preference ordering. In chapter 4 we explained how preferences are measured. Only respondents who are able to rank the four show cards that describe the outcomes of an environmental dilemma (for instance Chemical Waste) qualify as rational on Arrow's thin-theory: they have reported one of the twenty-four possible (complete and transitive) preference orderings. In chapter 5, the respondent's strategies of choice were measured, and choices were related to orderings by the test of rational choice. That test uses a weak definition of rational choice, which is borrowed from game theory: the dominance rule. Respondents are said to make a rational choice if, and only if, their preference ordering is associated with a dominant strategy to cooperate or defect, and their actual choice of a strategy is consistent with the dominant strategy. In this respect, the test of rational choice is a first test of consistency in the model of practical reasoning.

The measurement of motives on the two dimensions of Valuation and Willingness will be described below. While choices are linked to preferences by the definition of rational choice, motives are to be linked to preferences by a definition of consistent preferences. This definition uses a concept of consistency which models the actor's deliberative capacity to form preferences that are coherent with his motives. The definition is discussed in section 6.3. It leads to a second test, the test of consistent preferences. To get an intuitive sense of the consistency notion, consider a respondent with the familiar Prisoner's Dilemma ordering PQRS. This ordering is consistent only with motives which express (a) the respondent's resolute unwillingness to cooperate in the environmental dilemma, and (b) his positive evaluation of collective action (by the Others).

The two-stage model of the reasoning process in figure 6.1 runs from motives to choices, via preferences. In the first stage, preferences are related to motives by the test of consistent preferences. Respondents who qualify for this test are ones who satisfy Arrow's minimal definition of rationality, since they must have reported one of the twenty-four possible preference orderings. But what is captured by the test of consistent preferences is not part of the respondent's rationality, as here defined. The test of consistent preferences measures an aspect of practical reasoning that lies outside the ambit of rationality as we have conceived it here, namely as a property of strategy choice given the actor's preferences over outcomes. The test of consistent preferences checks whether or not a respondent successfully uses his powers of deliberation to rank the outcomes of the environmental dilemma in accordance with his stated motives. The second stage of the reasoning process does deal with the rationality of respondents. In this stage, preferences are related to choices by the test of rational choice. Again, respondents who qualify for this test should be rational actors, in Arrow's minimal sense. But the test of rational choice additionally checks an aspect of practical reasoning which likewise belongs to the concept of rationality: the capacity to choose according to the dominance rule, which guarantees that given preferences will be satisfied better than they would be under any alternative choice.

The point of this model is not only that it is informationally richer than a rational choice model, which operates exclusively from given preferences; it also serves to judge the *reliability* of the measured choice intentions, by going one step beyond preferences. This additional step is motivated by the thin-theory. Since that theory admits any complete and transitive preference ranking of the four outcomes of an environmental dilemma as a valid basis of a rational choice, it stands in need of testable assumptions concerning the motives that underlie preferences and choices. As we remarked in section 3.4, Green and Shapiro correctly note that the thin-theory of rationality imposes additional demands on 'measurement and empirical testing of rational choice-hypotheses'. We intend to take this suggestion seriously.

The notion of a 'reliable' choice is spelled out as follows, following the model of figure 6.1. Choices satisfying the dominance rule as well as the test of consistent preferences are choices that an actor can endorse, by reasoning from his individual values in the circumstances of an environmental dilemma. As long as these values remain the same, and provided that the circumstances do not change, a consistent actor has no incentive to choose differently. Choices that violate the dominance rule are subject to pressures of revision. Rational choices made on the basis of an inconsistent preference ordering may likewise be subject to pressures of revision, once the actor realizes that his motives require a different ranking of the outcomes of the dilemma.

6.2 The motives of Valuation and Willingness

In order to explain the variety of preference orderings in terms of the reasoning process outlined above, we need to examine the relationship between preferences and individual values. The individual values of a person are many-sided and diverse. Charting the full complexity of a person's individual values would require a separate study, for which the survey method may not be the most appropriate tool. For our purposes, the following operationalization of individual values will be sufficient. As was mentioned earlier, we select two independent dimensions of motivation in environmental dilemmas: the person's evaluation of voluntary collective action to reduce pollution, and the person's own willingness to bear the personal cost of cooperating in collective action. The measurement of the person's individual values is thus reduced to his responses on two dimensions of motivation, which are called the Valuation and Willingness dimensions, respectively. The operationalization of individual values proceeds by recording the respondent's agreement or disagreement, in each case of the dilemma, with two statements, the 'Valuation statement', and the 'Willingness statement'. In the survey, these statements are presented, following the measurement of the preferences. The interviewer hands out a card with the text: (1) fully agree, (2) agree, (3) neither agree nor disagree, (4) disagree, or (5) fully disagree and says: 'I will now present a number of statements to you. Could you indicate with the help of the following card to what extent you agree or disagree with the following statements?'

Chemical Waste

The Valuation statement: 'I believe that collecting toxic household waste at a recycling point for the sake of a cleaner environment is a good thing.'
   The Willingness statement: 'I am willing to spend the extra time and effort of bringing my toxic household waste to the recycling point for the sake of a cleaner environment.'

Energy Saving

The Valuation statement: 'I believe that saving energy in the household for the sake of a cleaner environment is a good thing.'
   The Willingness statement: 'I am willing to save energy in my household for the sake of a cleaner environment.'

Holiday Destination

The Valuation statement: 'I believe that spending the holiday close to home for the sake of a cleaner environment is a good thing.'
   The Willingness statement: 'I am willing to spend my holiday close to home for the sake of a cleaner environment.'

Before introducing the notion of consistent preferences, we present the responses to the Valuation and Willingness statements, and briefly compare them to the preference responses of table 4.2. This comparison shows that motives and preferences are indeed related systematically, in ways that one can intuitively grasp. For reasons of tractability, the five-point Valuation and

Table 6.1 *Motives on the Valuation scale*

		Chemical Waste		Energy Saving		Holiday Destination	
		N	%	N	%	N	%
V1	positive Valuation	974	98	950	96	523	54
V2	intermediate Valuation	14	2	26	3	225	23
V3	negative Valuation	3	0	16	2	220	23
Total		991	100	992	100	968	100

Willingness scales are reduced to two three-point scales, by drawing together the response categories 'fully (dis)agree' and '(dis)agree'. Table 6.1 thus lists three categories on the Valuation scale: (1) agreement, (2) neither agreement nor disagreement, and (3) disagreement. Each of these categories distinguishes a particular stance on the Valuation dimension, or in short a 'motive'. 'Agreement' is labelled as the motive of 'positive Valuation' (V1), 'neither agreement nor disagreement' as the motive of 'intermediate Valuation' (V2) and 'disagreement' as the motive of 'negative Valuation' (V3).[1]

The cases of Chemical Waste and Energy Saving show a remarkably high percentage of respondents who indicate that they positively value voluntary collecting of toxic waste and economizing on energy in the household. Almost none disagree with the Valuation statement in Chemical Waste and Energy Saving. By contrast, in Holiday Destination just over half of the respondents agree with the statement that spending the holiday close to home is a good thing, while 23 per cent disagree. This shows that protecting the environment from being polluted by voluntary reduction of recreational travel is perceived as a more problematic form of collective action than getting rid of toxic waste in the appropriate way, or cutting down on energy consumption.

Next, consider the responses to the Willingness statements. Table 6.2 lists three categories on the Willingness scale: (1) agreement, (2) neither agreement nor disagreement, and (3) disagreement. Each of these categories distinguishes a particular stance on the Willingness dimension, or in short, a 'motive'. 'Agreement' is labelled as the motive of 'positive Willingness' (W1), 'neither agreement nor disagreement' as the motive of 'intermediate Willingness' (W2) and 'disagreement' as the motive of 'negative Willingness' (W3).[2]

Again, Chemical Waste and Energy Saving show very high percentages of respondents who indicate that they are willing to bring away their toxic household waste to the recycling point, or to save energy. Few disagree with the Willingness statement in Chemical Waste and Energy Saving. By contrast, in

---

[1] The response category of 'no opinion' is listed as 'missing', and is not included in the table.
[2] The response category of 'no opinion' is listed again as 'missing'.

Table 6.2 *Motives on the Willingness scale*

		Chemical Waste		Energy Saving		Holiday Destination	
		N	%	N	%	N	%
W1	positive Willingness	918	92	895	90	318	33
W2	intermediate Willingness	48	5	71	7	207	21
W3	negative Willingness	25	3	25	3	442	46
Total		991	100	991	100	967	100

Holiday Destination, just under a third agree with the Willingness statement, while over 40 per cent disagree. This shows that the respondents are far less ready to participate in collective action when it comes to cutting down on their recreational travel than when their household activities of toxic waste disposal or saving of energy are at issue.

These results are now combined. Table 6.3 presents the joint answers to the Valuation and Willingness statements in cross-tabulations for each of the cases. The combination of motives reported by a respondent (Vi, Wj) (i,j = 1, 2, 3) is called the respondent's 'motive structure'.

In the table of Chemical Waste, a total of 990 respondents has reported a motive (positive, intermediate, or negative) on each of the two scales. In the upper-left cell (V1, W1), for instance, 909 of these have a motive structure of positive Valuation and positive Willingness. This frequency may, for instance, be compared to the corresponding cell of Holiday Destination, where only 244 out of a total of 951 respondents positively value collective action for the environment, and are willing to take part in it themselves.

At this point it is helpful to compare some of the motive structures in the three cases of the dilemma to some reported preferences. Intuitively, the motive structure of positive Valuation and positive Willingness corresponds to a type of preference ordering that puts universal cooperation (Q) in first place, and has a dominant strategy to cooperate. Conversely, motive structures of negative Valuation and negative Willingness may be expected to go together with non-cooperative preference orderings, in which the universally non-cooperative outcome (R) is preferred, and which have a dominant strategy to defect. We shall elaborate on this in the next section. But when the motive and preference data are regarded in this loose way, the patterns of cooperative attitude revealed by table 6.3 are pretty much in line with the reported frequencies of typically co-operative preference orderings.[3] These frequencies were recorded in table 4.2.

---

[3] In terms of *preferences*, the first two cases are highly cooperative when they are characterized by the percentages of the two most frequently reported orderings with a dominant strategy to cooperate, QPSR and QPSR. In Chemical Waste and Energy Saving, these two orderings occur

Table 6.3 *Motive structures of Valuation and Willingness*

Chemical Waste

	Willingness scale			
Valuation scale	W1	W2	W3	Row total
V1	909	43	21	973
V2	8	5	1	14
V3	—	—	3	3
Column total	917	48	25	990

Energy Saving

	Willingness scale			
Valuation scale	W1	W2	W3	Row total
V1	881	60	7	948
V2	12	6	8	26
V3	2	4	10	16
Column total	895	70	25	990

Holiday Destination

	Willingness scale			
Valuation scale	W1	W2	W3	Row total
V1	244	130	139	513
V2	46	59	115	220
V3	22	16	180	218
Column total	312	205	434	951

In general, the results from tables 4.2 and 6.3 seem to confirm that the Valuation and Willingness dimensions can usefully capture aspects of individual values relevant for explaining reported preference orderings. This can be shown by examining some other motive structures as well. Empirically, the two motive dimensions tend to correspond strongly with each other, at least for many respondents, as table 6.3 demonstrates. But conceptually, a person's

in 650/811 or 80%, and 589/813 or 72% of reported preferences (as calculated from table 4.2). By contrast, Holiday Destination is clearly the least cooperative case, with only 308 QSPR or QPSR-orderings out of 759 reported preferences (41%). In terms of *motive structures*, a similar pattern emerges from the frequencies of positive Valuation and positive Willingness of table 6.3. In Chemical Waste and Energy Saving, the percentages of motive structure (V1,W1) in the total of reported motive structures are 909/990 or 92%, and 89%, respectively, while in Holiday Destination the corresponding percentage is only 244/951 or 26%.

willingness to cooperate need not necessarily run parallel with his or her positive Valuation of environmental collective action. The two motives may be inversely related. Olson's logic of collective action provides a good example of this. His point is that an individual actor attaches high value to the benefit of achieving the common interest, while as a member of a large group, his or her willingness to contribute is completely absent. As we already remarked above, motives of positive Valuation and negative Willingness are intuitively consistent with the Prisoner's Dilemma ordering PQRS. Taking this for granted for the moment, then, one can compare the frequencies of the Prisoner's Dilemma ordering in each case of the dilemma to the frequencies of the corresponding motives. Table 4.2 showed that this ordering occurs very rarely in each of the three cases, and most frequently in the case of Holiday Destination. Now as table 6.3 shows, the motive structure (V1, W3) occurs relatively rarely as well, and again most frequently in Holiday Destination. At the level of motives, this confirms what was said earlier when we commented on the distribution of preference orderings in table 4.2: none of the three cases can be plausibly regarded as cases of an *actual* social dilemma, in which cooperation fails, because free-riding attitudes predominate.

6.3 The test of consistent preferences

As noted, the three-point scales of Valuation and Willingness generate nine possible motive structures (Vi, Wj) (i,j = 1, 2, 3). We are not claiming any-thing substantive, at this point, about the personal reasons that might underlie someone's decision to report a particular combination of motives. Since the two dimensions are logically independent, any motive structure can be regarded as a valid response, from the actor's perspective, just as any of the twenty-four possible preference orderings is regarded as a valid response. The question is: how should one assess the relationship between the motive structures and the preference orderings which the respondents have reported? To show how this may be done is the topic of the present section. Following the model of practical reasoning explained in section 6.1, we suppose that a person's pref-erences are a reflection of how his or her individual values guide rational ac-tion, under specified beliefs about causal connections in the world. Here, these beliefs are standardly given by the circumstances of the Potential Contributor's Dilemma.[4]

The linkage of the twenty-four preference orderings to the nine motive struc-tures is based on the following idea. The motives that a *consistent* respondent chooses on the dimensions of Valuation and Willingness (positive, intermediate,

---

[4] Note, however, that respondents may entertain different beliefs concerning the effectiveness of collective action for achieving a less polluted state of the environment, in each of the three cases. We shall take up some of the survey evidence for this in chapter 13.

		Column player: The Others	
		Waste recycled (C)	Waste thrown away (D)
Row player: Individual	Waste recycled (C)	**Q**	**S**
	Waste thrown away (D)	**P**	**R**

Figure 6.2 The Potential Contributor's Dilemma of Chemical Waste.

or negative) will commit that respondent to obey specific *constraints* on how the four outcomes of the dilemma should be ranked in order of preference. The constraints of a particular motive, for instance V2, or W1, reflect what it signifies to adopt that motive, given the proper meanings of the Valuation and the Willingness statements in the cases at hand. Once these constraints have been spelled out, each of the nine motive structures will be consistent only with some of the twenty-four possible preference orderings. The preference orderings that satisfy the constraints imposed by a given motive structure form the *consistent set* of that motive stucture.

A respondent is consistent, then, if and only if his or her reported preference ordering is in the consistent set of his or her reported motive structure. Our task is now to determine the consistent sets of the nine motive structures. We start by separately discussing the constraints on preference orderings for the three motives on the dimensions of Valuation and Willingness.

Ideas about the consistency of motives and preferences obviously depend on one's substantive assumptions about the constraints that the motives impose on the ranking of the four outcomes of the dilemma. As we just said, such assumptions arise from notions about the meaning of the Valuation and Willingness statements. It should be recognized that such notions are contestable, up to a point. In the present analysis, therefore, we shall make only very weak assumptions regarding the meanings of the two statements. Our assumptions are placed within the Potential Contributor's Dilemma, in which the respondent is supposed to identify with the row player, Individual. Figure 6.2 reproduces the dilemma in an appropriate form, with Chemical Waste as example.

We now specify the constraints of the three positions on the Valuation scale, starting at the positive end. The Valuation statement, for the case of Chemical Waste, says: 'I believe that collecting toxic household waste at a recycling point for the sake of a cleaner environment is a good thing.' If a consistent respondent agrees with this statement (positive Valuation, V1), then he or she is bound to prefer outcome Q to outcome S, and outcome P to outcome R. On this first assumption, agreement with the Valuation statement expresses a positive evaluation of achieving a less polluted environment through collective action, in the following sense: *for the same strategy of Individual*, Individual prefers the cooperation of the Others to their defection.

This assumption is explained as follows. Positive Valuation means that the respondent believes it to be good that collective action, of the kind specified by the case at hand, is undertaken for the sake of the environment. The collective action may or may not include Individual's own cooperation, but it must always include that of the Others. Hence, Individual positively values the cooperation of the Others. Now there are two plausible ways of translating this meaning of positive Valuation into constraints on the ranking of outcomes. The first one is the weakest, and it runs as follows: if Individual were to cooperate (either Q or S), then he or she would prefer the Others to cooperate (Q > S), and if Individual were to defect (either P or R) then he or she would also prefer the Others to cooperate (P > R). These weak constraints are the ones we adopt. They say that Individual prefers the cooperation of the Others to their defection, on condition that Individual's own strategy is held constant. The second way of translating positive Valuation into constraints on the ranking of outcomes is more demanding. It says that Individual prefers *any* outcome in which the Others cooperate to *any* outcome in which they defect. This implies the pairwise rankings Q > S and P > R, in which Individual's own strategy is held constant, but it also implies Q > R, and P > S, in which Individual's own strategy switches between the outcomes he or she is evaluating. We here reject the more demanding constraints, and are thus content to assume that a consistent respondent with positive Valuation will always prefer Q to S and P to R, whatever else he or she may prefer.[5]

Next, the constraints of 'disagreement' with the Valuation statement are assumed to be the *mirror image* of the constraints of agreement. Thus, if a consistent respondent disagrees with the Valuation statement (negative Valuation, V_3), then he or she is bound to prefer outcome S to outcome Q, and outcome R to outcome P. The motive of negative Valuation should not be misconstrued. It does not necessarily mean that the respondent thinks that a more polluted environment is more valuable than a less polluted one, considered in isolation from the (costly) collective action needed to produce either of these states. The respondent may *either* hold that a more polluted environment is to be preferred, and thus reject collective action for the sake of a less polluted environment. *Or* hold that a more polluted environment is indeed the worse of the two states, but that it is not worth having collective action to reduce pollution,

---

[5] The more demanding assumption mentioned in the test has been tried. It leads to a more complex analysis of the consistent linkages between motives and preferences, while not much affecting the empirical results to be presented below on the basis of the weak assumption. See van der Veen, 1996. For different tests of consistency, see Aarts, Pellikaan and van der Veen, 1995, and van der Veen and Pellikaan, 1994.

on balance, independently of his or her personal willingness to participate in any such action. In both of these cases of negative Valuation, the respondent will prefer S to Q, and R to P. As we show in chapter 10, the distinction between these two ways of construing negative Valuation is important for assessing the response on motives and preferences in the context of Dutch self-regulation policies that appeal to the environmental responsibility of citizens.

Finally, we specify the constraints of 'neither agreement nor disagreement' with the Valuation statement (intermediate Valuation, V2). These constraints reflect the logical possibilities of occupying the position in between positive and negative Valuation, given the constraints of each of these extremes. Intermediate Valuation is therefore defined disjunctively by two alternative constraints, either of which may be in force. The respondent with intermediate Valuation *either* prefers Q to S (in line with positive Valuation) and R to P (in line with negative Valuation) *or* prefers S to Q (in line with negative Valuation) and P to R (in line with positive Valuation). Under the first alternative, the respondent in Individual's position wants the Others to cooperate in case he or she were also to cooperate. It is also desired that the Others defect in case he or she were also to defect. Under the second alternative, the respondent wants the Others to defect, were he or she to cooperate, and wants the Others to cooperate, were he or she to defect. The two alternative constraints on the ranking of the four outcomes show that intermediate Valuation reflects an ambivalent attitude towards the desirability of obtaining a less polluted environment through collective action, though each of the two does so in a different way. From the actor's perspective, these two ways of ranking the four possible outcomes of the dilemma cover different aspects of a respondent's individual values, as these are activated by his intermediate response V3 to the Valuation statement.

Our assumptions on the constraints of the motives on the Valuation scale are summed up in figure 6.3, together with the consistent sets of orderings that belong to each of these motives.

We now consider the meaning of the Willingness statement in the context of the dilemma, as illustrated in figure 6.2. Again we make minimal assumptions as to what the gradations of agreement with that statement impose by way of constraints on preference orderings. The Willingness statement, for the case of Chemical Waste, says: 'I am willing to spend the extra time and effort of bringing my toxic waste to the recycling point for the sake of the environment.' A consistent respondent who agrees with the Willingness statement (positive Willingness, W1) is assumed to prefer outcome Q to outcome P, and outcome S to outcome R. Agreement with the Willingness statement expresses willingness to contribute to a less polluted environment, in the following sense: *for the same strategy of the Others*, Individual prefers his own cooperation to his own defection.

Motive	Constraints on orderings	Consistent sets of orderings
V1	Q > S and P > R	QSPR, QPSR, QPRS, PQSR, PQRS, PRQS
V2	either Q > S and R > P	QSRP, QRSP, QSPR, RQPS, RQSP, RPQS
	or S > Q and P > R	SQPR, SPQR, SPRQ, PSQR, PSRQ, PRSQ
V3	S > Q and R > P	SRQP, SQRP, SRPQ, RSQP, RPSQ, RSPQ

Figure 6.3 Constraints and consistent sets of Valuation motives.

This assumption is explained as follows. In the Potential Contributor's Dilemma, Individual's cooperation always involves a cost to himself, for instance in Chemical Waste, the time and effort spent on bringing toxic household waste away to the recycling point. But the state of the environment (more or less pollution) in effect only depends on the cooperation or defection of the Others. The Willingness statement, however, does not mention anything regarding the actions of the Others. Thus agreement with this statement means that the respondent is willing to bear the cost of cooperating, regardless of what the Others do. There are again two plausible ways of translating positive Willingness into constraints on the ranking of outcomes. The weaker of these two is the one we adopt. It says that Individual prefers to cooperate, holding constant the strategy of the Others. Hence if the Others were to cooperate (either Q or P), then Individual would prefer to cooperate himself (Q > P), and if the Others were to defect (either S or R), then Individual would still prefer to cooperate (S > R). The more demanding way of interpreting positive Willingness says that Individual prefers *any* outcome in which he cooperates to *any* outcome in which he defects. This implies Q > P, Q > R, S > P and S > R. We reject this more demanding set of rankings, and are thus content to assume that a consistent respondent with positive Willingness will always prefer Q to P and S to R, whatever else he may prefer. The constraints of positive Willingness have strong behavioural consequences for rational actors, since the pairwise rankings Q > P and S > R define a dominant strategy to cooperate, as we noted in section 5.3.

Next, the constraints of 'disagreement' with the Willingness statement are assumed to be the *mirror image* of the constraints on agreement. Thus if a consistent respondent disagrees with the Willingness statement (negative Willingness, V3), then he is bound to prefer outcome P to outcome Q and outcome R to outcome S. Once more, the behavioural consequences of this assumption for rational actors are strong, since the pairwise rankings P > Q and R > S define a dominant strategy to defect.

Motive	Constraints on orderings	Consistent sets of orderings
W1	Q > P and S > R	QSPR, QPSR, QSRP, SQRP, SQPR, SRQP
W2	either Q > P and R > S	QRPS, QRSP, QPRS, RQPS, RQSP, RSQP
	or P > Q and S > R	PSRQ, PQSR, PSQR, SRPQ, SPQR, SPRQ
W3	P > Q and R > S	PRQS, PQRS, PRSQ, RSPQ, RPSQ, RPQS

Figure 6.4 Constraints and consistent sets of Willingness motives.

Finally, the constraints of 'neither agreement nor disagreement' with the Willingness statement reflect the logical possibilities of occupying the position in between positive and negative Willingness, given the constraints of the last two motives. The constraints of intermediate Willingness (W2) are defined disjunctively by two alternatives, either of which may hold. The respondent *either* prefers Q to P (in line with positive Willingness) and R to S (in line with negative Willingness) *or* he prefers P to Q (in line with negative Willingness) and S to R (in line with positive Willingness). Under the first alternative, the respondent in Individual's position wants to cooperate in case the Others cooperate, and he wants to defect in case the Others defect. Under the second alternative, the respondent wants to defect if the Others cooperate, and he wants to cooperate if the Others defect. The orderings consistent with the constraints of intermediate Willingness have no dominant strategy attached to them. The alternative constraints on the ranking of the four outcomes show that intermediate Willingness reflects a *conditional* attitude to taking part in a scheme of collective action, though each alternative will let the preferred strategy depend on the prospective actions of the others in a different way. From the actor's perspective, the two alternative ways of ranking the four possible outcomes of the dilemma express different aspects of a respondent's individual values, as these are activated by his intermediate position W3 in response to the Willingness statement.

Our assumptions on the constraints of the motives on the Willingness scale are summed up in figure 6.4, together with the consistent sets of orderings that belong to each of these motives.

After having specified the different constraints of the motives on the Valuation and Willingness dimensions, we are now in a position to deal with the question posed at the beginning of this section. Which of the twenty-four possible preference orderings are consistent with each of the nine possible motive structures (Vi, Wj) (i,j = 1, 2, 3)? Fortunately, the answer is straightforward. On our assumptions, the Valuation and Willingness constraints are mutually

Willingness scale

Valuation scale	W1		W2		W3	
	Dominant C		No dominant strategy		Dominant D	
V1	QSPR	QPSR	QPRS	PQSR	PRQS	PQRS
V2	QSRP	SQPR	QRPS	QRSP	PRSQ	RPQS
			PSQR	PSRQ		
			SPQR	SPRQ		
			RQSP	RQPS		
V3	SRQP	SQRP	SRPQ	RSQP	RPSQ	RSPQ

Figure 6.5 Consistency between preference orderings and motives.

compatible for each of the nine motive structures. Thus, to be consistent with a given motive structure, say (V2, W3), a preference ordering must satisfy the constraints defined by the Valuation position (V2), as well as the constraints defined by the Willingness position (W3). In general, it follows that the consistent set of any motive structure (Vi, Wj) is the *intersection* of the consistent sets of its component motives Vi and Wj.[6] The nine consistent sets of preferences are shown in figure 6.5.

It may be noted that each of the twenty-four possible preference orderings is consistent with only one of the nine possible motive structures. As shown in figure 6.5, the orderings in the Willingness columns are of the same type with respect to the dominance rule of rational choice, whereas the orderings in the Valuation rows are of different types. This reflects the fact, noted above, that the gradations along the motive dimension of Willingness record definite dispositions to act, whereas the gradations along the motive dimension of Valuation record different evaluative attitudes towards environmental collective

---

[6] To show this informally, we consider motive structure (V1, W1). As was summarized in figure 6.3, the constraints of motive V1 are Q > S and P > R. The constraints of motive W1 are Q > P and S > R, from figure 6.4. By transitivity of the ordering relation, Q > P and P > R implies Q > R. Thus, the constraints of V1 and W1 jointly fix five of the six possible ordered pairs of outcomes in a preference ordering of four outcomes, leaving only the pair (P,S) unspecified. These constraints are satisfied by only two orderings, QSPR and QPSR. Hence the consistent set of motive structure (V1, W1) consists of these two orderings only. As can further be seen from figures 6.3 and 6.4, QSPR and QPSR belong to the consistent set of motive V1, together with four other orderings. These same two orderings belong to the consistent set of motive W1 as well, again together with four other orderings, which, moreover, are different from the four others in the consistent set of motive V1. Hence the orderings QSPR and QPSR in the consistent set of (V1, W1) form the intersection of the consistent sets of motives V1 and W1. The consistent sets of the eight remaining motive structures can be derived in the same way.

action, without thereby committing a rational actor to act in a certain way. Finally, it can be seen that the upper left cell of figure 6.5 only has orderings with the universally cooperative outcome Q as first preference and the universally non-cooperative outcome R as last preference. This cell corresponds to motive structure (V1,W1), which combines positive Valuation and positive Willingness. Following the diagonal to the lower right cell (V3,W3) in figure 6.5, which combines negative Valuation and negative Willingness, the reverse holds: the orderings in this cell rank the universally non-cooperative outcome first, and the universally cooperative outcome last.

Similarly, the consistent orderings with the free-rider outcome P and the sucker outcome S as first or last preference are oriented along the diagonal running from the upper right cell (P first preference) to the lower left one (S first preference). The corner cells of this diagonal thus show the preferences belonging to motive structures in which the responses on the Valuation and Willingness dimensions are inversely related.

The test of consistent preferences can now be stated. First we define which respondents *qualify* for the test. These are only the respondents who report one of the twenty-four preference orderings, as well as one of the nine motive structures. We now stipulate that respondents who do not qualify for the test fail it. These respondents have not expressed a definite opinion about the Valuation and Willingness statements. Or they have not been able to rank the four outcomes of the dilemma, according to the instructions of the interview. Or, possibly, they have failed on both counts. The failure of these respondents to pass the test of consistent preferences is not that they give inconsistent answers, but rather that they do not satisfy the informational conditions for judging their consistency in the first place.

Secondly, we define which respondents who do qualify for the test pass or fail. Those whose reported ordering is (is not) in the consistent set of their reported motive structure, as specified by figure 6.5, pass (fail) the test. As noted above, there are several ways to construct a test of consistent preferences. Depending on the assumptions on how the respondents interpret the meaning of agreeing or disagreeing with the motive statements of the interview, one can build up a configuration of the twenty-four preference orderings in the two-dimensional space of Valuation and Willingness. As a consequence of this variety, it becomes difficult in some respects to evaluate the performance of the respondents on the consistency test which was presented in this section.

Below we shall address this problem indirectly, by asking to what extent consistency, as defined by figure 6.5, makes a difference for rational choice. It will be found that respondents who pass the test of consistent preferences are more likely to follow the dominance rule of rational choice than respondents who fail the test. Meanwhile, in the next section, we present and discuss the empirical results of the consistency test.

Table 6.4 *Consistent preferences compared to the motive-preference response*

Chemical Waste (Consistency ratio: $617/810 = 76\%$)

Valuation scale	Willingness scale			Row total
	W_1	W_2	W_3	
V_1	747 (612)	36 (2)	15 (1)	798 (615)
V_2	6 (1)	2 (0)	1 (0)	9 (1)
V_3	—	—	3 (1)	3 (1)
Column total	753 (613)	38 (2)	19 (2)	810 (617)

Energy Saving (Consistency ratio: $565/812 = 70\%$)

Valuation scale	Willingness scale			Row total
	W_1	W_2	W_3	
V_1	724 (553)	53 (6)	6 (1)	783 (560)
V_2	6 (0)	5 (1)	5 (1)	16 (2)
V_3	2 (0)	2 (0)	9 (3)	13 (3)
Column total	732 (553)	59 (7)	21 (5)	812 (565)

Holiday Destination (Consistency ratio: $204/741 = 28\%$)

Valuation scale	Willingness scale			Row total
	W_1	W_2	W_3	
V_1	187 (129)	111 (8)	106 (15)	404 (152)
V_2	40 (3)	41 (2)	95 (17)	176 (22)
V_3	14 (0)	12 (0)	135 (30)	161 (30)
Column total	241 (132)	164 (10)	336 (62)	741 (204)

6.4 Consistent preferences in the three cases

How well do the respondents perform on the test of consistent preferences in the three cases? In the present comparison, we are interested in the performance of respondents who qualify for the test. Our overall measure of performance in a case is the 'consistency ratio': the total number of consistent preferences divided by the total number of respondents with a valid motive structure and a valid ordering. This last number is called the 'motive-preference' response.

In table 6.4, the consistency ratio of the cases is calculated from the figures in the 'totals' cell, located at the lower right of each case matrix. In this cell, the motive-preference response is mentioned first, and the number of consistent orderings is mentioned second, in brackets. In the nine cells of the three matrices

(Vi, Wj) of table 6.4, the motive-preference response and the bracketed number of consistent orderings are also specified separately for each motive structure.

To get a grip on these numbers, consider the case of Chemical Waste. In total, 810 of the 811 respondents who reported a complete preference ordering (see table 4.2), have reported a complete motive structure as well. Thus the total motive-preference response is 810, and it is distributed among the nine different cells of Chemical Waste. For instance, in cell (V1, W1), 747 respondents have reported motive structures of positive Valuation and positive Willingness. All of these respondents also reported a complete preference ordering. However, only 612 of them have reported either of the two orderings QSPR or QPSR, which are the only ones consistent with motive structure (V1, W1). The preference orderings of those 612 respondents are thus in line with what follows from their motives V1 and W1, given the assumptions we have made about how the 'agreement'-response to the Valuation and the Willingness statement constrains preference orderings.

Next, Energy Saving has 724 instances of positive Valuation and Willingness in a motive-preference response of 812. Of these 724 respondents, 553 are consistent. Likewise in Holiday Destination, 187 out of a total motive-preference response of 741 are in cell (V1, W1) and of these 187 respondents, 129 are consistent.

Table 6.4 shows a pattern which will be familiar by now. In terms of their distribution of the motive-preference response, Chemical Waste and Energy Saving look very much alike. Both predominantly show motives of positive Valuation and Willingness. Also, the consistency ratios of these cases do not differ largely. Of the 810 respondents in Chemical Waste who qualify for the test of consistent preference, 617 or 76 per cent actually pass it. In Energy Saving, the ratio is roughly similar, 565/812 or 70 per cent. Moreover, in both cases, virtually all of the consistent orderings are located in the upper left cell (V1, W1). The numbers of consistent orderings in the other eight cells of Chemical Waste and Energy Saving are quite small.

In Holiday Destination, the ratio of consistency is far smaller than in the other two cases. Of the 741 respondents who qualify for the test, only 204 or 28 per cent manage to pass it. Moreover, the configuration of consistent preferences in the matrix of Holiday Destination is different. Even though the majority of consistent orderings occurs in the cell of positive Valuation and positive Willingness (V1, W1), as it does in the other two cases, it is a far smaller majority in Holiday Destination, while consistent orderings occur more frequently in the remaining eight cells, unlike in the other two cases. As can be seen from the table also, the (disaggregated) consistency ratio between motives and preferences in cell (V1, W1) is higher than it is in the other cells, in every case.

Thus the low performance of Holiday Destination is due to the fact that the overall consistency ratio is strongly affected by how the consistent motive-preference response is distributed among the nine motive structures. Compared to Chemical Waste and Energy Saving, Holiday Destination is clearly a case in which collective action for a less polluted environment, as exemplified by motive V1, gets far less consistent support from respondents, and the consistent willingness to take part in such action (motive W1) is far less widespread as well. In chapter 13, we analyse the policy significance of this in some detail.

6.5 Does motive-preference consistency matter?

One way of looking at the significance of the test of consistent preferences is to causally relate it to the test of rational choice. The test of rational choice was introduced in chapter 5. Only respondents who have orderings with a dominance rule qualify for the test, and it requires that the reported choice of the respondent (to cooperate or defect) must follow the dominant strategy (cooperative or non-cooperative) which is associated with his reported ordering. In section 5.4, we noted that in all cases of the dilemma, orderings with a dominance rule are positively associated with the corresponding choices, as measured by the Somers' D asymmetric coefficient, with the dichotomous variable Choice as the dependent variable and the dichotomous variable Dominance Rule as the independent one. The positive dependence of Choice upon Dominance Rule is strongest for the case of Chemical Waste, followed by Holiday Destination. It turns out to be much weaker in the case of Energy Saving, as table 5.3 shows.

To see whether consistency between motives and preferences matters, we now split the respondents who have reported a motive structure, an ordering with a dominant strategy, and a choice to either cooperate or defect, into two groups. The first group includes respondents with *consistent* orderings, and the second group includes respondents with *inconsistent* orderings. The question we want to examine is the following. Do respondents in the first group perform better on the test of rational choice than respondents in the second one?

There is a theoretical reason for asking this question. Respondents in both groups are rational, in the minimal sense that they are capable of reporting a transitive and complete preference ordering of the outcomes of the dilemma. However, respondents in the first group are also able to match their preference orderings with their motives of Valuation and Willingness, unlike those in the second group. The matching instructions are defined by the test of consistent preferences. Now if this test is reasonably well-constructed, then passing rather than failing the test should certainly make a difference to rational choice, according to the model of practical reasoning which we described in section 6.1 above.

In particular, one would then expect that the first group of respondents, whose preferences cohere with their motives, will be better placed to use their cognitive powers of making a rational choice than respondents in the second group, whose preferences are unrelated to their motives, according to the test. From this we deduce a proposition that can be subjected to statistical analysis. The proposition says that members of the first group (consistent preferences) will perform significantly better on the test of rational choice than members of the second group (inconsistent preferences).

The proposition is analysed with the aid of a three-variable cross-tabulation. Table 6.5 shows the relationship between the dichotomous variables Dominance Rule (either orderings with dominant cooperative strategies or orderings with dominant defect strategies) and Choice (either cooperate or defect), controlling for the dichotomous variable Consistent Preferences, which distinguishes the first group from the second one.

In Chemical Waste, the association between Dominance rule and Choice is very strong.[7] The variable Consistent Preferences explains part of this relationship. The respondents with consistent preferences do much better, and those with inconsistent preferences do only slightly less well than the bivariate relationship displayed in table 5.3 (Choice dependent 0.89). In this case of the dilemma, the respondents with consistent preferences have almost a perfect score (0.97), and those with inconsistent preferences are still doing very well (0.83). This suggests that passing the test of consistent preferences in Chemical Waste tends to improve the power to make a rational choice, while failing the test does not seriously weaken it.

The case of Energy Saving shows a completely different picture. In table 5.3, the strength of the bivariate relationship between Dominance rule and Choice is not very strong (Choice dependent 0.25). But now, controlling for Consistent preferences has a remarkable effect, as table 6.5 shows. Respondents with consistent orderings do indeed tend to choose rationally far more often than respondents with inconsistent preferences. In Energy Saving, the consistency of motives and preferences makes a substantial difference as far as facilitating rational choice is concerned. Holiday Destination, finally, shows a pattern similar to Energy Saving. Here too, the control variable Consistent Preferences has a profound effect on the relationship between Dominance Rule and Choice.

The results of table 6.5 thus do not refute our proposition that respondents with consistent preferences tend to use their cognitive powers to make a rational choice significantly better than do respondents with inconsistent preferences. In other words, the consistency between motives and preferences has a significant effect on rational choice.

---

[7] We use the same measure of association as in table 5.3, Somers' D asymmetric, with Choice as the dependent variable. The entries in the cells which are marked with an asterisk (*) denote the numbers of respondents who pass the test of rational choice and the test of consistent preferences in each of the cases.

Table 6.5 *Consistent preferences as control variable*

Chemical Waste	Consistent preferences			
	Choice			
Dominance Rule	Defect	Cooperate	Row total	
Defect	2*	0	2	
Cooperate	16	593*	609	*Somers' D .97*
Column total	18	593	611	*T-value: 1.42*

Chemical Waste	Inconsistent preferences			
	Choice			
Dominance Rule	Defect	Cooperate	Row total	
Defect	12	1	13	
Cooperate	12	112	124	*Somers' D .83*
Column total	24	113	137	*T-value: 3.92*

Energy Saving	Consistent preferences			
	Choice			
Dominance Rule	Defect	Cooperate	Row total	
Defect	5*	0	5	
Cooperate	33	519*	552	*Somers' D .94*
Column total	38	519	557	*T-value: 2.26*

Energy Saving	Inconsistent preferences			
	Choice			
Dominance Rule	Defect	Cooperate	Row total	
Defect	9	29	38	
Cooperate	16	125	141	*Somers' D .12*
Column total	25	154	179	*T-value: 1.64*

Holiday Destination	Consistent preferences			
	Choice			
Dominance Rule	Defect	Cooperate	Row total	
Defect	58*	1	59	
Cooperate	15	105*	120	*Somers' D .86*
Column total	73	106	179	*T-value: 14.8*

Holiday Destination	Inconsistent preferences			
	Choice			
Dominance Rule	Defect	Cooperate	Row total	
Defect	152	17	169	
Cooperate	90	127	217	*Somers' D .48*
Column total	242	144	386	*T-value: 11.78*

* Entries marked with an asterisk refer to responses that pass both consistency tests.

To conclude this section, it is worth looking separately at the cross-tabulations 'consistent preferences' in table 6.5. These cross-tabulations record the strategy choices of respondents who have reported consistent preferences with dominant strategies. Hence they enable one to scan the numbers of respondents in each case who pass both of the two consistency tests of rational choice and consistent preferences. The entries of these *fully consistent* respondents are marked with an asterisk in table 6.5. The fully consistent cooperator is a respondent who reports a cooperative choice which matches his reported ordering with a dominant strategy to cooperate. This ordering, in turn, is matched by a reported motive structure showing positive Willingness, since the constraints of positive Willingness (W1) imply a dominant strategy to cooperate, as defined in section 6.3. Likewise, a fully consistent defector is a respondent whose reported choice to defect matches his reported ordering with a dominant strategy to defect, and that ordering is in turn matched by a motive structure displaying negative Willingness (W3).

Both in Chemical Waste and Energy Saving, virtually all of the fully consistent respondents are of the cooperative type. Chemical Waste has 595 fully consistent entries (this is 82 per cent of the total response of 611 + 137 respondents), of which only 2 are defectors. Energy Saving has 524 fully consistent entries (76 per cent of the total), of which only 5 are defectors. In Holiday Destination, the ratio of full consistency is much lower: only 163 fully consistent responses in a total of 565, or 29 per cent. However, the bias in favour of cooperation is much less marked in this case. Of the 163 fully consistent entries, 105 are cooperators and 58 are defectors.

When discussing the results of the rational choice test in section 5.4, we noted that the case of Holiday Destination stands out from the other two cases of the dilemma, in the sense that rational choices to cooperate and rational choices to defect are distributed more evenly. The same observation holds for the distribution of fully consistent cooperators and defectors. On the other hand, Holiday Destination does far less well than the two other cases in terms of the ratio of full consistency. This is explained by the lesser performance of Holiday Destination with respect to rational choice (section 5.3), and with respect to consistent preferences (section 6.4). The significance of this finding will be taken up in chapter 13.

6.6 Conclusion

In chapter 3, we discussed the view of Green and Shapiro. This view attributes the 'pathologies of rational choice' to 'the characteristic aspiration of rational choice theorists to come up with universal theories of politics' (Green and Shapiro, 1994: 6). We have a somewhat different diagnosis. In many cases, the failures of rational choice theory to deal adequately with politically significant decisions are the result of choosing the wrong perspective. This is the observer's perspective. It is based upon a thick-theory of rationality, exemplified by Olson and Hardin's analysis, which models the preferences of a rational actor in the environmental dilemma by the criteria of effectiveness and efficiency, as we noted in chapter 3. To advance the empirical study of social dilemmas in which citizens rather than profit-maximizing firms, are involved, we have strongly argued in favour of the actor's perspective. This perspective follows the thin-theory of rationality of Arrow and Riker, and the dominance rule of game theory. It provides a formal structure that defines conditions of rational choice, while leaving it entirely open how rational choices are related to the citizen's individual values. The actor's perspective, moreover, requires a substantive empirical application of this formal structure. In the previous chapters, we have proposed a method for explaining the diversity of observed preference orderings in environmental dilemmas.

Figure 6.1 shows the conceptual model of our approach. It accepts the importance of the formal definitions of rationality and rational choice in empirical research. The formal framework enables us to drop the constricting assumptions of homogeneous actors and equivalent social dilemmas that belong to the thick-theory. We accept the diversity of the actor's individual values, as well as the implication that a rational individual is able to form any of the twenty-four possible preference orderings in an environmental dilemma, instead of just one, the Prisoner's Dilemma ordering. Furthermore, we allow the possibility that a rational individual may be willing to make a voluntary contribution in one specific setting of collective action, while at the same time refusing to cooperate in another situation.

The core of our approach is the assumption that the individual values of an actor can be represented by general motives, which explain the actor's preferences. This assumption is the crucial part that separates the actor's perspective from the observer's. The assumption of the observer's perspective is that all individuals are motivated by the criteria of effectiveness and efficiency, by virtue of being rational. As we admit, this assumption is often useful for studying the behaviour of entrepreneurs. But for the study of the behaviour of ordinary citizens, it is far too restrictive. It is not at all plausible to model the rational choices of citizens by imposing upon them the motivations of profit-maximizing economic agents. From our point of view, the behaviour of citizens must be studied from the assumption that they have a degree of freedom to form their preferences similar to the freedom that consumers have in microeconomic theory. Of course we do not want to rule out the possibility that some citizens sometimes think and act like entrepreneurs in a Potential Contributor's Dilemma. But we wish to stress that they can have other motives as well, and that it is therefore of importance to operationalize the link between motives and preferences in an empirically valid way. We shall put our approach to the test in part III, in the context of assessing policies that aim to promote the environmentally responsible behaviour of citizens.

But, before entering into the realm of practical policy in part III, we want to analyse the three environmental dilemmas from a different viewpoint, in the next two chapters. So far, we have examined the responses to the three dilemmas, without looking at the actual behaviour that the respondents have reported in the survey in each of the three corresponding areas of environmental behaviour. The question we wish to examine is whether our model of motives, preferences, and choice intentions in the Potential Contributor's Dilemmas provides a better explanation of reported behaviour than the ruling macro-sociological approach. That approach attempts to explain reported behaviour in terms of the respondents' background characteristics, and their general attitudes toward environmental issues. We have reasons to believe that reported behaviour may be better explained when one takes account of the non-equivalence of environmental dilemmas. The following two chapters will enable us to study the macro-sociological approach, and compare it to a model which is sensitive to the contextual differences between cases of the environmental dilemma.

7

The non-equivalence of the cases

7.1 Hard and easy cases of the dilemma

Modern theories of institutions recognize that 'the traditional behavioral assumptions have prevented economists from coming to grips with some very fundamental issues and that a modification of these assumptions is essential to progress further in the social sciences'.[1] Douglass North argues in favour of important modifications of the behavioural assumptions. His starting point is the complex causal relationship between the subjective perception of individuals operating in an institutional environment. He is concerned with the existence of institutions over time, i.e., of the workings of formal and informal constraints on behaviour. These constraints define the opportunity set of individuals. They also partly shape the way people choose in the various social contexts that give meaning to the constraints.

The actor's perspective provides one important modification of the economic approach by accepting that different people can have different preferences and motives. In line with institutional approaches, it is then of interest to ask to what extent our three cases of the dilemma may have contextual qualities which facilitate or hinder environmentally friendly attitudes and behaviour. In previous chapters, it was repeatedly shown that the aggregate level of cooperation differs among the environmental cases. In this chapter we take a closer look at the characteristics of the individual response patterns across the three cases.

The question is whether the three Potential Contributor's Dilemmas somehow demand different intensities of cooperative attitude. In other words, do we observe that it is more difficult to be willing to 'do the right thing' in choosing one's holiday destination than in handling one's household chemical waste? Do

[1] See North, 1990: 17.

124

the respondents give evidence of valuing collective action for the environment more in the area of household energy saving than in accepting restrictions on recreative air travel? Can it be verified that an individual's rational decision to cooperate can be expected to occur most frequently in Chemical Waste? These are the questions to be studied here. Only in the final chapter shall we be addressing the possible explanations, by comparing the different costs, benefits, and the beliefs that can account for observed differentials of cooperation between cases. This chapter lays some of the groundwork. It is devoted to establishing the non-equivalence of the cases, with the aid of the Mokken technique of scale analysis, in the next two sections.

This technique allows us to model the intuitive notion that Chemical Waste is the *easiest case* of the three, and Holiday Destination is the *hardest case*, in respect of the motives, preferences, and strategy choices of the respondents. Modelling this notion is of importance for environmental policy. For as we shall explain below, the 'hardest case' is the case which requires the highest intensity of cooperative disposition from individuals. In particular, if a respondent is observed to be cooperatively disposed in the hardest case, then this means that it is statistically likely that he will also be so disposed in the easier cases, both of which then require a less intense disposition to cooperate.

The significance of the non-equivalence of environmental dilemmas will be briefly discussed in the concluding section. From the viewpoint of self-regulation policies, the intensity structures identified below may require corresponding degrees of citizen commitment for handling the environmental problems effectively. The case that requires the highest intensity to cooperate at the individual level – Holiday Destination – may also turn out to be the hardest case to solve for the government, once the contextual properties of this case have been properly accounted for. But as we have said, this is a further issue which can only be studied later, in part III, after it has been securely established that environmental dilemmas can be compared in this way.

7.2 The model of the hardest case

In modelling the notion of the hardest case we have selected some core components of our survey: (i) the willingness to contribute for the sake of a cleaner environment; (ii) the evaluation of the way in which environmental pollution can be reduced by voluntary collective action; (iii) the six preference orderings that correspond to a dominant cooperative strategy; (iv) the cooperative strategy choice; and finally (v) the rational choice to cooperate. The dichotomous variables corresponding to these five components will be introduced below. Our task is to compare the response patterns on those variables, and identify the case that requires the highest intensity to cooperate as the hardest case.

In terms of social choice theory, the notion of the hardest requires one to establish the '*first element*' of the three cases with respect to some variable. The first element is a necessary but not a sufficient condition for placing the three cases on a single continuum. In order to establish a unidimensional scale, the response patterns in the three cases must also be *transitive*.

For example, denote the relation 'more difficult to cooperate' by the symbol '»', where 'cooperating' may refer to any of the five variables listed above. If Holiday Destination is the hardest case, then that means that in respect of this relation, the pairwise comparisons of Holiday Destination (HD) with Energy Saving (ES) and Chemical Waste (CW), must display the pairwise rankings: HD » ES and HD » CW. The meaning of this can be spelled out by saying: 'If an individual is willing to cooperate in HD, then he is willing to cooperate in ES and CW;' This 'hardest case assertion' may or may not hold true in a deterministic model. Or it may be shown to be statistically (un)acceptable in a probabilistic model.

In addition, consider the remaining pairwise comparison between Energy Saving and Chemical Waste. If that comparison satisfies either of the two rankings: ES » CW or CW » ES, then the relationship between the three cases is transitive, and they can be placed on a unidimensional cumulative scale, with HD as the hardest case, either of CW and ES as the easiest case, and the remaining case occupying the intermediate position. To illustrate the cumulative property of the scale, suppose that HD » ES » CW. This means that the following assertions are true (in a determinstic model) or statistically acceptable (in a probabilistic model): 'if someone is willing to cooperate in HD, then he is willing to cooperate in ES and CW' and 'if someone is willing to cooperate in ES, then he is willing to cooperate in CW'.

In this section we first present the deterministic structure of the hardest case model and then apply it to the dichotomized survey data, in a probabilistic model. Mokken's concept of *item homogeneity* is used for the statistical acceptability of pairwise comparisons between cases, and for the hardest case assertion. In section 7.3, we analyse the data concerning the five above-mentioned dichotomous variables to establish whether the three cases form unidimensional scales.

The investigation of the hardest case model must start from the assumption that any of the three cases might be the hardest case. The general model abstracts from the empirical cases. We introduce three different alternatives to be ranked in terms of the relation '»', x, y and z. If alternative x is the hardest case, then the following two conditions must be satisfied.

[1] $x \gg y$

[2] $x \gg z$

Case *y*

		Cooperate (1)	Not Cooperate (0)
Case *x*	Cooperate (1)	x_1, y_1	x_1, y_0 *error-cell*
	Not Cooperate (0)	x_0, y_1	x_0, y_0

Figure 7.1 The hardest case *x* and case *y*.

Given conditions [1] and [2], the alternatives x, y and z form a unidimensional scale only if one of the following conditions holds: either [3] or [4].

[3] $y \gg z$

[4] $z \gg y$

To establish that one of the three cases qualifies as the hardest case, it does not matter which of the conditions [3] or [4] is valid, or indeed whether either of them is valid. In this section we concentrate on the first two conditions, referring the issue of cumulative scales to section 7.3. In the deterministic model, conditions [1] and [2] imply that individuals who are willing to cooperate in the hardest case x must certainly be willing to cooperate in the relatively easier cases y and z. From condition [1] the following properties of a so-called 'perfect' response pattern are deduced.[2]

The possible responses on the variable 'cooperate' that defines the relation $\gg$ ('more difficult to cooperate') between the alternatives x and y are dichotomized. That is, these responses are limited to two categories: Cooperate or Not Cooperate. The first category, Cooperate, includes all responses that are considered to be a 'positive response'. The second category, Not Cooperate is the non-positive response, which includes all other responses that were distinguished in the survey questions, depending on what 'cooperate' actually refers to. The dichotomization of the response alternatives in x and y into a positive response (denoted by '1') and non-positive response (denoted by '0') creates four cells in figure 7.1: $x_1 y_1$, $x_1 y_0$, $x_0 y_1$ and $x_0 y_0$.

Figure 7.1 shows that any individual in the set of n persons who is prepared to cooperate in case x must be willing to cooperate in case y. If someone cooperates in x, but not in y, then he or she violates the perfect response pattern. Thus in the perfect response pattern, the so-called 'error-cell' x_1, y_0 is empty. The figure also indicates that if an individual does not cooperate in case x, both possible actions in y, to cooperate or not, are consistent with the notion of the hardest case. The same applies to condition [2]. The ranking $x \gg z$ implies that individuals who

---

[2] See table 2.2 *Two perfect items*, Mokken, 1971: 35.

Case z

Cooperate (1)   Not Cooperate (0)

Case x	Cooperate (1)	x_1, z_1	x_1, z_0 *error-cell*
	Not Cooperate (0)	x_0, z_1	x_0, z_0

Figure 7.2 The hardest case x and case z.

cooperate in the hardest case x must also cooperate in the relatively easier case z. Figure 7.2 illustrates the perfect response pattern of condition [2].

The perfect response patterns constitute the deterministic model of the hardest case. When we apply this theoretical model to the data, it will become clear that in reality the error-cell will seldom have zero frequency. The next step is to specify how many imperfections are admissible in a probabilistic model. Mokken's concept of the *pairwise item homogeneity coefficient* (H_{ij}) defines the acceptable number of violations. The probabilistic model does not require that the error-cell has zero frequency. The pairwise item coefficient is defined as follows: $H_{ij} = 1 - (fo) / (fe)$, where fo is the observed frequency and fe is the expected frequency in the error cell of the cross-table of two alternatives i and j. Mokken has argued that the probabilistic model requires an acceptability limit of .30 for the pairwise item coefficient H_{ij}.[3]

The probabilistic model can be used to decide which case, Chemical Waste, Holiday Destination, or Energy Saving, fits the profile of alternative x, the hardest case according to the above general conditions [1] and [2]. Of course the probabilistic model does not presume in advance that one case is the hardest case. First, the cases are compared in pairs so as to establish which case has the lowest frequency of cooperation. The case with the lowest frequency of cooperation must be the hardest of the two, provided that the number of violations of the perfect response is acceptable. Second, the pairwise item coefficient is calculated in order to determine whether the appointed hardest case satisfies the minimum requirement: $H_{ij} \geq .30$. If the same case is appointed twice by the probabilistic model as the hardest case and both pairwise item coefficients are sufficiently high, then we can conclude that this case is indeed the hardest case.

As mentioned above, our hardest case analysis dichotomizes the core components of the survey, which are here listed with the name of the dichotomous variable in parentheses: (i) the Valuation scale (Valuation), (ii) the Willingness scale (Willingness), (iii) the six preferences with dominant Cooperate (Dominant Cooperate), (iv) the strategy Cooperate (Choice Cooperate), and (v) the rational

---

[3] This means that the ratio of observed to expected frequencies in the error cell must not exceed 70%. See Mokken 1971.

Table 7.1 *Chemical Waste vs. Holiday Destination*

		Holiday Destination		
		(1)	(0)	Row total
Chemical Waste	(1)	519	455	974
	(0)	*4	15	19
Column total		523	470	993

choice to cooperate from an ordering with dominant Cooperate (Rational Choice Cooperate). The results of these five variables are summarized in table 7.4.

We first describe the dichotomous variables, starting with Valuation. Category V1 (fully agree and agree) of the Valuation scale is the positive response '1' All other categories, including the missings, are labelled as the non-positive response '0' of Valuation (see table 6.1). The same dichotomizing is used for the Willingness scale, with W1 as the positive response of Willingness (see table 6.2). Six preference orderings are included in the variable Dominant Cooperate: QPSR, QSPR, QSRP, SQPR, SQRP, and SRQP (see table 5.2). Together, these form the positive response, while the remaining eighteen orderings (including the non-valid answers) form the non-positive response. For the variable Choice, the positive response is the choice of strategy Cooperate. The choice Defect and No Choice are the non-positive response (see table 5.1). The positive response of the variable Rational Choice Cooperate conjoins the positive responses of Dominant Cooperate orderings with those of Choice. All other answers are marked as the non-positive response.

The procedure of the probabilistic model of the hardest case will now be illustrated for the dichotomous variable of Valuation. Tables 7.1 to 7.3 present the three possible cross-tabulations of Valuation for the cases Chemical Waste, Energy Saving, and Holiday Destination. First, we scan the frequencies of the positive response to see which cell is to be assigned as the error-cell in each of these tables. Only the lower left cell and the upper right cell can be appointed as the error-cell, because by definition the error-cell combines a positive response of case x with a non-positive response of case y or z (compare figures 7.1 and 7.2).

In table 7.1 Chemical Waste is compared to Holiday Destination. The column total of Holiday Destination's positive response (category (1)) is lower (523) than the row total of Chemical Waste's positive response (974). Thus the error-cell in table 7.1, marked with the symbol '*', is the lower left cell, and Holiday Destination is the candidate for the hardest case in this comparison.

The second pairwise comparison, in table 7.2, shows Chemical Waste and Energy Saving. The difference between the number of respondents with motive

Table 7.2 *Chemical Waste vs. Energy Saving*

| | | Energy Saving | | |
		(1)	(0)	Row total
Chemical Waste	(1)	937	37	974
	(0)	*13	6	19
Column total		950	43	993

Table 7.3 *Holiday Destination vs. Energy Saving*

| | | Energy Saving | | |
		(1)	(0)	Row total
Holiday Destination	(1)	513	*10	523
	(0)	437	33	470
Column total		950	43	993

V_1 in these two cases is relatively small, but the row total of category (1) of Chemical Waste (974) is still higher than the column total of category (1) of Energy Saving (950), which means that in this comparison Energy Saving is the candidate for the hardest case.

The final pairwise comparison must decide which of the two cases, Energy Saving or Holiday Destination, qualifies as the hardest case. Table 7.3 shows that the row total of category (1) of Holiday Destination (523) is much lower than the column total of category (1) of Energy Saving (950). The response patterns of Valuation across the three cases thus show that Holiday Destination is the final candidate for the hardest case.

The next step is to establish whether the number of individuals who violate the perfect response pattern is sufficiently low, i.e., whether the pairwise item coefficient H_{ij} of Holiday Destination is sufficiently high in both of the tables 7.1 and 7.3. The calculation of the pairwise item pair coefficient H_{ij} is as follows:

$HD \gg CW$ $\quad H_{ij} = 1 - (f_o)/(f_e) = 1 - 4/10 = .60$

$HD \gg ES$ $\quad H_{ij} = 1 - (f_o)/(f_e) = 1 - 10/23 = .56$

Both of these pairwise item coefficients lie well above the acceptable value of .30. This means that in respect of the variable Valuation, Holiday Destination

Table 7.4 *Results of the hardest case analysis*

Variable	Comparison	H_{ij} pairwise item coefficient	Hardest case
Valuation	HD » CW	.60	Holiday
	HD » ES	.56	Destination
Willingness	HD » CW	.38	Holiday
	HD » ES	.65	Destination
Dominant Cooperate	HD » CW	.53	Holiday
	HD » ES	.47	Destination
Choice Cooperate	HD » CW	.42	No
	HD » ES	.21	
Rational Choice Cooperate	HD » CW	.48	Holiday
	HD » ES	.35	Destination

is the hardest of the three cases. The same procedure is used to analyse the other five dichotomous variables. Table 7.4 shows the results.

The first column of the table lists the selected variables. The second column presents the results of the comparison that verifies which case satisfies conditions [1] and [2]. The third column gives the pairwise item coefficients of the cross-tabulation, and the last column presents the case that statistically qualifies as the hardest case.

Table 7.4 shows that Holiday Destination is the hardest case for Valuation, Willingness, and Dominant Cooperate. The fourth variable in the table, Choice Cooperate, meets the requirements of the conditions [1] and [2], but in the comparison between HD and ES, the pairwise item coefficient is below the lower limit of .30. However, when we examine the variable Rational Choice Cooperate, we see that Holiday Destination emerges as the hardest case once again. This fact confirms our guess that there is a connection between a positive result on the consistency test of rational choice and the intensity structure of the response pattern with respect to the variables Dominant Cooperate and Choice Cooperate, even though the latter fails to mark out Holiday Destination as the hardest case.

7.3 The scalability of the cases

The basic assumption of the hardest case model is that alternative x must satisfy the general conditions [1] and [2], discussed in 7.1 above. We have confirmed that Holiday Destination is alternative x. Given the conditions [1'] HD » CW and [2'] HD » ES, the cases Chemical Waste, Energy Saving,

Table 7.5 *Coefficients of scalability*

Variable	Comparison	Pairwise item coefficient	Scale coefficient
Valuation	HD » CW	.60	.47
	HD » ES	.56	medium scale
	ES » CW	.28	
Willingness	HD » CW	.38	.39
	HD » ES	.65	weak scale
	ES » CW	.28	
Dominant Cooperate	HD » CW	.53	.51
	HD » ES	.47	strong scale
	ES » CW	.53	
Choice Cooperate	HD » CW	.42	.27
	HD » ES	.21	no scale
	ES » CW	.24	
Rational Choice	HD » CW	.48	.45
Cooperate	HD » ES	.35	medium scale
	ES » CW	.48	

and Holiday Destination will form a unidimensional scale only if one of the following conditions holds.

[3'] CW » ES, or

[4'] ES » CW

The cross-tabulation of Energy Saving and Chemical Waste in table 7.2 gives the answer to the question concerning which of these two conditions holds for the dichotomous variable of Valuation. It shows that the response patterns of Valuation satisfy condition [4'] ES » CW. Although the pairwise item coefficient is just below the lower limit of .30 of the hardest case model ($H_{ij} = .28$), it is still high enough to form a scale with the other two item coefficients of the variable Valuation in table 7.4. This is because the Mokken procedure of scale rules that three items form a unidimensional scale if the overall scalability coefficient H is at least .30.[4] Table 7.5 gives the coefficients of scalability of the variables that were analysed.

---

[4] In the present case, the *scale coefficient H* evaluates the statistical acceptability of the three assertions 'HD » CW, HD » ES, and ES » CW', taken jointly. Likewise, Mokken distinguishes another composite coefficient, the *item coefficient*. For example, the item coefficient of the hardest case H_i ($i = HD$) evaluates the joint acceptability of the first two of the above-mentioned assertions, in one single figure, which must also be at least .30. The item coefficients of Holiday Destination are not shown in table 7.5. However, we will make use of this coefficient in conducting hardest case analysis with respect to several other variables in part III below.

Mokken's classification of scales distinguishes between the 'degrees of scalability in terms of the overall coefficient H':[5]

Weak scale	$.30 \leq H < .40$
Medium scale	$.40 \leq H < .50$
Strong scale	$.50 \leq H$

The response patterns in table 7.5 show that the cases Holiday Destination, Energy Saving, and Chemical Waste can be ranked on a unidimensional scale. The variables of Valuation (medium scale), Willingness (weak scale), Dominant Cooperate (strong scale), and Rational Choice Cooperate (medium scale) show distinct intensity structures, varying from the easiest case Chemical Waste to the hardest case Holiday Destination. Taking into account that Rational Choice Cooperate combines the variables Cooperate (just under the limit of .30) and Dominant Cooperate (strong scale), it can be concluded that the core components of the survey have a transitive ranking of the cases: HD » ES » CW.

7.4 The non-equivalence of social dilemmas

Based on the above results, we can elaborate the model described in the previous chapters. By measuring motives, preference orderings, and choices in the context of a Potential Contributor's Dilemma, we can regard these variables as the components of a cognitive process of practical reasoning, as summarized in section 6.1. The actor's perspective has led us to trace the consistency between the individual motives that shape preference orderings and the rational choice to cooperate from these orderings. The data analysed in this chapter very strongly suggest that the three cases of the environmental dilemma are truly non-equivalent, as we have already asserted in chapter 2, when discussing differences in the preference response. We now also see that the cases elicit a systematically different response when the data on each of the three components of practical reasoning are scrutinized by means of scale analysis. Figure 7.3 summarizes the cognitive process and the intensity structure of the cases with respect to the corresponding dichotomous variables.

From left to right, figure 7.3 shows the cognitive process leading to a cooperative rational choice in each of three cases, starting with motives, and ending with the strategy choice. From top to bottom, the figure pictures the intensity structures of Holiday Destination, Energy Saving, and Chemical Waste, with respect to the corresponding dichotomous variables. The hardest case of Holiday Destination is at the top, showing that it requires a high intensity of cooperative disposition for an individual, statistically speaking, to score positively on these

---

[5] See Mokken, 1971: 185.

Cognitive process

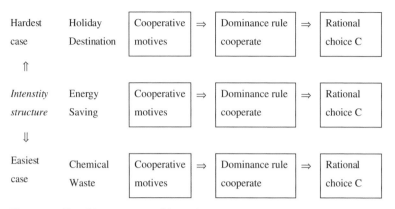

Figure 7.3 Cognitive process and intensity structure.

variables, while the easiest case of Chemical Waste requires only a low intensity of cooperative disposition.

These observed intensity structures of environmental dilemmas are examples of how informal and formal constraints and incentives shape the subjective motives and choices of individuals. To illustrate some of the flavour of this, when people buy their groceries in the supermarket, they can run up free Air Miles-points on a chipcard, and save for a great variety of holiday arrangements which are lavishly adverstised in the Air Miles catalogue. This provides an incentive to regard flying out to a distant holiday destination as something legitimate and normal, the fare of which one conveniently accumulates while procuring one's dairly fare. Without wanting to moralize here, it is clear that this sort of practice makes it harder to associate air trips with environmental pollution. It is, as we have mentioned in section 2.3, a prominent instance of a commercial counterpoint to the kind of 'social instrument' that the Dutch government would want to use in order to make people aware of the link between holidays and pollution. On the other hand, for toxic household chemicals listed in the municipal arrangements of separate waste collection, it has become very clear to most people that these are a hazard for the environment. At the same time, these arrangements provide all sorts of public facilities so that people can dispose of the chemicals in a relatively easy way. Awareness of the problem and low cost go together here.

We accept the notion that motives of individuals are not completely self-centred, i.e., individuals do not necessarily respond to environmental dilemmas on the basis of effectiveness and efficiency criteria. But obviously, this rejection of the observer's perspective has not prevented us from recognizing that different cases of the dilemma have different intensity structures. When we try to understand environmental behaviour, we have to accept some 'stylized facts'. One of these stylized facts is that returning a battery to the shop, or to a recycling facility, in order to prevent its substances from polluting the environment, is not as difficult as abstaining from a cheap flight to the family's favourite holiday destination. If so, this differential in costs will show up in the intensity structure of the corresponding cases. In chapter 13, we shall have much more to say about the relevant differentials of such costs of cooperation, as well as about the different beliefs concerning effective voluntary cooperation for environmental goals. Meanwhile, in the next chapter, we turn to the large issue of explaining the actual and reported behaviour of individuals, when they are faced with environmental dilemmas.

8

Reported behaviour

8.1 Determinants of behaviour

Economic growth in the nineties has led to increased consumption and more household chemical waste, rising energy consumption, and more traffic to holiday destinations. The Dutch government and its environmental advisory boards acknowledge the fact that the share of environmental pollution caused by consumers is rising. They also realize that traditional economic and legal tools for regulating the producers will not serve to change the behaviour of consumers, at the end of the chain. Given political mandate, government has the means of controlling the environmental behaviour of producers (at least in principle), while it has no firm grip on the actions of households (not even in principle). One reason that policymakers have found it difficult to influence the behaviour of consumers is that policy in the past was based on the standard Olson assumption that consumers react as a single group to environmental collective action problems, with a tendency to free ride.

Recent studies by the Netherlands Social and Cultural Planning Office (SCP) have shown that consumers cannot be addressed as a single group, and that they may sometimes be disposed to act cooperatively: 'People will behave in an environmentally friendly way only if they are willing and able to do so.'[1] The willingness and ability of consumers to cooperate is subject to a large variety of conditions. As we have shown, observed motives, preferences, and choice intentions in situations involving waste disposal, energy consumption, or holidays suggest that different people respond differently to each of these environmental

---

[1] See SCP, 1999: 115. The Social and Cultural Planning Office was created in 1973 as a complement of the Economic Planning Office. Both of these institutions serve a highly important function as advisory bodies to the government.

dilemmas, and, moreover, that the same people behave differently, depending on the dilemma they are faced with.

But what, then, are the relevant determinants of reported environmental behaviour? The first step of any market researcher is to look for subgroups with shared social, economic and cultural characteristics. In this chapter we shall attempt to show, however, that the context of environmental dilemmas matters a lot as well in explaining the environmental behaviour of consumers.

In 1994 the SCP launched a project entitled 'determinants of environmentally relevant consumer behaviour'. It analyses a conceptual model that includes social, cultural, and economic attributes, such as age, gender, religion, education, environmental involvement, political orientation, and income. The model takes these 'sociocultural' attributes of respondents as independent variables to explain their reported behaviour in concrete settings, for example 'refusal of plastic bags when offered, disposal of small-scale chemical waste and choice of transport'. Recent results of the project give some important insights. Plastic bags are more readily accepted by men than by women, and more often refused by the highly educated. Disposal of household chemical waste hardly seems to have any relationship with the sociocultural variables. Here environmentally friendly behaviour is related to the availability of facilities, and the extent to which people regard the separation of household waste as successful.

Likewise, in the choice of transport, the sociocultural variables fail to account for the variations in reported behaviour. The factor of accessibility seems to have an important influence in the choice between public transport and private car. The SCP concludes that its model was not able to explain behaviour in all of these cases with a common set of sociocultural variables, and that environmentally relevant behaviour is not determined by one common (environmental) dimension.[2] As an avenue of further research, the SCP recommends analysing environmentally relevant behaviour with the traditional sociocultural variables in combination with data on the personal preferences of consumers, and on their cognitive-motivational strategies.[3]

In section 8.2 we present a model of reported behaviour which strongly resembles the SCP model, using our own survey data. This model includes most of the sociocultural variables, as well as reported behaviour in various cases, among which are ones corresponding to the three environmental dilemmas of the previous chapters. Our results confirm the conclusions of the SCP model: sociocultural characteristics do not adequately explain reported behaviour. Next, in section 8.3, we follow the above recommendation. We

---

[2] See SCP, 1996: 170. A later study of the SCP led to the same conclusion: 'It is not possible to provide a comprehensive account of all environmentally relevant behaviour, and indeed to study each action or set of actions individually would provide us with no insight into the environmental impact of broader patterns of behaviour' (SCP, 1999: 116).

[3] See SCP, 1996: 171.

combine the sociocultural variables with the choice intentions that our respondents have reported in the three environmental dilemmas. This move brings in the element required by the SCP, to take account of personal preferences and motives. For, given that there is a reasonably tight relationship between motives, preferences, and choices in the three dilemmas, the new independent variable of Choice (to cooperate or defect) may be regarded as a proxy of the respondents' 'personal preferences' and 'cognitive-motivational strategies'. When the variable of Choice is added to the model presented in section 8.2, the explanation of reported behaviour is improved considerably.[4] The last section of the chapter comments on the significance of this exercise.

8.2 The sociocultural model

In our survey the respondents were questioned on six different situations of environmental behaviour. Four of these correspond to the cases of the Potential Contributor's Dilemma described in earlier chapters. We asked the 993 respondents to report how often they threw away household chemical waste with the rest of the garbage. They were also asked how many times they took account of the energy consumption in the purchase of new electrical appliances. Another aspect of energy saving behaviour, likewise related to the case of Energy Saving, is the question of how often one economized on the use of warm water, when showering and washing the dishes. The last question corresponds to Holiday Destination: how often did the respondents choose to spend their holiday abroad, rather than in their own country. The two remaining questions deal with organic waste (how often does one throw leftovers and garden waste away with the rest of the garbage, instead of depositing it in special bags for separate weekly collection) and shopping (how often does one use the car while shopping).

Table 8.1 shows the response in these six cases of reported behaviour. Most respondents report environmentally friendly behaviour in the handling of chemical waste (91 per cent) and organic waste (72 per cent). Their reports are less friendly concerning use of warm water (57 per cent) or buying new electrical devices (50 per cent), and even less so regarding the use of a car when shopping (49 per cent) and choice of holiday destination (46 per cent).[5]

These findings on reported behaviour in table 8.1 roughly correspond with the outcome of the hardest case analysis of the last chapter. In addition to the six questions about reported behaviour, our survey includes most of the social, cultural, and economic characteristics used in the SCP model. Attributes such

---

[4] As measured by the adjusted coefficient of determination R^2.
[5] The responses listed in the rows of table 8.1 are to be read as environmentally friendly, or the reverse, according to the interpretations of the response categories in each case. For example, in Chemical Waste and Organic Waste, as well as in Shopping with car and Holiday Destination, 'Never' and 'Mostly not' indicate cooperative behaviour, whereas in the two Energy cases, these same response categories indicate non-cooperative behaviour.

Table 8.1 *Six cases of reported behaviour*

	Chemical Waste		Organic Waste		Energy Electric		Energy Water		Shopping with Car		Holiday Destination	
	N	%	N	%	N	%	N	%	N	%	N	%
Never	779	78	602	61	185	19	115	12	354	36	307	31
Mostly not	127	13	105	11	187	19	164	17	126	13	150	15
Sometimes	45	5	53	5	127	13	157	16	200	20	213	22
Mostly	24	2	86	9	285	29	343	35	149	15	177	18
Always	18	2	146	15	204	21	214	22	140	14	133	13
Missing	—		1		5		—		24		13	
Total	993	100	993	100	993	100	993	100	993	100	993	100

as age, gender, income, education, religion, and vote for political party are measured by a single questionnaire item. Several forms of religious convictions are put into one category, to distinguish them from non-religious people. We also dichotomized the answers of the question: 'for which party did you vote in 1994 Parliamentary Elections?' The individuals who voted for the Green Party (GroenLinks) or for the Liberal Democrats (D66) are taken together in the class 'vote for a greenish party', while all others respondents were classed as 'not vote for a greenish party'.

For cultural attributes such as value orientation, environmental involvement, environmental faith, and environmental interest, we combined several items into a single measure.[6] The social, cultural, and economic attributes form ten determinants (X_1 to X_{10}) to explain six types of reported behaviour – Chemical Waste (Y_1) to Holiday Destination (Y_6) – in the multiple regression analysis of equation [8.1].

$$[8.1] \quad ZYi = \beta_1 ZX_1 + \beta_2 ZX_2 + \cdots + \beta_{10} ZX_{10} \quad [i = 1, \ldots, 6]$$

Only one dependent variable (Y), Chemical Waste, is identical in our model and that of the SCP. The question on the use of a car is similar, but in the SCP study it concerns choice between public transport and private car in general, while in our survey the use of a car is narrowed down to shopping. The other four cases,

---

[6] For example, 'value orientation' is a scale based on six Flanagan-items indicative of a postmaterialist attitude. 'environmental involvement' is formed by six statements indicating how concerned people are about pollution. 'Environmental faith' is based on three statements which say that environmental pollution has been reduced in the past, that reduction of environmental pollution at present is satisfactory, and that it is expected to be further reduced in the future. Finally, 'environmental interest' is defined analogously to the questions on political interest, where respondents indicate whether they take an interest in environmental issues by reading articles, watching television programmes, and discussing the issues.

organic waste, choice of holiday destination, and the two forms of energy saving are different from the cases in the SCP study. Despite these differences, all cases involve disaggregated areas of environmental behaviour. This is why we regard our model as an approximate replication of the SCP's sociocultural model.

In equation [8.1], the measurement units of the variables are dissimilar. This makes the interpretation of the regression coefficients difficult. We therefore transform the original distribution of the variables to standardized scores (Z-scores) in the multiple regression analysis. For each of the six cases we used the same multiple regression equation. The standardized regression coefficient 'β' of each (Z-transformed) independent variable (X) in equation [8.1] can be seen as a determinant of the (Z-transformed) dependent variable (Y). The coefficient β_1 shows the effect of independent variable X_1 on cooperative reported behaviour Y_1. In other words, the beta coefficient (β) expresses the weight of this independent variable – as compared to the other ten determinants – in explaining the dependent variable.[7]

Table 8.2 gives the results of the six multiple regression analyses. The rows list the ten independent variables X_1 (age) to X_{10} (value orientation 'postmaterialism'). The columns show the beta coefficients of these independent variables for each of the six cases.

The determinants that explain behaviour in most of the six cases are age, gender, religion, environmental involvement and environmental interest. The multiple regression analysis shows that especially the elderly, women, people with a religious conviction, and those with a high involvement and high interest behave more cooperatively than younger people, men, the non-religious, and those with a low involvement and low interest. Some independent variables are ambiguous. For example, people who are highly educated cooperate more in respect of their of warm water and use of a car for shopping, than those who are not. This relation is reversed in the handling of food and garden waste, and the choice of a holiday destination. At first sight, there seems to be no plausible explanation why education would have a different effect in these cases.

Another variable that gives mixed outcomes is income. High-income respondents cooperate more than low-income ones in handling organic waste and buying electric appliances, but they cooperate less than low-income people in shopping with a car and choosing a holiday destination. A possible explanation is that handling organic waste is an easy case (beta = .19), in which high-income people have no difficulty in cooperating, while Holiday Destination and Shopping with a car are hard cases, and especially so for people who earn a lot (beta coefficients respectively −.29 and −.18, in table 8.2). The percentages of cooperative behaviour of Chemical and Organic Waste in table 8.1 are consistent

---

[7] When the condition of significance of p < .05 is not satisfied, the beta coefficient is not given in table 8.2.

Table 8.2 *Determinants of behaviour*

	Chemical Waste	Organic Waste	Energy Electric	Energy Water	Shopping with Car	Holiday Destination
	beta	beta	beta	beta	beta	beta
(X_1) Age 18–89	.06	.13	.14	.13	.09	.13
(X_2) Gender Man–woman	.07	*	*	.09	.14	*
(X_3) Education Low–high	*	−.08	*	.13	.11	−.13
(X_4) Religion Yes–no	−.12	*	*	*	*	−.09
(X_5) Income Low–high	*	.19	.15	*	−.29	−.18
(X_6) Green party No–yes	*	*	*	*	.08	*
(X_7) Involvement Low–high	.12	*	.15	.17	*	*
(X_8) Trust Low–high	*	*	*	*	*	*
(X_9) Interest Low–high	.10	*	.21	.25	*	.11
(X_{10}) Value Mat–postmat	.09	*	*	*	.07	−.08
Adjusted R^2	.08	.07	.12	.15	.14	.12

with this guess, since they show that over 70 per cent of the respondents never throw their organic waste away with the other garbage, or mostly refrain from doing so. However, the figures of table 8.1 do not support the notion that Energy Electric is a particularly easy case. For this behaviour we must look at another explanation. People with a high income are rather cooperative in worrying about the energy consumption of their electrical appliances, as shown by beta .15 in table 8.2, while at the same time being markedly non-cooperative in car shopping and choosing holiday destinations. But this does not deter them from buying a lot of electrical appliances, even though they are concerned about the power consumption of each separate item of equipment. This would be consistent with the unfriendly environmental behaviour of high income respondents towards shopping with a car, and holiday choice.

Most standardized regression coefficients in table 8.2 are relatively small. The largest determinant of environmental behaviour is income. People with a high income use their money to buy the means of pleasure and convenience, and understandably, this claims more energy and waste production. They thus impose larger environmental damage, despite the fact that more money also allows them to purchase environmentally efficient durables.[8] In sum, the result of the multiple regression analyses of the six cases is not impressive. In all six cases the coefficient of determination R^2 is not high at all.[9] This confirms the conclusion of the SCP that sociocultural variables do not explain environmentally friendly behaviour very well.

8.3 An alternative model

As we mentioned above, the poor results of the traditional characteristics in the study of the SCP have led to a recommendation to analyse environmentally relevant behaviour by taking account of the consumers' 'personal preferences' and 'cognitive-motivational strategies'. We will now follow this recommendation, by extending the multiple regression analysis of the last section to include an additional independent variable, called 'Choice' (X_{11}). This variable refers to the strategic choice between Cooperate and Defect in the three dilemmas which were studied from the actor's perspective. In view of the consistency between motives and preferences, and the even stronger consistency between preferences and choices, we here assume that the variable of Choice represents the preferences and motives of the respondents in the three cases. Choice is thus taken as a proxy of the consumers' personal preferences and cognitive-motivational strategies, which the SCP would want to have included in a model of reported environmental behaviour. Figure 8.1 summarizes the conceptual model used in the above multiple regression analysis – from X_1 to X_{10} – with our extra determinant 'Choice' (X_{11}) added.

In section 5.3, we presented a consistency test for the respondent's preference ordering and strategy choice. An individual makes a rational choice if his or her preference ordering has a dominant strategy Cooperate (or Defect), and he or she actually reports the strategy Cooperate (or Defect). For each of the three cases we have measured the intended behaviour or choice of strategy in the setting of the Potential Contributor's Dilemma. The interviewer presents the cards which describe the four cells of the Contributor's Dilemma of each case. The interviewer then poses the questions of valuation and willingness, and finally, asks the respondent to state his or her intended behaviour. The questions in the survey were formulated as follows.

Chemical Waste: 'I will ask you a couple of questions about chemical household waste, such as batteries, leftovers of paint, and motor oil. What would you

---

[8] Similar conclusions are drawn in the most recent study of the SCP. See SCP 1999.
[9] The adjusted coefficient of determination R^2 measures the extent to which the variation of a dependent variable Y is explained by all independent variables.

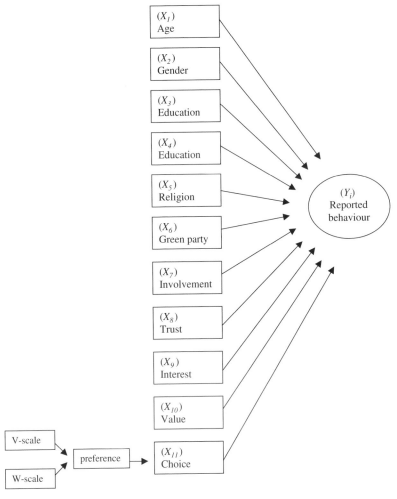

Figure 8.1 The extended sociocultural model.

do yourself with chemical household waste? Do you throw the waste away with the regular garbage or do you bring it to the collection point?'
– I would throw the chemical household waste away with the rest of the garbage
– I would take the chemical household waste to the collection point
– Don't know / no answer

Energy Saving: 'I will ask you some questions about environmental pollution due to the use of energy in the household, such as heating, lighting or warm

water. What would you do yourself? Are you going to save energy in your household or are you not going to save energy?'
– I would not save energy
– I would save energy
– Don't know / no answer

Holiday Destination: 'I will ask you a couple of questions about environmental pollution due to the traffic (cars, buses or aeroplanes) to a holiday destination abroad. What would you do when you take a holiday? Would you stay close to home to reduce environmental pollution, or is your holiday destination far away?'
– I would go far away on holiday
– I would stay close to home on holiday
– Don't know/no answer

Most individuals (93 per cent) are prepared to bring their chemical household waste to a special collection point, where toxic waste is processed properly. Likewise most individuals (90 per cent) are willing to save household energy. Only a small number of these individuals (37 per cent) was willing to spend their holidays close to home (see table 5.1).

It should be noted that the 'Choice' variable can be used only for the cases of reported behaviour in which the respondents have stated their motives, preferences, and choices in the corresponding Potential Contributor's Dilemmas. As we have noted above, however, these correspondences, while presenting no problems in the cases of Chemical Waste and Holiday Destination, are less than perfect in the case of Energy Saving. We comment on this below.

Table 8.3 shows the result of the new multiple regression analyses for Chemical Waste, Energy Saving (electricity consumption and warm water use), and Holiday Destination. The introduction of the new determinant has quite a large effect in the polar cases – the easiest case Chemical Waste and the hardest case Holiday Destination. It has no effect, however, in the two Energy Saving cases. First we discuss the results of the two energy cases which did not match our expectation that the introduction of the new determinant would make a difference. The standardized regression coefficients of Energy Electric and Energy Water in table 8.3 are almost the same as in table 8.2. The independent variable Choice has some weight in explaining behaviour there, but compared with the other independent variables the effect is not impressive.

Furthermore, adding the new independent variable of Choice in the multiple regression analysis hardly improves the explanation of the variation of behaviour in Energy Saving. The lack of impact of Choice in the multiple regression analysis raises questions about our original wording of the environmental decisions in this case. In the questionnaire regarding this environmental

Table 8.3 *A new determinant 'Choice'*

	Chemical Waste	Energy Electric	Energy Water	Holiday Destination
	beta	beta	beta	beta
(X_1) Age 18–89	.08	.15	.13	.07
(X_2) Gender Man–woman	.07	*	.09	*
(X_3) Education Low–high	*	*	.12	*
(X_4) Religion Yes–no	−.08	*	*	−.08
(X_5) Income Low–high	*	.15	*	−.16
(X_6) Green party No–yes	*	*	*	*
(X_7) Involvement Low–high	.06	.14	.17	*
(X_8) Trust Low–high	*	*	*	*
(X_9) Interest Low–high	.06	.19	.25	*
(X_{10}) Value Mat–postmat	*	*	*	−.08
(X_{11}) Choice Defect–cooperate	.51	.12	.08	.51
Adjusted R^2	.32	.13	.16	.35

dilemma, the issue of watching the energy consumption of new electrical appliances and the issue of economizing on warm water are combined in one single case. In hindsight, this may not have been sufficiently discriminating, since it lumps together decisions regarding the use of *given* household equipment, such as electric boilers or gas heating of water, with decisons concerning the electricity used by *newly purchased* durables. For a more accurate measurement of motives, preferences, and choices in these areas of household activity, it might have been better to present the respondents with a single (electrical equipment or warm water) Potential Contributor's Dilemma and not a compound one (electrical equipment and warm water).

Despite this imperfection, the results of the polar cases give reasons to be optimistic about the impact of the new determinant for explaining behaviour. Not only are the regression coefficients of Choice in Chemical Waste and Holiday

Destination high ($\beta = .51$), the introduction of this independent variable in the model of section 8.2 also improves the explanation of reported behaviour considerably. As tables 8.2 and 8.3 show, the adjusted coefficient of determination R^2 increases with .24 and .23, respectively, in these two cases.

To sum up, both the SCP model and our own model in section 8.2 come to the same conclusion. Sociocultural characteristics on their own provide no adequate explanation of reported environmental behaviour. The results of the second multiple regression analysis in this section demonstrate that choices based upon personal preferences and motives in environmental dilemmas of specific cases can increase the explained variation. This confirms the intuition of the SCP about the importance of personal preferences and motives.

8.4 From motives to behaviour

By extending the sociocultural regression model with the new determinant of 'Choice', we established the connection between motives and reported behaviour. The actor's perspective, as operationalized in chapters 4 to 6, was fitted into the sociocultural model. This is graphically illustrated in figure 8.1. To summarize the procedure, we measured motives, preferences, and strategy choices in survey questions pertaining to Potential Contributor's Dilemmas that match the real-life situations in which environmental behaviour is reported. The connections run from motives to reported behaviour, as shown in figure 8.2. Each individual was asked to understand the choice to handle household chemical waste, as an n-person collective action problem. Also, the choice of holiday destination and the choice to save energy in the household were presented as an n-person game. To avoid a systematic influence of one case over the other two cases, the three cases were randomized during the survey. And to prevent the answers on real-life behaviour from being contaminated by the answers on intended behaviour in the Potential Contributor's Dilemmas, we made sure that both sets of questions were widely spaced in the interview.

Chapter 4 shows that most individuals were able to construct transitive preference orderings for each of the four possible outcomes of the dilemma. In the same chapter we showed that only 148 respondents have identical preference orderings in all of the cases. The overlap of the easiest case Chemical Waste and the hardest case Holiday Destination is 63 identical orderings. This means that the individuals did not give one standard answer to the three Contributor's Dilemmas.[10]

---

[10] In other surveys we have presented the case Chemical Waste to university students, and the pattern of preference orderings are similar to the ones of table 4.2. The case Chemical Waste is presented as a Potential Contributor's Dilemma in a face-to-face survey in the Dutch Parliamentary Election Panel Study in 1994. See H. Anker and E.V. Oppenhuis, 1995.

Figure 8.2 The actor's perspective model.

In chapters 5 and 6, we established consistency tests which link motives to preferences, and preferences to strategy choices. And finally, in order to show that those strategy choices do contribute to explaining what respondents report concerning their behaviour in the real world, we incorporated the variable 'Choice' into the sociocultural model. The results of our analysis have methodological and policy implications. First we discuss the methodological implications of our study and then we explain what the policy consequences are for handling environmental problems. The diversity of preference orderings for the three cases indicates that individuals have different views on particular environmental problems. This simply means that Mancur Olson was wrong in assuming that all problems of collective action are equivalent and can be viewed as identical free-rider problems. Olson is right in assuming that there are important similarities in different problems of collective action. These similarities make it possible to present the three different cases in the same way in the survey as an n-person game, i.e., the Potential Contributor's Dilemmas.

However, the similarity and the equivalence of social dilemmas end with the modelling of Hardin's n-person game. Every particular social dilemma generates its own pattern of preference orderings. If some specific environmental problem turns out to be an easy case, such as Chemical Waste, then this potential social dilemma will not turn into an actual dilemma. If the preference orderings of a Potential Contributor's Dilemma are largely non-cooperative, as in Holiday Destination, then we are dealing with a so-called hard case. Whether or not some new social dilemma will be an easy or a hard case, cannot be decided in theory. Only by measuring the preferences of the individuals are we able to recognize the nature of a concrete collective action problem.

Some individuals will always be prepared to make sacrifices for a clean environment, and other individuals will never cooperate in a collective action situation. In real-life situations most people will evaluate each problem of collective action on its own merits. Although our model is based on the assumption that each person has his or her own reasons for cooperating (or not), it is obvious that a concrete social dilemma has inherent characteristics that, on a macro level, make it more (or less) likely that individuals have cooperative attitudes.

[11] Chemical Waste is also presented in a written survey. See Pellikaan, 1994 and van der Veen and Pellikaan, 1994.

A first implication of our study is that social dilemmas are only equivalent as far as we study them as an abstract concept. A concrete problem of collective action can turn out to be an actual dilemma or it presents no real difficulties. Environmental policy designed to influence consumer behaviour must be based on the notion that each potential social dilemma can be an easy or a hard case. This means that there is no general solution for the variety of environmental problems. For each case, the policymakers must come up with a tailor-made solution.

The distinction between easy and hard cases is very important for solving problems of environmental pollution. No less important is the fact that there is a strong coherence between motives, preferences, choices, and behaviour. The arrows in figure 8.2 illustrate the connection between the several elements of the actor's perspective. The connection is especially strong in the two polar cases of Chemical Waste and Holiday Destination. On the one hand, most respondents with cooperative preference orderings have consistent motives (table 6.5), and choose to cooperate, in line with their dominant strategy (table 5.2). On the other hand, respondents with non-cooperative orderings often have consistent motives, and rationally choose to defect. Moreover, respondents with consistent preferences are more likely to choose rationally than respondents whose preferences are not consistent with their motives (table 6.5). And finally, as shown in section 8.2, the addition of the variable 'Choice' to the sociocultural model significantly increases the explanation as reported behaviour in the polar cases. The implication for environmental policy is that one cannot simply change environmental behaviour by telling the people that they have to do the 'right thing'.

In order to change behaviour, the decision-makers have to work on both sides of the model in figure 8.2. Environmental policy must try to influence the valuation of the environmental goal and also try to advance the willingness to make a voluntary contribution for a clean environment. At the same time, individuals must be convinced that their environmentally friendly behaviour is really effective for reducing pollution. In part III we discuss these considerations for environmental policy in more detail.

Part III

Conclusions: theory and policy

9

Do people accept self-regulation policy?

9.1 Introduction to part III

This part of the book deals with the policy lessons suggested by our study of environmental dilemmas. In the last part, we have been led by the question to what extent and in what ways the attitudes and behaviour of our respondents deviate from the self-interested stance that characterizes an actual contributor's dilemma, taking due account of the differences presented by the three cases of environmental collective action. Now we want to focus on what may follow from this in respect of the design of policies that attempt to deal with these and similar problems. While the general direction of these two questions may seem straightforward enough, the last question is set against the particular background of Dutch environmental policy. The results of part II thus need to be reconsidered in the light of self-regulation policies. As we described in chapter 2, such policies seek to convince citizens that their environmental behaviour presents problems of voluntary collective action, and that they have a moral responsibility to cooperate towards the solution of these problems, at least to the extent sufficient for meeting the quantitative targets for reducing various emissions of pollutants. In the national environmental plans, several of these specific targets have been assigned to the group of consumers. A hallmark of the self-regulation approach is to address the consumers in their roles as citizens in order to obtain active compliance with the objectives of the plans.[1]

---

[1] The targets for for the group of consumers are regularly updated in the ongoing planning process, and the performance of consumers is likewise published in the official documents. For example, as this book goes to press, the Ministry of the Environment's Annual Progress Report (*Milieuprogramma 2000–2003*, a document that charts progress according to the guidelines stated in the latest 1998 national environmental plan) starts the chapter entitled 'Citizens' with a graph showing the performance of consumers on the environmental themes of climate change

In chapter 3, we discussed the actor's perspective on rational choice. It asserts that individuals are capable of acting rationally upon diverse values in the Potential Contributor's Dilemma. This is why we have stressed the importance of measuring the actual preferences that actors hold, and hence admitted all possible reported orderings of the four outcomes of the dilemma as potentially valid bases of rational action in our survey. In view of this generality, the actor's perspective is also concerned to connect observed preference orderings to independent information reflecting the individual values of actors. In the survey, that information is represented by the motivational dimensions of Valuation and Willingness. In relating motive structures to preferences by means of a consistency test, we were able to assess the empirical relevance of the standard Prisoner's Dilemma view to the predominance of self-interested motivation in collective action. The same method will now be used to assess the Dutch self-regulation approach to environmental policy.

In this chapter, we first present survey data regarding the *acceptance* of self-regulation policies addressed to citizens, taking care to distinguish this from the respondents' actual *agreement* with the substantive content of the messages that the government wants to put accross. This distinction will be considered in the next section. Chapter 10 deals with the agreement issue. Here we return to our discussion in section 2.4, about the 'strategy of internalization' enunciated by the first national environmental policy plan of 1989. We then identify the motives and preferences that express the public ethos of environmental responsibility, and re-analyse the observed motives and preferences of the respondents in the three cases of the dilemma, with the purpose of finding out to what extent the individual values of respondents are congruent with the ethos that the government strives to promote. From these two chapters, it may be concluded that respondents both accept self-regulation policy and agree with the underlying ethos to a quite substantial extent, but that this acceptance varies significantly across the cases of the dilemma, with Holiday Destination as the hardest case and Chemical Waste as the easiest one.

These conclusions, especially the one about agreement with the ethos, raise two wider theoretical issues that we discuss in chapters 11 and 12. First, the prevalence of cooperative motives, and the preference responses that are consistent with those motives on the consistency test of chapter 6, suggest that respondents often show a systematic commitment to the environmental ethos put forward by policymakers. This leads us, in chapter 11, to compare our empirical approach with the theory of rational cooperation from moral commitment developed by Amartya Sen in the seventies. Sen's main innovation here is the concept of a *moral meta-ranking of preferences*. We argue that

and waste disposal, before listing several new initiatives, including the devolution of social instruments to local governments (*Milieuprogramma 2000–2003*: part 2, ch. 3, Second Chamber no. 27404/1–2).

our consistency tests refine and empirically extend Sen's analysis of moral commitment, by showing, among other things, that responses to the three environmental dilemmas of the survey can be graded on an *environmental meta-ranking of motives*, which exactly corresponds to the substance of the public ethos.

Secondly, the agreement responses of chapter 10 also show that unconditionally cooperative motives and preferences are reported far more often than conditionally cooperative ones are. We examine this finding in the context of some literature on moral cooperation in theories of rational choice. According to a dominant line of argument, recently summarized by Elinor Ostrom, rational agents who are sensitive to moral motives are likely to engage in conditional cooperation in situations of collective action, in a 'virtuous triangle of trust, reciprocity and reputation'. Morally disposed rational agents, however, would not normally be willing to cooperate unconditionally. This is contrary to what our findings suggest. In chapter 12, we critically examine Ostrom's line of argument and discuss the evidence she cites. Our conclusion is that the incidence of conditional response to social dilemmas is in part a function of their size, and also depends on 'common-pool' or 'common-sink' characteristics. We argue that in large-scale dilemmas, such as our environmental cases, an individual's moral disposition to act cooperatively need not follow the logic of reciprocity. It can take the form of unconditionally cooperative motives and preferences, depending on the cost of cooperative action involved in the case at hand.

Finally, chapter 13 draws together the findings of these four chapters on policy and theory, in an assessment of Dutch self-regulation policy. Our strategy of assessment is based on the construction of a summary indicator of 'consistent ethical cooperation', which combines the two tests of consistent preferences and rational choice. Noting that the three cases form a scale on this indicator, with Holiday Destination as the hardest case, we then seek to explain the reasons for this dimensionality in terms of salience, cost, and efficacy factors. These factors enable us to evaluate the chances and limitations of the self-regulation approach.

9.2 Acceptance and agreement

Success in achieving self-regulation of citizens depends on how well-conceived the policies actually are, and how well they are implemented at the ground level of specific cases. We cannot here address the details of the specific policies that were discussed in section 2.3. More generally, however, the effectiveness of self-regulation policy depends on people's *acceptance* of the social instruments, as well as on their *agreement* with the basic moral message which is being communicated. These are things on which our study can shed some light. In this and the following chapter, we examine the issues of acceptance and agreement.

The next section presents new survey data on the first issue. To what extent do the respondents accept that governmental agencies, or their fellow citizens, engage in persuading them to take account of the environment in their daily lives? And how does this compare to their acceptance of legal or economic sanctions on that behaviour? While the results will be seen to vary across the three cases, as a whole they indicate that the role of government as initiator of environmental persuasion was widely accepted in Dutch society, at the time of the survey.

To what extent are attitudes in the three dilemmas congruent with what the government is trying to put across? In the next chapter we ask how many of our respondents are in line with the two stages of the environmental ethos, after having re-examined the official documents in which that ethos is expressed. This second issue of agreement is one of content. It should be distinguished from people's acceptance of the medium of environmental reform, the social instruments. Even if one thinks there is nothing objectionable about government campaigns to save energy, or even if one enthusiastically welcomes subsidized discussion platforms on global warming, one is still free to evaluate what is being said on its merits, and one can decide to follow the official advice in some cases, but not in others. Thus, measuring substantive agreement with the public ethos is important for policy purposes regardless of the acceptance of self-regulation policy. It shows how people have reacted to the relatively novel idea that they are to be held responsible for contributing to a diverse set of environmental qualities in the decisions of everyday life. Nevertheless, while issues of acceptance and agreement are conceptually distinct, they may also be causally interrelated.

In Dutch policy literature on self-regulation, it is suggested that the likelihood of a cooperative attitude in a given case is positively affected by a 'normalizing' effect. This means that the behaviour of actors has been exposed to (socially) regulative intervention in the past. In Chemical Waste, especially, to a lesser extent in Energy Saving, and hardly at all in Holiday Destination, such exposure could lead people to regard environmental persuasion by government agencies and informal social control as normal events, the occurrence of which they tend to accept as a matter of course. This, in turn, may create the perception that such interventions are socially appropriate, from which it is only a relatively small step towards an unthinking agreement with their purposes. In such a mechanism of agreement by acceptance, the 'medium is the message'.

There is some empirical evidence of the normalizing effect on attitudes in the environmental dilemmas.[2] Yet we think that it is a mistake to place great reliance on the normalizing effect. It would be rash to think that bringing official campaigns up to speed in the case of Holiday Destination would induce people

[2] See Bartels, 1994.

to change their environmental behaviour in the area of recreational travel as a matter of accepted routine, rather than as a matter of reasoned behaviour, in the genuine sense of that term. The normalizing effect is independent of any definite link between reasons and action, if we mean by 'reasons' an intellectually convincing set of factual beliefs and normative prescriptions. Of course it is difficult to measure the respondents' reasoned agreement with the environmental ethos in a mass survey, but one can try to obtain indirect evidence. This is what we will be after when we ask the following questions about agreement: do the motives, preferences, and choice intentions of the respondents indicate that they hold the social project of taking responsibility for the environment through voluntary collective action to be a valuable one, in the areas of saving energy, disposing of toxic household waste, and choosing a place to spend their holiday? And are they willing to contribute to the social project, in each of those cases?

9.3 The acceptance of legal regulation and self-regulation

Following the core survey questions on the social dilemma, we included items on the acceptance of three types of behavioural regulation for the three cases. These questions distinguish between two kinds of self-regulation on the one hand (self-regulation by government agencies, as opposed to self-regulation by citizens), and legal regulation on the other.

Self-regulation by citizens

To what extent do you consider it desirable or undesirable that people remind each other more often to:

(1) bring their toxic household waste to the collection point?
(2) save energy in the household?
(3) spend their holiday close to home because of the environmental consequences?

Self-regulation by government

To what extent do you consider it desirable or undesirable that government agencies remind people more often to:

(1) bring their toxic household waste to the collection point?
(2) save energy in the household?
(3) spend their holiday close to home because of the environmental consequences?

Legal regulation

To what extent do you consider it desirable or undesirable that government agencies take measures that make it compulsory for people to:

(1) bring their toxic household waste to the collection point?
(2) save energy in the household?
(3) spend their holiday close to home because of the environmental consequences?

The categories presented on a show card were: 'very desirable', 'desirable', 'neither desirable nor undesirable', 'undesirable', and 'very undesirable'. Before analyzing the response in summary form below, we want to discuss the meaning and relevance of gathering this kind of data on the acceptance of policy types. Compared to the diverse categories of social instruments listed in our overview in section 2.3, the present survey questions are rather crude. They are designed to capture two main distinctions. First, the difference between legal regulation and self-regulation (either by citizens or by government agencies) simply turns on *compulsion* versus *persuasion*. A respondent's acceptance of self-regulation, or of legal regulation, tells us nothing more than his assent to either of these methods of intervention. The answer does not speak to the respondent's view on the desirability of the different concrete policies under either of these methods, many of which he may not even know about. For our present purposes, then, the first distinction concerns the acceptance of measures that either affect the agents' parameters of choice ('legal regulation') or try to change their preferences for choosing between available options ('self-regulation').

It is important to know whether self-regulation policies meet with less resistance than efforts at regulating behaviour legally. This is certainly a matter in which policymakers are interested, given the high compliance cost of the latter type of regulation. One could argue that the matter is easy to decide. Citizens, it might be said, will prefer social regulation to legal regulation, because it simply leaves them more freedom of action. But this is not always true. For one thing, there will be a clear reason to prefer effective legal regulation of noxious pollutants, such as PCBs and heavy metals, from entering the soil and water, and in so far as such substances are under the control of consumers, one might not want to count on the responsible behaviour of citizens. But even in the absence of clear and present health risks, it is still not straightforward that legal regulation would be less preferable than social regulation. Some may think that if the government is really concerned to set people on environmentally friendly courses, then it should seek firm democratic authority to restrict undesirable behaviour by laws and incentives of taxation, rather than by badgering the public to be morally responsible and do the right things voluntarily. So the issue of charting differences in acceptance between legal regulation and self-regulation is empirically important, not only because it gives some insight into the possible effectiveness of the latter type of policy, but also because it addresses the wider question of what is commonly thought about the scope of legitimate government intervention on behalf of the environment.

The first two survey questions make a second distinction that needs to be explained: self-regulation by citizens versus self-regulation by government agencies. Our aim here is to find out whether the respondents are sensitive to just who engages in persuasion. Each of these types of self-regulation can take a variety of different forms, which people may react to differently. As said above, we here abstract from that. Yet there is an ambiguity to be noted. The questions presume that the two types of self-regulation can be more or less clearly distinguished by the respondents: is it the government, or is it basically the neighbour next door who is telling us these things about the environment? For policymakers however, both kinds of self-regulation may be regarded as types of state intervention. As we noted in section 2.3, the government uses social instruments of self-regulation of the *direct* or the *indirect* type. The indirect social instruments devolve moral persuasion from government to intermediary organizations, including local citizen groups, for instance Agenda-21 initiatives. As a consequence, the answers to the questions on 'self-regulation by government' and 'self-regulation by citizens' may to some extent be considered as measuring acceptance of direct and indirect governmental policies of self-regulation. The relevance of posing the two self-regulation questions is related to this point. If self-regulation by citizens is accepted, while self-regulation by government is rejected in a particular case of the dilemma, then the respondents are in favour of being held to account by their peers, but resist being spoken to by an almighty government on the environmental issues in question. If in another case it were to be the other way round, then this could mean that people think it proper, in that area of behaviour, to rely on the state rather than on their peers. It might even show, on further inquiry, that they trust the state more than their fellow citizens to provide relevant facts about environmental risks, and to provide guidance on how to reduce those risks.

In view of the above considerations, one might expect to observe unsystematic responses on acceptance across the cases of the environmental dilemma, with respect to each type of regulation. But on the contrary, table 9.1 shows a remarkably systematic pattern. In this table, the response categories are interpreted as follows: '(very) desirable' indicates acceptance, and '(very) undesirable' indicates rejection of a given type of regulation. The middle category 'neither desirable nor undesirable' indicates a neutral attitude. It will be left out of the picture, together with the 'do not know/no opinion' category.[3]

[3] The percentages of answers lost in this operation are 16% for Chemical Waste, 15% for Energy Saving, and 7% for Holiday Destination. This last case thus evokes the highest degree of unequivocal response.

Table 9.1 *Acceptance and rejection of three regulation types*

N = 993		Chemical Waste	Energy Saving	Holiday Destination
Legal regulation	acceptance (%)	53	33	8
	rejection (%)	31	46	80
Self-regulation	acceptance (%)	77	70	31
by citizens	rejection (%)	9	12	39
Self-regulation	acceptance (%)	89	83	42
by government	rejection (%)	4	7	38

We shall start by examinimg the differences in acceptance of regulation types by looking first at the *columns* of table 9.1. In all cases of the dilemma, the three types display a *common percentage ranking of acceptance*: self-regulation by government is ranked first, self-regulation by citizens is ranked second, and legal regulation is ranked last. Moreover, the types also approximate the reverse percentage ranking of *rejection* in all of the cases: legal regulation is ranked first, self-regulation by citizens second, and self-regulation by government last (except in the case of Holiday Destination, where self-regulation by citizens and by government are almost equally rejected at just under 40 per cent). Thus, one can legitimately characterize the differences in response to types of regulation between cases by looking at the ranking of acceptance figures only, since the rejection of regulation follows the reverse ranking.

Is legal regulation the hardest of the three types for an individual to accept? Can it be said, in other words, that a respondent who accepts legal regulation in any given case will be quite likely to accept social regulation as well? This is indeed confirmed by scale analysis of the kind we discussed in chapter 7. Moreover, in every single case, the three types of regulation form a scale, with legal regulation at one end, and self-regulation by government at the other.[4]

---

[4] Following the procedure of scale analysis outlined in chapter 7, nine dichotomous items are constructed, one for each of the three types of regulation, and for each of the three cases. To take just two examples, the item 'Acceptance of legal regulation in Chemical Waste' ranges over all 993 respondents, with Value 1 for the ones who accept legal regulation in this case, and Value 0 for those who respond otherwise. In all, 525 respondents score Value 1, and the remainder (993 − 525 = 468) then scores Value 0. Likewise, 'Acceptance of self-regulation by government in Holiday Destination' has 413 respondents scoring Value 1 and 580 respondents scoring Value 0. The remaining seven Acceptance items are constructed similarly. Applying scale analysis to the assertion that legal regulation is the hardest type, involves comparing the positive scores of the items along the columns of table 8.1. It is indeed confirmed that respondents who accept legal regulation are likely to accept each of the two types of self-regulation as well, in each case. The item homogeneity coefficients for Acceptance of legal regulation, which express the strength of the hardest type assertion, exceed .5 in each case and

This implies that self-regulation by citizens is a harder type than self-regulation by government with respect to acceptance.

These results are in some ways good news for the viability of self-regulation policy. Respondents are much more opposed to legal governmental intrusions into their free action space than they are to accepting normative guidance from their fellow citizens, or from the government, on how to behave in that free space. Judging from the aggregate response to the acceptance questions in table 9.1 (reading down the columns), the government's role of initiating self-regulation policies in the Netherlands seems to be one that the respondents feel comfortable with. Even in the troublesome case of Holiday Destination, 42 per cent still think it is (very) desirable that the government regularly reminds them of the environmental benefits to be had from spending their holiday close to the home, while only 8 per cent would accept legal regulation of holiday travel. And while the acceptance of legal regulation is rather high in Chemical Waste (53 per cent), the acceptance of self-regulation by government in that case is widespread indeed (89 per cent).

Table 9.1 also indicates that state efforts in persuading citizens are accepted somewhat more than mutual persuasion among citizens. This may reflect a perception of the leading role played by the government in promoting environmental qualities. However, though these differences in acceptance are significant, they are not spectacular. This shows that the effort to engineer a broad discussion on environmental aspects of daily life may also have a considerable role to play, just as the advocates of self-regulation policy think it should. The results of the scale analysis lend support to each of these conclusions.

Next, we shall examine the differences between cases. Now the acceptance figures are examined across the three *rows* of table 9.1. It is easy to see that acceptance of regulation differs significantly across the three environmental cases, irrespective of the type of regulation involved. For all three types, the percentage acceptance ranking of cases is: Chemical Waste, Energy Saving, Holiday Destination, with the last case registering a rather lower level of acceptance than the other two. The acceptance rankings suggest that individual respondents find it harder to accept regulation of any kind in Holiday Destination than they do in the other two cases. Following chapter 5 once again, the hardest case assertion is tested. It says that respondents who accept a given type of regulation in the case of Holiday Destination will also accept that type of regulation in the cases of Chemical Waste and Energy Saving. The assertion is statistically confirmed

thus meet the criterion of strong scalability: .52 in Chemical Waste, .65 in Energy Saving and .67 in Holiday Destination. Moreover, all the pairwise item coefficients in each of the cases are well above the minimally acceptable value of .30. In each case also, the three items – Acceptance of legal regulation, Acceptance of self-regulation by citizens, and Acceptance of self-regulation by government – form a strong scale as well. The scale coefficient of homogeneity exceeds .50. In Chemical Waste it is .51, in Energy Saving .62, and in Holiday Destination .65.

by scale analysis. Moreover, for any type of regulation, the three cases form a scale, with Holiday Destination at one end, and Chemical Waste at the other.[5] This implies that Energy Saving is a harder case than Chemical Waste with respect to acceptance.

9.4 Conclusion

To sum up, the case of Holiday Destination displays appreciably more resistance to regulation than the other two cases do. When the choice of holiday is at stake, respondents are much less inclined to tolerate incursions into the domain of free choice than when they are being asked (or would perhaps be forced) to take the time and trouble in the household to save on energy, or dump their batteries in a special container. The normalizing effect may partly explain this difference in acceptance of regulation, as was suggested in section 9.2 above. But as we shall demonstrate in chapter 13, there is more to it than that: differences in the cost of cooperating between cases of the dilemma also exert a major influence. In general, though, the survey confirms that there is scope for the pursuit of policies of self-regulation, as far as the acceptance of such policies by the public is concerned. In view of the monitoring and compliance costs associated with legal regulation of household behaviour, this is of some importance. If government wants to make people's behaviour environmentally more friendly, it must start talking to them, as Dutch policymakers have realized. The response patterns that we just reported strongly suggest that people in the Netherlands are not averse to being talked to. This raises the issue of the next two sections. Do people actually agree with what is said by government about how valuable a common good an unpolluted environment is? And, if so, are they inclined to cooperate, taking to heart the governmental slogan 'A better environment begins at your own doorstep'?

---

[5] A scale analysis here involves comparing the positive scores on the items Acceptance of legal regulation, Acceptance of self-regulation by citizens, and Acceptance of self-regulation by government along the rows of table 9.1. The item homogeneity coefficient for Holiday Destination, which expresses the strength of the hardest case assertion for each type of regulation, is at the level of strong scalability (exceeding .5): .62 for Acceptance of legal regulation, .71 for Acceptance of self-regulation by citizens, and .61 for Acceptance of self-regulation by government. Moreover, the pairwise item coefficients of each of the regulation types are well above the minimally acceptable value of .30. The Acceptance of regulation items for the three cases also form a strong scale. The scale coefficient of homogeneity for Acceptance of legal regulation is .66, for Self-regulation by citizens .64, and for Acceptance of self-regulation by government .55.

10

Do people agree with the environmental ethos?

10.1 Introduction

The issue of reasoned agreement with a social ethos is an intricate one. In contrast to the acceptance issue, we do not present new survey material here. Instead we shall spend time in reviewing observed attitudes in environmental dilemmas. The results were presented in part II, from the actor's perspective. It was shown that respondents rationally cooperate or defect in the stylized game form of the dilemma, in their role of 'Individual' versus 'The Others', depending on their preferences over the game's four outcomes. The observed diversity in preferences is linked to the respondents' diverse stances on the motivational dimensions of Valuation and Willingness, according to criteria of internal consistency. Moreover, diversity of response occurs not only between individual respondents, but between the same respondent's stances in different dilemmas as well. In short, different people respond differently to the general challenge of the dilemma, and the same people may also respond differently, depending on the area of social behaviour in which that general challenge is posed. Chapters 7 and 8 have focused on this last source of diversity.

In what follows below, we try to bring order into the diversity of responses, by interpreting the data in light of the environmental ethos. Taking up the suggestions of chapter 2, we argue in some detail about how the environmental ethos can be *decomposed into two cumulative stages*, the first stage concerning the 'internalization of environmental value', and the second stage concerning the 'internalization of personal responsibility'. Having laid out the content of the ethos in these two components in section 10.2, we briefly revisit the typically Dutch policy aim of drawing on people's moral resources in order to obtain compliance, in section 10.3. Then we go on to show in section 10.4, how gradations of agreement with the first stage of the ethos can be measured by the response on the motivational dimension of of Valuation, while gradations of agreement with the second stage (which presupposes agreement with the first) are measured by the joint response on the dimensions of Valuation and Willingness. Next, we identify the preference orderings that reflect gradations of agreement with the environmental ethos, according to our test of consistent preferences. This finally leads us to present the motive and preference responses for the cases of the dilemma in an appropriate form in section 10.5, and to grade the difficulty of giving a cooperative response by means of scale analysis. We conclude with a summary overview of the results of this and the preceding chapter.

10.2 The two stages of the environmental ethos

In explaining the content of self-regulation policies, we discussed the significance of a programmatic policy statement in the first national environmental plan. This statement, which was quoted at length in section 2.4, spells out the government's decision to launch the 'strategy of internalization', which aims at making individual responsibility for the environment count in people's minds. As this document says, 'individuals will have to give substance to this responsibility by doing everything reasonably within their capacities to prevent environmental degradation as the direct or indirect result of their activities'. To appreciate the structure of the ethos which is invoked here, it will be necessary to quote the passages immediately following this statement:

> The large scale at which some environmental problems occur does not reduce the responsibility for making a contribution to these problems. Every link in the chain of production-consumption-waste reduction can be scrutinized in terms of this responsibility . . . In principle, therefore, our environmental behaviour must be justified. This includes consideration of alternatives for activities that may pose large risks to the environment. A problem with such justification of behaviour is the fact that isolated activities often contribute only slightly to the total deterioration or improvement of environmental quality. Thus, in justifying an activity, a recalculation must take place: one has to answer the question concerning what the effect would be on environmental quality once a number of people undertake the same actions, given the physical and market conditions of such actions. This implies that one must be aware of the possibility that specific actions may elicit a great number of similar actions which adversely affect environmental quality in the aggregate. If this is the case, then it should be factored into the justification of individual activities. If such individual recalculation is not made, then one is assuming in effect that one person may claim licence to pollute more than another, given the desired quality of the environment.
>
> (NMP1, 1989: 86–8)

To prepare the ground for a fresh look at the results of part II in this chapter, we analyse the content of the environmental ethos, by looking at the above passage in conjunction with the one preceding it, which was quoted in section 2.4. As there suggested, the message of what the government is saying about responsibility for the environment can be decomposed in two cumulative stages, with the first stage presupposing the second. The two stages correspond to the collective and the individual aspects of the social dilemma, respectively. The first stage of the ethos focuses on what Dutch environmental policy language calls the *internalization of environmental values*. 'Internalization' here has the distinct meaning of a *positive valuation of environmental quality* (biodiversity, clean soil, water and air, a stable climate, and so on). This valuation is informed by reasons for affirming the importance of various environmental qualities, reasons which may be either instrumental or intrinsic, depending on one's conception of environmental good. However, as we noted in discussing the liberal character of the ethos (section 2.5), the communicative policies of social regulation that address such questions of value are predominantly oriented towards an instrumental outlook on environmental quality. In keeping with the conception of sustainable growth, they are concerned to stress the well-being of present and future generations, as the passages of the environmental plan that we quoted in section 2.4 clearly indicate.

A positive orientation towards features of environmental quality is a necessary condition for the second stage of the environmental ethos, which will be discussed in a moment. But first, it is necessary to point out that the internalization of environmental values is linked, in principle, to a conception of voluntary collective action, which is directed to achieving the values in question. This link is evident from the judgement, again quoted in section 2.4, that the actors of civil society should not think that the solution of pollution problems can simply be left to the government, as a matter for the environmental policy sector to deal with. For example, consumers might well agree that emissions of fluor from aerosol cans, or the phosphorous substances emanating from some detergents, should be reduced to protect the ozone layer, or respectively to improve water quality. But they might also hold that it is really up to the government to regulate the producers, so that they themselves can buy whatever they want from a menu of environmentally approved goods, without having to engage in 'recalculating' their own actions. Whatever may be said in favour of such an attitude, it is clearly one that the environmental ethos sets out to change, by suggesting that the citizens take it upon themselves, as a matter of course, to select more environmentally friendly patterns of consumption, even in the absence of environmental product regulations.

Given these elaborations of what is involved in the part of the ethos that deals with the internalization of environmental values, then, it is possible to see that the survey questions on the motivational dimension of Valuation are capable of capturing this first stage of the ethos. This may be seen from our presentation of the Valuation motive, for the case of Chemical Waste (section 6.2). There, a respondent who agrees with the statement: *'I believe that collecting toxic household waste at a recycling point for the sake of a cleaner environment is a good thing'*, is said to display a positive Valuation to addressing the social dilemma in question, by means of voluntary collective action. This is fully compatible with endorsing the first stage of the environmental ethos as described above. In agreeing to the Valuation statement of the survey, the respondent is not merely indicating that he or she attaches value to local reduction of toxic waste by means of the recycling scheme, but also implicitly affirming that it is a good thing that a sufficient number of local households would actually take the trouble to bring their chemical household waste to the recycling point, quite independently of whether he or she would personally want to contribute. With respect to that last point, of course, the question is whether someone who has internalized the good of collective action for a designated environmental value will also be willing to assume personal responsibility by participating in the collective action. This is where the second stage of the environmental ethos comes in.

The second stage explicitly introduces the concept of personal responsibility. In Dutch policy jargon, it is called *the internalization of environmental responsibility*. This is the responsibility of the individual for shouldering a reasonable burden of contribution to some voluntary scheme. What is at issue in this second stage are the norms of proper conduct that regulate individual choice in situations of environmental collective action. Such norms may not always be firmly established, and it is often uncertain what they would demand of the individual in any given context. In its official rhetoric, the environmental ethos assumes individual responsibility to refer to some kind of willingness to contribute to collective action, as the campaign slogan 'A better environment starts at your own doorstep' testifies. Thus in its unqualified form, the second stage of the ethos wants to instil the following kind of maxim in citizens: 'the environment is important, therefore I ought to contribute to it'. We shall take this further in the next chapter, in the context of Sen's analysis of moral commitment.

For the present purposes of clarifying the second stage, however, it is worth noting that the normative requirement of personal contribution in a scheme of collective action must always be subject to qualifying conditions of 'reasonableness'. Such conditions are inevitably subject to ambiguity. For one thing, what it is reasonable to ask from somebody in a given case of environmental collective action will depend on the opportunity cost of cooperative behaviour. Now the rhetoric of the first national environmental plan boldly asserts that individuals should be prepared to contribute 'within their capacities', as the passages quoted in section 2.4 have it. This is saying, presumably, that individuals should be willing to incur considerable costs in forgone welfare or comfort, in view of the great urgency of environmental problems. But as we have also seen in section 2.2, the doctrine of sustainable growth, which motivates the policy drive of 'internalization', clearly recognizes that the objectives of reducing pollution at source, however urgent, always have to be weighed against legitimate non-environmental interests.

What counts as a 'reasonable cost' is thus largely a matter of social judgement. The ethos of responsibility cannot address this source of ambiguity in general. It can only build upon contextually contingent, and partly contested, notions of reasonable contribution in specific cases of environmental dilemmas. But independently of this, there is a second source of ambiguity in the above-quoted passages from the 1989 plan. Notions about what is 'reasonable' in matters of voluntary collective action under a norm of cooperation may vary, depending on the general state of compliance to that norm, even if the cost of compliance remains within reasonable bounds for everybody concerned. What the ethos has to say about this second source of ambiguity needs to be explicated with some care. Given the above-quoted passages, we argue that the second stage of the ethos is compatible with a *demanding* and a *lenient* version of the individual's own responsibility to cooperate. For the sake of clarifying that distinction, let us suppose for the moment that most share the view that in general, it would be good if people were to participate in Chemical Waste's voluntary scheme for separately collecting toxic waste. They are aware, that is, in what ways toxic substances dumped in unseparated household waste present an environmental problem, for which the scheme is at least a partial solution. They also agree that bringing toxic waste to the recycling point is well within 'the capacities' of the individual members of households, and that it does not impose too great a burden, at least in standard cases. On these suppositions, the first stage of the environmental ethos is linked to the second by the following kind of appeal:

You seem to agree that it is good if people in the neighbourhood do something about the problem of toxic household waste. You know what it is you can do yourself, and you also know that if a sufficient number of us do it, then the problem will at least have been satisfactorily addressed. Now, even though the isolated actions within your own household in this case hardly affect the environment, you ought to pause and 'recalculate' the effect of those actions, by asking: 'What would happen to the environment if we all went on dumping our batteries and old paint in the household garbage can?' You already know the answer to that question. Therefore it is reasonable that the members of your household should take an individual responsibility for the proper handling of the problem, just as other households should.'

This reasoning is clear enough, but it glosses over an important normative point. It is indeed not unreasonable to say, in this case, that I should be responsible and start recalculating the effects of my own actions, provided that everyone else can be expected to show the same kind of responsibility. But the reasoning may be less persuasive if it is an entirely open question to me whether others will actually bother to recalculate, let alone act accordingly. In view of this, the requirement of internalizing environmental responsibility can be interpreted in two ways, as either demanding or lenient.

In the *demanding* interpretation, the person's acknowledgement of a collective responsibility for an environmental quality that can be obtained without excessive cost to citizens, leads to a strong assignment of personal responsibility. In this case, internalization passes from: 'we all ought to contribute to a worthwhile environmental good' to 'I ought to contribute', without pausing to ask the troublesome question: 'but what ought I to do if the others do not in fact contribute?' The demanding interpretation thus requires *unconditional compliance* to the norm of cooperation. In the *lenient* interpretation, by contrast, the duty of personal responsibility for making a contribution precisely depends on the answer to that troublesome question. Its demands are weaker, since it requires *conditional compliance* with the norm of contribution, that is, it requires someone to contribute only if others do so as well. Both of these interpretations are compatible with what is being advocated in the passages quoted above.

To see this, consider the injunction to recalculate the significance of relatively innocent individual actions, which harm the environment in the aggregate. On the demanding interpretation, the injunction sets up an unqualified prohibition of such actions, whatever the others may do. On the lenient one, it only forbids a person to take a free ride on the others, or as the text says, 'to claim licence to pollute more than others do, given the desired quality of the environment'. This last prohibition implicitly assumes that there is at least a significant number of others who do in fact refrain from going all the way in their polluting activities. It does not cover the case of what the individual ought to do in case these others were to defect in the environmental dilemma at hand. Thus, the prohibition says *no more than* that one should not act as a free-rider. Hence the prohibition implies conditional, but not necessarily unconditional, compliance with the norm of cooperation. This establishes that the lenient and the demanding interpretations of the ethos are both compatible with the official text.

Taken together, the first and second stages of the environmental ethos may be related to the responses on the motive dimension of Willingness in our survey. Referring once more to the presentation of Chemical Waste in section 6.2, a respondent who agrees with the statement: *'I am willing to spend the extra time and effort of bringing my toxic household waste to the recycling point'*, is taken to display a positive Willingness to contribute. In and of itself, this response does not necessarily indicate that the respondent's willingness is due to the 'recalculation' considerations that characterize the ethos. However, if the respondent has also reported agreement with the Valuation statement, then the response as a whole (i.e., the motive structure of positive Valuation and positive Willingness) is compatible with the substance of the ethos in its demanding unconditional interpretation, while the response exhibiting a motive structure of positive Valuation and intermediate Willingness is compatible with the ethos in its lenient conditional interpretation. We shall take up this proposal in the next section.

To conclude, we look ahead to some of our conclusions in the final chapter, by making one comment on the logic of the programmatic policy statement which was analysed in section 2.4 and then further pursued above. That statement strongly suggests that Dutch environmental policy-thinking must be rather preoccupied with the phenomenon of the social dilemma. In itself, this is probably true. Strangely, however, the policy writings on self-regulation in the Netherlands do not analyse the general structure of social dilemmas in detail. And indeed, what is said about the social dilemma, as applied to environmental problems, often ignores the logic of the two stages of the environmental ethos set out above. In particular, as we shall demonstrate in more detail later, it is assumed that if citizens stick to environmentally harmful behaviour in various areas, while at the same time they are observed to be well aware of the aggregate consequences of their behaviour, then they are supposed to be succumbing to the 'social dilemma', in the sense that they value collective action for environmental goals, but refuse to contribute personally. This diagnosis may be misleading. The two-stage logic of the environmental ethos suggests that the problem may lie deeper. Those who are unwilling to cooperate, while yet being aware of their harmful behaviour, may be unwilling because they simply deny the value of collective action for the sake of the environment, given the high costs they associate with cooperative behaviour *for everyone concerned.* On the basis of further analysis of the survey results, we shall suggest that this possibility is one that helps to explain the distinction between hard and easy cases of environmental dilemmas.

10.3 Knaves, pawns or knights?

The government addresses the population at large, explicitly asking individual actors, either producers or consumers, to *justify* their environmental behaviour. What is more, the government also asks individual actors to account for their behaviour in terms that identify the tasks of reducing pollution, waste, irreversible resource depletion, and other forms of environmental degradation, as ones involving a personal contribution to schemes of *voluntary* collective action. Of course, this is not to say that the government wishes to withdraw entirely as a legal regulator, and leave it up to the goodwill of civil society to solve every environmental collective action problem in sight. Our reason for stating the issue in terms of voluntary collective action was explained in section 2.5. Dutch policymakers have come to see that the urgency of environmental problems, as revealed by their highly ambitious planning goals, makes it necessary to enlist the actors of civil society to collaborate with the state. This is done by promoting informal mechanisms of social obligation for protecting the environment. When describing the principles of Dutch environmental planning in section 2.2, we noted that the key premise underlying the internalization strategy is the assumption of a 'capability for self-regulation'. This assumption states that producers and consumers, whose joint behaviour is at the root of the environmental problem, are also capable of responding in responsible ways to the challenge which that problem poses.

The significance of that assumption can be grasped by referring to a distinction made by Julian LeGrand. The policy outlook of Dutch environmental planning is one which sees fit to regard the actors of civil society not merely as *knaves*, who will take every opportunity to pollute, if that happens to be in their self-interest and if they feel they can get away with it; nor as *pawns*, who will tend to obey clear directives, but who cannot be expected to do more than comply passively. The actors of civil society are, at least in large part, regarded as *knights*, possessing moral resources of environmental virtue, which it is the task of good governance to activate.[1] This is why the Dutch government feels entitled to ask citizens and corporate actors to show active compliance, in accordance with an ethos of environmental responsibility. We have argued that this appeal to the ethos, while it can certainly be described as part of a policy of moral reform, is not motivated by a wish to create a more virtuous citizenry. The appeal to citizens is decidedly result-oriented, as is shown by the shares of environmental performance demanded from the target group of consumers in the quantitative planning objectives of the national environmental plans.

In this chapter, we shall take the aims of self-regulation policy at face value, and ask whether the respondents in the survey give evidence of agreeing with the substance of the ethos. We assume that what the government has to say to the citizens, concerning the right way to handle environmental problems, has not gone unnoticed by the respondents. Thus, we regard the substance of the ethos, as spelled out in the previous section, as a relevant 'thick' description of motivation, on which rational choices to cooperate or defect in the three environmental dilemmas could possibly be based.

In chapter 3, we criticized the notion of a 'thick-theory' of rational choice. The target we focused on is the account of self-interested motivation, which lies at the heart of the standard interpretation of a Potential Contributor's

---

[1] See LeGrand, 1997.

Dilemma as an *actual* dilemma. As noted several times before, the standard interpretation assumes that a rational actor will invariably follow the Prisoner's Dilemma-ordering (PQRS), and hence invariably acts on the dominant strategy to defect which is associated with that ordering. In chapter 6, it was seen that motivations of self-interest can be recorded on the two dimensions of Valuation and Willingness. The self-interested rational actor of the thick-theory will then be someone who regards the environmental result of (nearly) universal cooperation in a scheme of collective action as a desirable thing, but is nevertheless unwilling to participate in that scheme, by taking on the cost of cooperating himself. This corresponds to motive structure (V_1, W_3), in which such an actor would agree with the Valuation statement, and would disagree with the Willingness statement.

As we have been keen to explain, our objection against the thick-theory does not deny that rational actors with these particular self-interested motives may in fact be very numerous, and so produce the unhappy result of the actual Contributor's Dilemma in any number of cases. What we have been denying is that it is justified to regard such motives as the only ones that characterize the outlook of a rational actor in a Potential Contributor's Dilemma. To put it more generally, what we are objecting to is not the use of a 'thick' description of rational choice as such. One may freely assume that in particular cases of the dilemma, rational actors will be predominantly, or even exclusively, motivated to free ride on an environmental collective good in ways that produce an actual dilemma. But it is not legitimate to lay down in advance that such motivations – however plausible they seem to an outside observer – must be accepted as an integral part of the theory of rational choice. Substantive assumptions about motivation properly enter at the level of applying rational choice theories. That is to say, they must be subject to empirical scrutiny.

Below we shall spell out the motive structures that characterize the ethos of environmental responsibility, and the preference orderings that are consistent with these. It will also be seen that various motive structures and preference orderings run counter to the environmental ethos in various ways, including those of the free-rider in the thick-theory who populates the universe of standard rational choice applications.

10.4 The ethical interpretation of motives and preferences

We now return to the two-tiered structure of the ethos. Its first stage aims at an *internalization of environmental value*. Its second stage, which builds upon the first one, tries to bring about the *internalization of individual responsibility*. The attitude corresponding to an individual's endorsement of the first stage requires the motive of positive Valuation (V_1). This is because someone who has internalized environmental value must always hold that voluntary collective action for the sake of an environmental quality is a good thing. The second stage of the ethos invokes the personal responsibility to live up to a norm of cooperation. This norm is predicated on the evaluative judgement of the first stage. It says that one should be willing to bear the cost of cooperating, because voluntary collective action for the sake of the environment is a social good. In section 10.2 we distinguished a demanding interpretation of the ethos, which imposes a duty to cooperate unconditionally, from a lenient interpretation, which only imposes a duty to cooperate conditionally on the good behaviour of others. Because agreement with the second stage of the ethos presupposes agreement with its first stage, this norm of cooperation applies to individuals who have internalized environmental value, and who therefore must have motives of positive Valuation. Given this linkage, we distinguished the demanding interpretation of the ethos from the lenient one, by defining the former as the motive structure of positive Valuation and positive Willingness (V_1, W_1), and the latter as the motive structure of positive Valuation and intermediate Willingness (V_1, W_2).

Can the other seven motive structures (V_i, W_j) be interpreted in these terms as well? This is the question we now address. The policy statement quoted in section 10.2 does indeed allow one to identify motive structures that express a partial or full rejection of the attitude exemplified by the ethos. Consider first positive Valuation and negative Willingness (V_1, W_3). These motives include the typical attitude of the free-rider in the thick-theory, as has been noted in the last section. Motive structure (V_1, W_3) can now be interpreted specifically as one which agrees with the first stage of the ethos, but rejects the second stage. The individual affirms that voluntary cooperation by others for the purpose of obtaining less pollution is indeed a good thing, as the first stage requires, but steadfastly refuses to take on board the personal responsibility of cooperating. Secondly, consider those who are likewise unwilling to cooperate, regardless of what the others may do. If this unwillingness derives from the judgement that voluntary collective action for the environment is no good, then we have motives of intermediate or negative Valuation, and negative Willingness: either (V_2, W_3) or (V_3, W_3). Both of these motive structures can legitimately be interpreted in opposition to the environmental ethos. Persons who report such motives clearly reject both stages of the ethos. Unlike the free-rider, their unwillingness to cooperate is based on a refusal to subscribe to the evaluative claim of the first stage, that voluntary cooperation for the environment is a social good. In other words, they reject the personal responsibility to cooperate because they think that others need not – or perhaps even should not – cooperate either. As we argue in chapter 13, there are specific reasons of recalcitrance that may explain this diehard stance of opposition to the environmental ethos. Such reasons are highly relevant to the assessment of self-regulation policy.

Of the nine possible motive structures, the remaining four are ones that combine intermediate or negative Valuation (either V_2, or V_3) with positive or intermediate Willingness (either W_1 or W_2). These motive structures defy interpretation in terms of the environmental ethos. According to the ethos, the willingness to cooperate oneself, whether unconditionally (W_1) or conditionally (W_2), must be motivated by the view that collective action for the environment is desirable, and this requires positive Valuation (V_1). The present motive structures reject this view, since each of them lacks positive Valuation. In these cases, the individual's willingness to cooperate must therefore be explained by other reasons. We shall not seek to spell out these reasons here.

As argued in chapter 6, every single motive structure corresponds to a set of consistent preference orderings, summarized in figure 6.5. This correspondence will now be used to characterize preference orderings by reference to the five motive structures which were just given a definite interpretation, in terms of the environmental ethos. Following the exposition above, these motive structures are labelled as (V_1, W_1): 'full agreement' with the ethos, (V_1, W_2) 'partial agreement' with the ethos, and (V_1, W_3) 'rejection of norm', that is to say, rejection of the cooperation norm of the second stage. Finally, both (V_2, W_3) and (V_3, W_3) are labelled as 'rejection of ethos', because they contradict the requirements of both stages. For the sake of convenience, figure 10.1 below identifies these five motive structures. The corresponding preference orderings are printed boldface, to distinguish them from orderings consistent with the four motive structures which are not interpretable.

In chapter 11, the theoretical background of this interpretation will be further discussed. At this stage we only comment on some points concerning the preferences of the partial agreement category, and the two 'rejection' categories. Orderings QPRS and PQSR reflect partial agreement with the environmental ethos (V_1, W_2). Both of them lack a dominant strategy to cooperate. However, the behavioural consequences of acting upon each of these orderings are rather different. An actor with ordering QPRS will satisfy his preferences best by co-operating in case the others cooperate, and by defecting in case the others defect. This ordering therefore exhibits a disposition to cooperate, conditionally on the cooperation of the others. Actors with the QPRS-ordering may thus be seen to satisfy the notion of partial (i.e. conditional) agreement with the environmental ethos. That is to say, their disposition to cooperate only on condition that the others do so too is in line with what we have called the *lenient interpretation* of the cooperation norm.

But now consider PQSR, the other consistent ordering of (V_1, W_2). An actor with this ordering will satisfy his preferences best by cooperating in case the others defect, and by defecting in case the others cooperate. Such actors certainly do not satisfy the notion of partial agreement with the ethos in the standard way. On the one hand, their disposition to cooperate only on condition that the others defect (making them end up in the sucker outcome S) may be taken to signal an attitude of self-sacrifice for the environmental cause, similar to what is implied by the motive of positive Willingness. But on the other hand, their disposition to defect only if the others cooperate (which gets them into the free-rider outcome P) is similar to what is implied by the negative Willingness of a self-interested actor. Thus, while motive structure (V_1, W_2) has here been labelled as 'partial agreement' with the ethos, the corresponding preference orderings QPRS and PQSR reveal that the ethos may be partially endorsed in different ways. We return to this point in chapter 11.

The second comment concerns the preferences which are consistent with rejection of the environmental ethos in various forms. Some of these preferences express free-ridership. Consider the orderings PQRS and PRQS in the category 'rejection of norm' (V_1, W_3). Of the two, PQRS is the familiar Prisoner's Dilemma-ordering. It is usually regarded as the paradigmatic case of the free-rider. But our account of consistent preferences suggests that PQRS is *not the only instance* of free-rider preferences. In the context of the Potential Contributor's Dilemma, a free-rider is ordinarily understood to be someone with a rational incentive to defect unconditionally, from the desire to take advantage of a collective good which comes about by the voluntary cooperation of a sufficient number of other people. On this understanding, the ordering PRQS in the consistent set of (V_1, W_3) reflects free-ridership as well, and, in fact, so does the (rather strange) ordering PRSQ, which is consistent with (V_2, W_3) in the category 'rejection of ethos'. This can be seen as follows.

Essential to the motivation of free riding on a collective good are two conditions of a rational actor's preferences. First, the free-rider is motivated to defect if the others cooperate, *because* this makes him as well off as he can possibly be (this implies that outcome P is preferred most). This condition captures the ordinary understanding that the free-rider regards it as a good thing for himself that the others voluntarily cooperate. Secondly, the free-rider is motivated to defect unconditionally *because* if the others likewise defect, then he will not end up in his least preferred position (this implies that outcome R is not the worst outcome). This second condition, jointly with the first, ensures that the actor has a dominant strategy to defect, and thus captures the ordinary understanding that a free-rider has a rational incentive to defect come what may. Of the three orderings (PQRS, PRQS, PRSQ) that satisfy these two conditions, the Prisoner's Dilemma-ordering PQRS is special in one respect, of course. It is the only free-rider's ordering which, if acted on universally, produces a collectively suboptimal outcome, and thus leads to an actual Contributor's Dilemma. For when all defect from PQRS, the resulting outcome R is collectively suboptimal.

Valuation scale	Willingness scale W1	W2	W3
V1	*full agreement* **QSPR** **QPSR**	*partial agreement* **QPRS** **PQSR**	*rejection of norm* **PRQS** **PQRS**
V2	 QSRP SQPR	QRPS QRSP PSQR PSRQ SPQR SPRQ RQSP RQPS	*rejection of ethos* **PRSQ** **RPQS**
V3	SRQP SQRP	SRPQ RSQP	*rejection of ethos* **RPSQ** **RSPQ**

Figure 10.1 Motives and preferences interpreted in terms of the ethos.

But when all defect from either PRQS or PRSQ, then that same outcome is collectively optimal. It follows that free-rider's orderings in general should not be identified with the preferences that produce an actual Contributor's Dilemma.

Finally, let us consider the remaining preferences corresponding to the motive structures that we have been interpreting, and which are printed boldface in Figure 10.1. These are the orderings RPQS (belonging to (V2, W3)) and RPSQ and RSPQ (belonging to (V3, W3)). Like free-rider preferences, these orderings have a dominant strategy to defect. But unlike free-rider preferences, the actor's rational incentive to defect is motivated by the judgement that universal non-cooperation (outcome R) would be the best outcome of interaction. From the actor's point of view then, it would be best if everyone desisted from co-operating. This is an attitude that rejects the environmental ethos most clearly. Motive structure (V3, W3) is the one that uniquely characterizes it.

To make a point that we shall return to later in the next chapter, it is natural to think that the motive of negative Willingness, and its consistent set of preferences with dominant non-cooperative strategies, should be associated with a *self-interested* denial of what the environmental ethos requires. But the variety of motives and preferences that we have just defined in opposition to the ethos show that self-interested motivations in environmental dilemmas are diverse, since they also depend on the Valuation dimension. As we noted in conclusion of section 10.2, the policy strategy of internalization is given by the government's aim of persuading citizens to adopt motives of positive Valuation and positive Willingness, and so counteract the tendency of self-interested consumer behaviour. It would be a mistake, however, to assume that the kind of self-interest that stands in need of correction by policies of self-regulation is invariably the one exemplified by free-rider orderings with positive Valuation, in particular the Prisoner's Dilemma-ordering PQRS.

10.5 The agreement response

To gain a preliminary impression of the impact of self-regulation policy in the three dilemmas, it is helpful to compare the responses in the two categories of full and partial agreement. This section summarizes the results, at the levels of motives and preferences. We also show that Holiday Destination is the hardest of the three cases with respect to full agreement. This is behaviourally the most relevant indicator of respondents' environmental responsibility, since it measures unconditional willingness to cooperate. Table 10.1 presents the *motive* response of the survey. For the sake of simplicity, we lump together the other seven categories as 'other motives'.

The first thing to note from table 10.1 is that the total agreement response (full and partial) is far less in Holiday Destination (40 per cent) than it is in the other two cases (96 per cent and 95 per cent, respectively). This is largely explained by two facts: the dimensions of Valuation and Willingness are positively correlated, and the share of positive Valuation motives in Chemical Waste and Energy Saving is close to 100 per cent, whereas it is just over 50 per cent in Holiday Destination. Both of these facts can be read off from table 6.3 in chapter 6, from which the figures in table 10.1 are taken. Clearly, the environmental ethos has trouble getting off the ground in Holiday Destination, although it seems to meet with considerable success in the two less problematic cases of the dilemma. The respondents do not seem to agree as much with the judgement of the first stage – that it would be a good thing if people voluntarily limited their holidays to places close to the home. Hence it is not surprising that they tend to agree even less with the next stage of the ethos – that it would be their personal responsibility to help protect the environment in such ways.

Secondly, in each case, it can be seen that the percentages of partial agreement with the ethos are considerably below those of full agreement. However, in Holiday Destination this is true to a much lesser extent than it is in the two other cases of the dilemma, as table 10.1 also shows. Both of these findings stand in need of some discussion. It is not at all obvious why so many respondents, who agree that collective action is a good thing, should be willing to contribute regardless of what they expect others to do. We take up some of the reasons for this in chapter 12, where we examine reasons for accepting norms of unconditional cooperation in social dilemmas, rather than reciprocity norms of conditional cooperation.

Table 10.2 gives the response on full and partial agreement with the ethos, now at the level of *preferences*. The figures have been taken from table 4.2 in chapter 4. To forestall misunderstanding here: it need not be that every respondent who has reported a preference ordering listed under full, or partial, agreement has *also* reported the matching motive structure (V_1, W_1), or,

Table 10.1 *Full and partial agreement with the ethos: motives*

		Chemical Waste		Energy Saving		Holiday Destination	
		N	%	N	%	N	%
Full agreement	(V1,W1)	909	92	881	89	244	26
Partial agreement	(V1,W2)	43	4	60	6	130	14
Other motives		38	4	49	5	577	61
Total		990	100	990	100	951	100

Table 10.2 *Full and partial agreement with the ethos: preferences*

		Chemical Waste		Energy Saving		Holiday Destination	
		N	%	N	%	N	%
Full agreement	QSPR	491	60	443	54	201	26
	QPSR	159	20	146	18	105	14
Partial agreement	QPRS	16	2	19	2	20	3
	PQSR	3	0	13	2	31	4
Other preferences		142	18	192	24	402	53
Total		811	100	813	100	759	100

as the case may be (V1, W2). In other words, not all respondents in table 10.2 are necessarily reporting the preferences that are *consistent* with their reported motives.

Yet, as table 10.2 shows, roughly the same features of the motive response on agreement in table 10.1 appear in the preference response as well. First, the total of preferences expressing partial and full agreement with the ethos in Holiday Destination lags considerably behind the high percentages reported in Chemical Waste and Energy Saving. Secondly, in all cases of the dilemma, the preferences of partial agreement (QPRS and PQSR) occur much less frequently than those of full agreement (QSPR and QPSR), while the proportion of the former in the total is appreciably higher in Holiday Destination than it is in the other two cases, in which it is very low indeed. This last point again shows that the majority of respondents who agree with the ethos are willing to cooperate unconditionally, even though this tendency is less marked in Holiday Destination.

Finally, we want to mention the hardest case-analysis of the dichotomized variables of *full agreement*. Respectively, these variables are defined as the positive scores of (V1, W1) at the level of motives, and the positive scores of either QSPR or QPSR at the level of preferences, as shown in tables 10.1

and 10.2. With respect to both variables, the hardest case assertion is amply confirmed. Individual respondents who fully agree with the ethos in Holiday Destination are quite likely to do so in the other two cases as well. The three cases also form a unidimensional scale, for both variables, with Holiday Destination at the hardest end, and Chemical Waste at the easiest.[2]

10.6 Acceptance and agreement: overview

The guiding thread of this and the preceding chapter was the question of how the respondents react to self-regulation policy. We first looked at the issue of acceptance. Do the respondents give evidence of accepting the *medium* of self-regulation, as this is shaped by the social instruments that the government brings to bear on people? We concluded that self-regulation policies go down rather well on the whole, compared to the acceptance of regulating household behaviour by legal means. We also found that there are significant differences in the acceptance of self-regulation policy between the three cases. The differences may be due to the fact that people have become used to having their environmental behaviour scrutinized. This seems to be true especially in the areas of waste disposal and household energy consumption, where social regulation commands high assent. People are far less accustomed to being held to account for their recreational choices, hence they may tend to regard intervention in that area as less desirable: the 'normalizing effect' of policy.

Nevertheless, we argued, policymakers should not place too much reliance on the mere force of habit in changing environmental behaviour for the better. And indeed, Dutch policies of self-regulation seriously try to convince citizens that a sustainable society starts at their own doorstep, as the official slogan has it. Hence it is of interest to look carefully at the substance of the *message* of self-regulation. This was the second issue we examined in this chapter. Do the respondents agree with the basic message of self-regulation, according to which one should accept personal responsibility to serve environmental goals in the business of everyday life? We studied the question by going back to the statement of intent in the first environmental policy plan, which launched the 'strategy of internalization'. A close look at that statement shows that this strategy relies on a specific set of moral appeals, which flow from an ethos of environmental responsibility. The ethos enjoins the actors of civil society, in their roles both as consumers and producers, to view the solution to environmental problems in terms of voluntary collective action. And building on this, the ethos asks every individual to make a responsible effort in contributing to the

---

[2] The item homogeneity coefficient for Holiday Destination, which measures the strength of the hardest case assertion, is .58 for motives, and .53 for preferences in full agreement. The scale coefficients of homogeneity are .39 (a weak scale) and .52 (a strong scale), respectively.

solution. In view of this deliberate policy strategy, it is important to obtain empirical evidence of the extent to which citizens actually agree with the moral injunctions of the government.

In the last two sections, we analysed the motive and preference data of part I, assuming that the respondents are actually aware of the ethos that the government tries to promote. This led us to apply the actor's perspective on rational choice, in order to test for gradations of assent with the two stages of the ethos in each case of the dilemma. The empirical results, as summed up above, are sufficiently interesting to pursue this path further. This we shall do in chapter 13, where we investigate the incidence of *rational choices* that reflect agreement with the environmental ethos. However, some of the theoretical moves we have made in order to get where we are at this point are in need of discussion in a wider framework of debate. The next two chapters address that need.

11

Moral commitment and rational cooperation

11.1 Ranking preference orderings

In this chapter we want to discuss how our perspective on rational cooperation fits in with the 'meta-ranking' framework, which was developed by Amartya Sen in the seventies. The analysis of motives and consistent preferences extends this framework, and applies it to environmental dilemmas. Sen has done much to defend the idea that cooperation in social dilemmas can be rational, not only in the philosopher's sense of being motivated by coherent reasons, but also in the economist's narrower sense adopted here, where choice follows the dominance rule. In pursuing this theme, Sen was concerned to show that morally committed rational behaviour is not easily accommodated by the standard account of utility maximization or preference satisfaction. But he convincingly argued that one can make good analytic sense of moral behaviour within a somewhat more complex structure of decision-making.

The last chapter interpreted the motives and preferences of respondents as reflecting gradations of agreement or disagreement with the environmental ethos, using the definition of consistency between motives and preferences that we developed in chapter 6. This exercise is closely related to Sen's account of moral commitment. The key concept in that account is a 'meta-ranking', a rank order of preference orderings which is based on an underlying structure of moral considerations. We introduce the concept in the next two sections, and then go on to compare it to our definition of consistent preferences in the context of the two-person Prisoner's Dilemma, as originally used by Sen. Our object is to show that the concept of a meta-ranking can be applied to the distinctly different game-theoretical structure of the Potential Contributor's Dilemma.

The issue of morally motivated rational behaviour in social dilemmas is a broad one. It raises not only formal questions concerning the proper framework for studying moral decisions, but controversial questions of a substantive, and in part empirical, nature about the kind of moral commitment that one could expect to emerge in social dilemmas of various kinds. Sen has also contributed to this side of the issue. One of his main suggestions has been that moral principles which demand unconditional cooperation may be favoured by policymakers for the purely instrumental reason of avoiding social dilemmas, and ensuring collective optimality. We shall also comment on this suggestion in section 11.3.

11.2 The meta-ranking approach

In a well-known 1977 article called *Rational Fools*, Sen commented on the typical economist's understanding of rational choice:

> Traditional theory has too little structure. A person is given one preference ordering, and as and when the need arises, this is supposed to reflect his interests, represent his welfare, summarize his idea of what should be done, and describe his actual choices and behaviour. . . . Economic theory has been much preoccupied with this rational fool decked in the glory of his one all-purpose preference ordering. To make room for the different concepts related to this behaviour, we need a more elaborate structure.
>
> (Sen, 1977: 335–6)

Noting that the 'all-purpose preferences' of *homo economicus* are resolutely self-interested, Sen went on to propose an account of rational choice, in which the individual is given a multiplicity of preference orderings over a distinct set of alternatives in the decision situation (either actions, or in case of strategic interdependence, action-related outcomes). Some of these orderings reflect different features of the person's self-interest. Self-interest may be conceived either narrowly, or more widely, so as to include the welfare of family, friends or larger groups with which the individual has ties of sympathy, or bonds of common identity. Other orderings may represent his ideas about what he should ideally feel committed to do, according to different codes of morality, which can vary all the way from conventional standards of dress at formal occasions, or business ethics, to universalistic rules of social justice. Such orderings, in contrast to the former ones, would be ones reflecting a commitment to renounce some aspects of self-interest in favour of morality. Hence they are described as orderings reflecting *commitment* rather than *sympathy*. Sen was especially concerned to bring an account of reasoned moral commitment into the framework of rational choice.

Given the multiplicity of ways to rank the alternatives of the decision situation, the person's actual choices may now be interpreted in two stages. Choice results from, first, a deliberate reflection concerning the selection of the most appropriate ordering on which to act under the circumstances, and secondly, from a rational reflection on how best to attain the most preferred outcomes under those circumstances, in terms of the selected ordering. The multiple preference format opens the possibility of introducing a criterion for the individual to guide the selection of a preference ordering. Sen calls this criterion a 'meta-ranking'. A meta-ranking is a socially salient, overarching set of considerations that enables the person to construct a ranking of the relevant orderings which he is in the process of evaluating, as possible bases for rational action in the choice situation.

Sen describes the notion of a 'moral meta-ranking' as follows. Suppose that a person is in the process of considering three preference orderings in a given situation, for instance one which would involve either donating money to a good cause like Oxfam, or spending it in various other ways. Ordering A represents the individual's personal welfare, which includes the interests of his family, ordering B his 'isolated' interests, ignoring sympathy, while ordering C is the one on which he has usually acted in similar situations in the past.

Now the 'most moral' ordering M could conceivably be any of A, B or C. Or else it could be some other ranking of the alternative actions quite distinct from all three. The last of these would be the case if none of these three orderings was the 'most moral' one, in terms of the moral system in question, and if the moral system required some sacrifice of self-interest, as well as 'isolated' self-interest. But even in the case where M is identified as the morally superior ordering which is distinct from A, B and C, the question would arise as to how A, B and C should be ranked relative to one another. For example, the particular moral system might tell the person that the pursuit of self-interest, including sympathy for loved ones, is to be commended over the pursuit of 'isolated' self-interest. This would put ordering A above ordering B. And suppose that the person had actually obeyed the moral system, but only up to a point. For instance, if the right thing were to donate 10 per cent of one's income to Oxfam, his or her habitual preference ordering C would tell that person to give 1 per cent, say, compatibly with his or her wish to fund the family holiday. In this case, then, the moral system in question would generate a complete and transitive ranking of the four orderings, in the sequence: M > C > B > A. This particular ranking of orderings would be an example of a (highly specific) moral meta-ranking for the person concerned.[1]

Of course, a meta-ranking might be based on overarching considerations other than those of morality. Also, whatever prescriptive considerations underlie a given meta-ranking, they might not be sufficently specific to allow the construction of a complete ranking of the orderings within the mental *repertoire* of the actor. Thus the meta-ranking notion is a general conceptual tool,

---

[1] Compare Sen, 1977: 338.

Player 2: The Other

Cooperate C   Defect D

		Cooperate C	Q	S

Player 1:   Cooperate C

Individual   Defect D

	Cooperate C	Defect D
Cooperate C	Q	S
Defect D	P	R

Figure 11.1 The game form of the Prisoner's Dilemma.

which can be specified to serve a variety of purposes. In earlier work, Sen had already applied the idea to the analysis of reasoned commitment in two-player Prisoner's Dilemma games.[2] To present his proposal of a moral meta-ranking in this context, we reproduce the 2×2 game form of Prisoner's Dilemma in figure 11.1.

The four outcomes P, Q, R and S will be italicized throughout, to prevent confusion with the corresponding outcomes of the Potential Contributor's Dilemma game form, where Individual is represented as if he is playing a game against the homogeneous collective of 'The Others'. The four outcomes of the decision situation are understood to be specified so that the narrow self-interest of the players is reflected by the PD-ordering, which is $PQRS$ for Individual and $SQRP$ for the Other, as in the classic story, where the orderings represent the rank order of the number of years in jail for each of the two prisoners. To illustrate the meta-ranking concept, Sen now imagines that the players both consider two alternative ways of ranking the four outcomes. The first of these is the so-called 'other-regarding' ordering (OR). It gives the players a dominant strategy to cooperate, and in particular OR is said to express the idea that 'each would appear to be adamant on not letting the other person down'.[3] Sen now specifies Individual's OR-ordering as $QSPR$. The Other's OR-ordering is then obtained by switching the outcomes P and R, i.e., $QPSR$. Interpreted morally, then, the 'other-regarding' preferences signify the player's willingness to put the other player's self-interest above his own, come what may.

The second ordering considered is the well-known 'Assurance-Game' (AG) ordering, which was originally introduced by Sen.[4] It is so called because the game characterized by it generates the problem of mutual assurance to cooperate. The AG-ordering simply reverses the PD-ordering's first and second preferred outcomes, hence for Individual it is $QPRS$, and for the Other it is $QSRP$. It expresses the idea that the player refuses to take advantage of the other's cooperation, because he or she considers that it is better to have the situation where both players are as well off as possible (Q) than the situation where one player maximizes his or her own self-interest (P for Individual; S for the Other). The AG-ordering does not have a dominant strategy, since it implies

---

[2] See Sen, 1974.   [3] See Sen, 1974: 60.   [4] See Sen, 1967: 112.

that the player gets the best result only by cooperating if the Other cooperates, and by defecting if the Other defects. It is, in other words, an ordering that exhibits a conditional disposition to cooperate, as we have also seen in section 10.4. If both players can absolutely assure each other of having these particular motivations, then they will both cooperate. If not, then they have an assurance problem. Without firm mutual assurance, there is no guarantee that a player will not find it prudent to defect in order to cover against the possible defection of the other player. Any one player, or both, might then adopt the conservative maximin strategy of avoiding the strategy that contains his or her worst outcome (S for Individual; P for the Other), thus placing the jointly best outcome out of reach.

In Sen's discussion of morality, the AG-ordering can be interpreted in two different ways. It could be considered either as a compromise position between the other-regarding norm of putting the other's self-interest above one's own on the one hand, and relentless pursuit of self-interest on the other; or the AG-ordering could be taken to express a specific moral view in its own right. This is the morality of reciprocity, which says that one should be prepared to give priority to the self-interest of the other, but only on condition that the other is willing to reciprocate.

Sen now proposes the moral meta-ranking $OR > AG > PD$. He does not spell out the substantive reasoning which underlies that proposal.[5] Judging from the way in which Sen described the OR-ordering, we assume that the moral system that would put OR above AG and AG above PD is simply given by the moral norm of not letting the other down, come what may. This is a norm that enjoins unconditional sacrifice of self-interest for the sake of one's fellow man, at least if he or she happens to be in the relevant reference group. In terms of that norm, then, OR is of course the 'most moral ordering' of the three, PD the least moral one, and AG is the compromise ordering which is 'halfway in between' the motivations behind OR and PD. This explanation of the proposed meta-ranking will suffice for the present purpose, but we will question Sen's characterization of the OR-ordering below.

Now of course, not everyone will necessarily agree with the strict requirement of ceding to the self-interest of the other which OR-morality imposes. Some might want to defend instead the morality of reciprocity, which makes one's willingness to refrain from letting the other down depend on a similar willingness on the other's part. According to that alternative moral norm, then, the AG-ordering would be the 'most moral one', and it would be all one needs to form a simple moral meta-ranking $AG > PD$. In that case, the other-regarding attitude would be regarded as being 'beyond the call of duty'. Be that as it may, we here proceed to discuss Sen's own proposed meta-ranking in the situation of the Prisoner's Dilemma game form. It is summarized by figure 11.2.

---

[5] Compare Sen, 1974: 60–2.

Orderings in the meta-ranking	most moral		compromise		self-interested
	OR	>	AG	>	PD
Player 1: Individual	QSPR	>	QPRS	>	PQRS
Player 2: the Other	QPSR	>	QSRP	>	SQRP

Figure 11.2 Sen's meta-ranking in the Prisoner's Dilemma.

Before we look into the details of Sen's proposal, there is one point to be clarified in this particular example. It is perhaps an obvious one, but important to mention nevertheless. The morality in question is here specifically defined in opposition to narrow self-interest, i.e., relative to the *PD*-ordering that leads us to label the structure of the 2 × 2 game form of figure 11.1 as a Prisoner's Dilemma-situation in the first place. Unlike the former example of a moral meta-ranking (M > C > B > A), the morality, as it is being construed in this particular example, does not set itself against extended self-interest of the kind that includes the narrow self-interest of others (either the other player, or someone else who is not part of the designated game). Sympathetic self-interest does not enter into the contrast between morality and self-interest that Sen is discussing here. Thus, the willingness to sacrifice one's own self-interest in favour of the Other's implies that when Individual considers acting upon *OR*-preferences, he is assuming that the Other actually *has* the self-interest which is reflected by the *PD*-ordering *SQRP*, even though Individual need not in general assume – at least not according to Sen's model of choice from multiple preference orderings – that the Other will automatically *act* to maximize his self-interest. The same goes, *mutatis mutandis*, for the Other's evaluation of Individual's interest.

11.3 Enlightened self-interest and moral commitment

At this point we should note two distinct problems that Sen meant to address with the meta-ranking exercise in the Prisoner's Dilemma. The first is the wider problem of adequately describing morally committed choices, which is the main purpose of *Rational Fools*. The second is a more specific problem. It concerns the usefulness of moral codes for promoting collective optimality in social dilemmas by means of social engineering.

In this chapter we shall be mainly engaged with the first of these problems. But the second problem merits a brief discussion in this section, since it is of obvious interest in the context of environmental self-regulation policies. Sen proposes to assess *OR*-morality from a purely instrumental point of view. His question is: to what extent can that morality help rational players to avoid the suboptimal outcome of the actual Prisoner's Dilemma game, and reach the jointly best outcome instead? He now proceeds to evaluate the moral meta-ranking from this point of view. In particular, Sen argues that the superiority of *OR* to *AG* and of *AG* to *PD* can be established on the criterion of *OR*'s superior performance in bringing about outcome *Q*, quite apart from the question of whether or not *OR*-morality is superior to other moralities, or to self-interest, on substantive moral grounds.

Sen's argument runs as follows. Collective optimality is defined by the outcome *Q*, as *Q* is evaluated in terms of the the 'true interests' of the players, that is to say *PD*-interests. Suppose first that both players are rational, at least in the sense of conforming to the dominance rule. And suppose, secondly, that both players were to act counterpreferentially with respect to their true interests, just *as if* they were both motivated unreservedly by the moral norm behind the *OR*-ordering. In that case, they would act to produce outcome *Q* without any problem, since the *OR*-ordering *QSPR* has a dominant strategy to cooperate. Now compare this to the case where both players were to act just *as if* they were motivated by the compromise stance that is reflected by the *AG*-ordering. Then one can see that *Q* would be by no means ensured. Short of absolute assurance, there would be no guarantee that both players with *AG*-orderings would want to cooperate. Finally, consider what would happen if the players were to follow their true interests, i.e., their *PD*-orderings. Then, of course, they would be led straightforwardly into the actual Prisoner's Dilemma, and outcome *Q* would be inaccessible.

On the basis of these comparisons, Sen concludes that the meta-ranking *OR* > *AG* > *PD* is supported by the criterion of promoting collective optimality. On that criterion, then, *OR*-morality would have to be recommended, independently of its moral defensibility. A noteworthy implication of the argument is that even if one could succeed in arguing that *AG*-morality (interpreted not as a compromise stance, but rather as a reciprocity norm in its own right) is morally more defensible than *OR*-morality, one would still have to consider the latter morality's superior conduciveness to collective optimality in one's final assessment of the two.

There are two problems with this conclusion. The first problem arises when we take the instrumental outlook exemplified by *as-if* morality for granted. Even then, it is not obvious that *OR*-morality will actually do any better in promoting collective optimality than *AG*-morality. For though acting on the *OR*-ordering generates no assurance problem, in the way that *AG*-ordering does, once the players *actually decide to act on a given ordering*, the *OR*-ordering does generate an assurance problem of another kind. For surely, the players need to convince one another that they will both be inclined to act just as if they embraced the rather strict morality of the *OR*-ordering. Compared to *AG*, *OR* is certainly more effective in assuring cooperation, once acted upon, but

OR-morality also creates the bigger problem of assuring one another that the game is going to be played in the *OR*-way in the first place. The reason is that *OR*-morality is much more demanding than *AG* in its requirement of renouncing the pursuit of self-interest, which, after all, is said to be the 'true interest' of the players concerned.

This objection is important because Sen himself makes it quite clear that the purely instrumental evaluation of the moral meta-ranking is not supposed to be adopted by actual players in real-life Prisoner's Dilemma situations. Rather, the results of Sen's imagined *as if* games are to be taken to heart by a society that tries to promote collective optimality in shaping its policies and institutions. Thus Sen says, for example, that a society might want to 'evolve traditions by which preferences of the OR-type are praised most, AG-type preferences next, and PD-preferences least of all'. And he goes on to discuss real-world cases in point, such as the political use of 'moral incentives' in eliciting work effort within Chinese communes during the Cultural Revolution.[6] This suggests that people in general, and players in Prisoner's Dilemma game forms in particular, are to be educated into accepting the recommended substantive morality itself as a basis for rational action.

Now with this last point clarified, the objection of demandingness which we raised above will have considerable force. It is not clear that a society would be well-advised to embark on the construction of moral 'traditions' that correspond to the rather demanding *OR*-morality, instead of trying to promote the less demanding *AG*-morality. If it is indeed the case that the strains of commitment involved in adopting *OR*-morality, rather than *AG*-morality, are far heavier, as we think it is, then it follows that the *AG*-ordering dominates the *OR*-ordering in respect of assuring that players will set aside their self-interest and adopt a cooperative attitude, whereas *OR* dominates *AG* when it comes to assuring that a cooperative choice will be made, once players decide to act on either of these orderings. Hence, if the problem is that players have to assure each other of their cooperative attitudes to begin with, it will be be much more difficult to get traditions of self-sacrificing *OR*-morality formed than traditions of reciprocal *AG*-morality. In such cases, the instrumentally motivated meta-ranking would then have to place *AG* above *OR*, contrary to Sen's proposal.[7]

But there is a second problem with Sen's recommendations to policymakers. The suggestion that societies can profitably engage in promoting one or another type of *as-if* morality in an attempt to engineer collective optimality is problematic, at least in societies that are also committed to the value of publicity. Exerting pressure on citizens to take a moral view in social dilemmas may be self-defeating if the citizens are made to realize, at the same time, that the public reasons for getting them to act morally are ones that are external to the point

---

[6] See Sen, 1974: 61–2, note 17.   [7] See van der Veen, 1981.

of the morality in question. This would certainly be the case if policymakers followed Sen's reasoning described above. Widespread recognition of the fact that institutions and policies that embody some type of moral code (either *OR* or *AG*) are being set up merely in order to avoid the trap of the universal pursuit of 'true' self-interests, may prevent the mobilization of genuinely moral resources in the society.

This point can be put in terms of LeGrand's distinctions, which we mentioned in section 10.3. The society might not get very far in its efforts at social engineering along the *as-if* moral line, if its policymakers were to take aside players engaged in an actual Prisoner's Dilemma game, and say: 'Look, of course we understand: you *do* want to act as a knave, and you *will* let the other down if you can get away with it. But he is a knave too. So both of you had better realize that you can't profitably get away with this behaviour. However, there is a way out: the two of you can at least end up in second-best position, given your knavish interests, if only you'd both be smart enough to act *as if* you were knights (which we jolly well know you aren't in fact).'

To revert to the setting of the first environmental policy plan, a public strategy devoted to the internalization of non-polluting forms of attitude and behaviour cannot simply depend on an appeal to *enlightened self-interest*, which is what the idea of enlisting *as-if* morality actually does. If such a public strategy is expected to work at all, then it must aim at getting across the attractions of a genuinely moral point of view. In our description of the strategy of internalizing environmental responsibility, it was seen that the policymakers have been well aware of this. They have tried to convince the Dutch public that it should view environmental problems under a dual challenge: as problems to be solved by voluntarily taking collective action for an environmental good, and as problems which require a morally responsible effort of cooperation to resolve them, given the availability of collective action.

Now as we have also seen in section 2.5, this is not to say that the environmental morality promoted under the policy strategy of internalization has nothing to do with collective optimality. On the contrary, we have taken care to stress that environmental policymakers in the Netherlands have launched their programme of moral reform in order to achieve the results envisaged by the planning objectives. The strategy, we said, is compliance-oriented, rather than virtue-based. Our present point, however, is that collective optimality cannot be serviced by *as-if* morality. Barring enforceable directives to cooperate, collective optimality can be had only if the policymakers succeed in appealing to genuinely moral motivations for overcoming the narrowly self-interested strategy to defect in environmental dilemmas. Such motivations may be given by notions of reciprocal fairness (which were being appealed to in the first environmental plan's injunction of 'not taking licence to pollute more than another, given the desired environmental quality'), or by the more demanding idea that it is sometimes right to risk the penalty of 'being suckered'. Which of the two kinds of moral appeal are most effective in concrete cases is an empirical matter, which we shall examine in section 12.3 below.

11.4 Consistent preferences in the meta-ranking

Having discussed the social engineering aspect of Sen's contribution, we now want to pay some attention to the more general issue he raised, of adequately describing the rationality of moral commitment. In this section, we shall be discussing this issue in the context of Sen's moral meta-ranking in the Prisoner's Dilemma. There are two comments we want to make. The purpose of these comments is to put our theory of consistency between motives and preferences in a wider perspective. First we discuss the conceptual status of the self-interested *PD*-ordering, and secondly, we take a closer look at the preference orderings that represent reasoned moral commitment of various kinds.

When moral commitment is not being regarded as handmaiden of collective optimality, it is no longer legitimate to regard the *PD*-rankings of the four outcomes as representing the 'true interests' of the players. Even so, the *PD*-ordering does have a privileged status in an analysis of reasoned moral commitment. For as noted in section 11.2, the *PD*-ordering is the one that identifies the structure of the Prisoner's Dilemma game form. By definition of that game form, it is the only possible ranking of the four outcomes that actually generates the conflict between individual rational action on the one hand and collective optimality on the other. In analysing the possible games that could be played within this structure of interdependent action, it is therefore in some sense natural to suppose that each of the players will be assuming the other always to have narrow self-interest in mind, or at least at the back of his or her mind.

Nevertheless, the supposed fact that each player assumes the other to have narrow self-interest in mind does not in general provide sufficient grounds for regarding narrow self-interest as the true interest, if what one means by a 'true interest' is the balance of reflections about how best to act on diverse and conflicting values in view of the different reasons that each player has for giving some of these values special weight. Within Sen's framework, to say that the player in a Prisoner's Dilemma-situation acts from reasoned moral commitment is to say that he or she is acting from some moral preference ordering which may possibly diverge from a self-interested ordering, where that last ordering may or may not include sympathetic identification with others. If the self-interest of the player happens to be of the narrow kind exemplified by the *PD*-ordering, as is supposed in the present meta-ranking example, then the moral preference ordering will in fact diverge from the *PD*-ordering. In that case, then, acting from reasoned moral commitment is acting from reasons that *include* a deliberate rejection of acting from narrowly self-interested reasons. Thus, in so far as the *PD*-ordering represents the relevant self-interest of the person, it is *analytically basic* to the notion of reasoned commitment. It is the ordering to be repudiated, in order for the person to commit to the moral point of view.[8] Hence, if the person in fact decided to act from reasoned moral commitment, then it is appropriate to regard the corresponding moral preference ordering as expressing his or her 'true interest', instead of the self-interested ordering that is always available in the background, but which has now been consciously rejected.

As noted earlier, one does not always need to suppose that the relevant self-interest of a person is represented by the *PD*-ordering, as a matter of empirical fact. However, if a person's relevant self-interest does happen to be represented by an ordering other than the *PD*-ordering (and also differs from the ordering reflecting commitment), then again, in the context of the Prisoner's Dilemma game form, the *PD*-ordering may be regarded as analytically basic. For in this case, the reasons that explain the kind of self-interest that the player actually would want to act on, short of acting on reasoned commitment, are once more defined in opposition to the *PD*-ordering.

For instance, Individual might hate the Other, and want to do him or her down, if need be at Individual's own expense. This sentiment of antipathy may be clarified, at the level of preferences, by the ordering *PRQS,* noting the reversal of outcomes *R* and *Q* in comparison with the *PD*-ordering. In respect of such 'vindictive' interests, Individual would of course be rationally driven to act in exactly the same way as on the basis of the *PD*-ordering, since both of these orderings have a dominant strategy to defect. However, the antipathetic player would now be understood to act from motives of extended interest, rather than from mere narrow self-interest. Both in cases of reasoned moral commitment and in cases of acting from extended self-interest, then, the narrowly self-interested *PD*-ordering may be regarded as the point of reference among the twenty-four possible preference orderings on which a player might care to act in the game form of Prisoner's Dilemma. Each non-*PD* ordering is understood as diverging from the *PD*-ordering in respect of a variety of reasons. It should be pointed out, though, that while the *PD*-ordering is analytically basic in the context of the two-person Prisoner's Dilemma game form, it is far less straightforward to regard it as such once one is dealing with the *n*-person Potential Contributor's Dilemma. We have noted this point in section 10.4, and return to it in the next section.

---

[8] Of course a person who is firm in his or her moral commitment to act might not even want to put the matter in this way, but might rather say that on beginning to consider a choice of strategy, he or she would already have set aside a self-interested view on the outcomes as simply irrelevant, so that the issue of 'repudiating the PD-ordering' would not even arise. However, this may be regarded as a limiting case of what we are describing in the text.

Staying within the situation of the two-person Prisoner's Dilemma, we now address the issue of representing reasoned commitment in the format of distinct preference orderings (such as *AG* or *OR*). We are concerned here to assess Sen's meta-ranking account by means of our notion of consistent preferences. As shown above, Sen's method of constructing a moral meta-ranking proceeds in three, largely intuitive, steps. First, the substantive content of a certain morality, which is to serve as the basis of the person's reasoned commitment, is translated into a 'most moral' preference ordering (this was ordering M in Sen's first example, and *OR* in the second one).

Secondly, a number of other preference orderings are considered. Each of these represents distinctly alternative considerations of the person's thinking about the situation (be they other moralities, or various forms of self-interest, or some compromise ordering habitually acted upon in the past). Thirdly, each of the other orderings is ranked in relation to the 'most moral' ordering, by registering the other ordering's extent of disagreement with the most moral one. This leads to the meta-ranking M > C > B > A in the first example, and *OR* > *AG* > *PD* in the second one.

In the previous chapters, we did not make use of the meta-ranking notion. But as will be demonstrated below, it is entirely possible to arrive at a meta-ranking by using the consistency relation between motives and preferences defined in chapter 6. Our way of constructing the appropriate meta-ranking in Sen's own Prisoner's Dilemma example follows the three steps of his own construction. First, the content of the morality serving as the basis of reasoned commitment for the person is analysed in the setting of the decision situation. This analysis takes place at the level of *motives*. The morality in question is regarded as a moral motive, which is characterized by a distinct set of pairwise ranking constraints on the four outcomes of the Prisoner's Dilemma. Each pairwise ranking represents an essential feature of the moral motive. Only preference orderings that satisfy these pairwise rankings are consistent with the moral motive, according to the procedure set out in section 6.3.

Secondly, in opposition to the moral motive, one other motive is considered. This other motive is supposed to be salient in the person's process of deliberation on whether or not to follow the moral motive, or strike a compromise. If the purpose of a meta-ranking is formally to express what goes on in processes of reasoned moral commitment, then the other motive may be the narrowly self-interested one, as in Sen's example. The content of the self-interested motive is likewise translated into a set of characterizing pairwise rankings, in order to determine which preference orderings are consistent with that motive.

Thirdly, in between the moral motive and the self-interested motive which stands in opposition to it, one can now construct one or several compromise motives. A compromise motive will always satisfy some pairwise rankings of the moral motive, and some pairwise rankings of the self-interested motive. Each compromise motive will then have its own consistent set of preference orderings. All motives in this construction are ranked in descending order, with the moral motive at the top, and the self-interested one at the bottom. In this way one arrives at the meta-ranking of the corresponding preference orderings. This method is a more general way of constructing a meta-ranking than the intuitive method used by Sen. Yet, because of its generality, it may lead to different conclusions.

To illustrate this, we now reconstruct the meta-ranking in the present example, assuming, as Sen did, that OR-morality is the basis for the player's reasoned commitment in the Prisoner's Dilemma situation. The first step is to consider Sen's OR-ordering, which is $QSPR$, in the notation of Individual, the row player. This ordering was identified above as being the 'most moral' ordering. As we have seen, Sen's stated reason for this was that players who follow the OR-ordering 'would appear to be adamant on not letting the other person down'. So we take this to be the relevant moral motive.

Now one may ask: why did Sen specifically choose to represent the OR-morality by the single ordering $QSPR$? On the face of it, there would seem to be other orderings which could express this morality as well. Indeed, any of the six possible orderings with a dominant strategy to cooperate is consistent with Sen's definition of OR-morality as the disposition of 'being adamant on not letting the other person down'. Hence, the constraints of OR-morality are given by the pairwise rankings that imply a dominant strategy to cooperate, i.e., $Q > P$ and $S > R$. Sen's ordering $QSPR$ is only one of the six orderings with a dominant strategy to cooperate. His selection of $QSPR$ is thus unexplained, so far.

The second step in the construction of the meta-ranking involves specifying the pairwise rankings of the self-interested motive. This is the motive that would have to be rejected by someone who is fully committed to OR-morality. In Sen's meta-ranking, this motive is narrow self-interest. In the Prisoner's Dilemma, the pairwise rankings of narrow self-interest are trivially given by the PD-ordering $PQRS$: $P > Q$, $P > R$, $P > S$, $Q > R$, $Q > S$, and $R > S$.

The third step in the construction defines the consistent sets of orderings belonging to the moral motive and the self-interested one, given the constraints of both motives. The consistent sets of possible compromise positions in between OR-morality and self-interest are also identified. In the present case, the consistent set of the OR-motive must contain orderings with a dominant strategy to cooperate, $Q > P$ and $S > R$. However, it must also satisfy the constraints of the self-interested motive *which do not conflict* with the constraints of the OR-motive. These non-conflicting constraints of the PD-ordering are $P > R$, $P > S$, $Q > R$, and $Q > S$. The only ordering that satisfies both the constraints of OR-morality, and these non-conflicting constraints of self-interest, is $QPSR$. This implies that according to our method of constructing a meta-ranking, the 'most moral ordering' that exemplifies OR-morality is $QPSR$, and not $QSPR$, as Sen proposed.[9]

Next, what about the possible compromise positions in the meta-ranking? As we have seen, Sen specified the AG-ordering $QPRS$ as the single ordering that would reflect a compromise between OR-morality and narrow self-interest. In order to see whether this is justified from the point of view of our method, we look once again at the constraints of OR-morality and self-interest. There is one compromise position in between the two. Its constraints are defined by ranking one of the two outcome pairs on which OR-morality and self-interest are *in conflict* (i.e the pairs (P, Q) and (R, S)) in accordance with OR-morality, and the other pair in accordance with self-interest. This means that the constraints of the compromise motive are defined disjunctively: *either $Q > P$ and $R > S$, or $P > Q$ and $S > R$.*[10] Moreover, the constraints of the compromise motive should also include the non-conflicting constraints of the PD-ordering which we just listed above, i.e., $P > R, P > S, Q > R$, and $Q > S$. From this, it follows that the consistent orderings of the compromise position are $QPRS$, as stipulated by Sen, and $PQSR$, which Sen does not mention. The four preference orderings in the reconstructed meta-ranking are given in figure 11.3.

There are certain advantages to constructing a meta-ranking in this rigorous way. For one thing, it shows that forging a link between a moral motive (here, OR-morality) and the preference orderings that are claimed to represent that motive, is less straightforward than Sen's method suggests. Quite a lot depends on the way in which the moral motive in question is to be understood in relation to the opposed motive (here, the narrowly self-interested one).

Secondly, the rigorous way of looking at the orderings that belong to a given meta-ranking focuses attention on the possible orderings that are consistent with the compromise motive, after the constraints of the compromise motive have been derived from the conflicting constraints of OR-morality and self-interest. The consistent orderings of the compromise motive are the AG-ordering $QPRS$, as well as the ordering $PQSR$. The counterparts of these orderings in the Potential Contributor's Dilemma were discussed in 10.4. Neither $QPRS$ nor $PQSR$ has a dominant strategy. However, $QPRS$ is a conditionally cooperative ordering, because of its pairwise rankings $Q > P$ (reflecting OR-morality) and $R > S$

---

[9] The rejection of $QSPR$ in favour of $QPSR$ is based on the observation that the pairwise ranking of S over P in $QSPR$ is not required by the constraints of OR-morality (which only specify $Q > P$ and $S > R$), while this ranking contradicts the self-interested constraint $P > S$ of the PD-ordering. Since the meta-ranking aims to characterize the orderings that represent the essence of the contrast between the two salient motives of OR-morality and narrow self-interest, it follows that the preferences which represent OR-morality in this contrast should not only obey that morality's ranking constraints, but should also maximally agree with the constraints of the opposing motive of self-interest. The only ordering that fits this dual requirement is $QPSR$.

[10] Compare the way in which we derived the constraints of the intermediate motives of Valuation and Willingness (V3 and W3) in 6.3.

Motives	OR-morality	Compromise		Self-interested
Orderings of the meta-ranking	*OR*	*AG* *CG*		*PD*
Player 1: Individual	*QPSR*	>	*QPRS, PQSR*	> *PQRS*
Player 2: the Other	*QSPR*	>	*QSRP, SQPR*	> *SQRP*

Figure 11.3 The reconstructed meta-ranking in the Prisoner's Dilemma.

(reflecting self-interest). By contrast, *PQSR* is a conditionally non-cooperative ordering, due to its pairwise rankings $P > Q$ (reflecting self-interest) and $S > R$ (reflecting *OR*-morality).

The orderings *PQSR* (for Individual) and *SQPR* (for the Other) will be labelled here as 'Chicken Game'-orderings (*CG*), because players following them are led into the well-known game of that name. It is an unstable game, in which rational players will satisfy their preferences best by cooperating, on condition that the other is certain to defect, and by defecting, on condition that the other is certain to cooperate. Unlike in the Assurance Game, the jointly best outcome *Q* cannot be ensured by making the players aware that each of them will act on the *CG*-ordering. Even with such mutual knowledge, anything may happen. The player who wants to play it safe will 'chicken out', that is to say cover against the other's possible defection, and hence cooperate. The player who wants to engage in brinkmanship will defect, hoping that the other player will chicken out. As a result, any of the four outcomes may occur, depending on the psychological dispositions of the two players.

Considered as a compromise between *OR*-morality and narrow self-interest, the *CG*-ordering might seem rather perverse when compared to the *AG*-ordering. Given that *AG* also reflects the distinct moral attitude of reciprocal cooperation, it could be said that the latter represents a more coherent and defensible compromise than the former. Yet, perverse as it may appear to be, the *CG*-ordering cannot be ruled out as a genuine compromise.[11]

---

[11] In the context of the original Chicken story, the willingness to chicken out in deference to the brinkmanship of the other does not of course represent any kind of moral motive whatsoever. But this is because the game form of that story is rigged so that the *CG*-orderings of the players represent their narrow self-interest, which is to show the bystanders that they come out gloriously in a contest of courting disaster (*R* is the outcome in which, for instance, both players in the contest run the risk of crashing their cars into a ravine, if they are unable to ram the brakes at the last split second, because the other did not hold back in time either). If the game form is that of a Prisoner's Dilemma, however, then the attitude of wanting to end up in *S* rather than in *R* does signify a sacrifice of self-interest, and given that the motive of *OR*-morality we are here considering is that of resolute care for the other, the *CG*-ordering does indeed represent a compromise, however unsatisfactory it may be from the point of view of either pure motive. In the next section we shall see that *CG*-orderings may have slightly less unsatisfactory features in the context of environmental Potential Contributor's Dilemmas.

11.5 An environmental meta-ranking

In our discussion of Sen's meta-ranking proposal so far, the focus has been on the Prisoner's Dilemma game form. But as we already mentioned, Sen certainly intended his approach to be of relevance for larger-scale interactions of the type that go under the name of social dilemmas. For example, Sen cited the case of Chinese communes as one where promoting norms of unconditional cooperation could provide the 'moral incentives' for eliciting work motivation in the absence of the economic incentive of wage payment.

More in general, it is helpful to regard the possible instances of the social dilemma as being located on a 'continuum of inclusiveness'. At the least inclusive end of it, one would find social interactions partitioned into many isolated two-person dilemmas of the kind illustrated by the classic case of the two prisoners. At the most inclusive end of the continuum, there are cases of society-wide collective action, the structure of which can be captured by the Potential Contributor's Dilemma, for instance the environmental case of Holiday Destination. In between, one can identify more local interactions. These can be modelled either in the format of the Potential Contributor's Dilemma or else, and more rigorously, as n-person Prisoner's Dilemmas. In the latter, each player faces more than one other *separately identifiable* player. The actors concerned are not, as it were, facing a crowd, but are instead able to single out the impacts of each of the other players' strategy choices.

We shall have more to say about the continuum of inclusiveness in the next chapter. For present purposes note that at both ends of it, the social dilemma is analysed in terms of an individual player, Individual, who is faced with the four possible outcomes that result from a two-actor, two-strategy matrix. In the Prisoner's Dilemma, the second actor is the other individual player, while in the Potential Contributor's Dilemma, the other actor is the (fictitious) collective of 'the Others'. This last representation, which was used in the survey questions of the three environmental cases, is the result of two simplifying assumptions, to wit, that each person in the position of Individual (a) decides either to cooperate or defect, given that all other persons either cooperate or defect, and (b) knows that his or her own action will not have a noticeable impact on the result of collective action. Notwithstanding this partitioning of the Potential Contributor's Dilemma into n separate personal decisions within a two-actor, two-strategy format, the dilemma remains a (hugely simplified) n-person Prisoner's Dilemma game form. For unlike the isolated two-person Prisoner's Dilemma of 'Individual versus the Other', here the n 'Individual–Others' interactions are bound together by the fact that each person who is not in the row position of a particular 2×2 matrix is assumed to be included in the homogeneous collective of $n-1$ 'Others'.

It is important to be aware that the two kinds of social dilemma are radically different in scope. And it may be expected, therefore, that the issue of reasoned commitment to a cooperative course of action is likely to appear in a different light when we go from the least inclusive to the most inclusive end of the continuum. In moving from a two-person Prisoner's Dilemma to a Potential Contributor's Dilemma, the interpretation of the four outcomes of interaction will change considerably. This is why we have taken care to label the outcomes of the former in italics, e.g. '*R*', while labelling those of the latter in normal type, e.g. 'R'. In particular, there is one difference that needs to be taken into account. The universally cooperative outcome of the Prisoner's Dilemma game form (Q) signifies the joint welfare of the players, in terms of (analytically basic, not necessarily 'true') *PD*-interests. In the the game form of the Potential Contributor's Dilemma, the universally cooperative outcome (Q) signifies something quite different. Just what Q does signify is subject to two closely related sources of variation.

First of all, a player is conceptually free to evaluate Q as either a desirable or an undesirable state of affairs, relative to R, the universally non-cooperative outcome. For instance, in one of the environmental dilemmas we have been discussing, it is entirely open to Individual to think that the result of universal restraint in choosing remote holiday destinations for the sake of reducing air pollution, or avoiding the devastations of mass tourism, is not, on balance, worth the limitations in personal freedom to all concerned. On that judgement, then, he or she may well prefer the universally non-cooperative outcome R to the universally cooperative outcome Q, and indeed to P and S as well. This attitude might show up in our survey as a preference response such as RPQS, corresponding to a motive response involving negative Valuation and negative Willingness (V_3, W_3). Of course, a respondent might also evaluate outcome Q in a highly positive way, thinking that it would truly be a great thing if 'we all manage to do something significant about global warming by voluntarily cutting down on unneccesary travel'. He or she would then be likely to respond by putting Q at the top of the table in his or her preference ordering, and report the corresponding motive structure with positive Valuation, and positive Willingness (e.g. V_1, W_1).

Secondly, as far as the person's narrow self-interest is concerned, there is another major difference with the Prisoner's Dilemma game form. As we have seen in section 10.4, any ordering with a dominant strategy to defect in the Potential Contributor's Dilemma can signify narrow self-interest. This diversity arises not only as a consequence of a narrowly self-interested person's conceptual freedom to evaluate Q positively or negatively, relative to R, but also from the structural difference in the impact of Individual's action between the two game forms. In the Prisoner's Dilemma, Individual's, or the Other's, defection will rule out collective optimality. In the Potential Contributor's Dilemma, on the other hand, Individual's defection will not noticeably affect collective optimality as long as the Others cooperate, but the defection of the Others will certainly rule it out (supposing, that is, that everyone positively values collective action for the sake of reducing pollution).

As a result of these two differences, the interpretation of narrow self-interest in the Potential Contributor's Dilemma is far less specific than it is in the Prisoner's Dilemma. As a result of this, the *PD*-ordering, which uniquely expresses narrow self-interest in the Prisoner's Dilemma (*PQRS*), is only one of several orderings expressing narrow self-interest in the Potential Contributor's Dilemma. In particular, the ordering PQRS is the only narrowly self-interested ordering which, if universally adopted, generates the divergence between individual rationality and collective optimality that characterizes the actual Contributor's Dilemma.

These differences between the two-person and the *n*-person dilemma affect the analysis of reasoned commitment. For as we have pointed out above, a person who commits to the requirements of some morality, within Sen's framework of analysis, thereby decides to reject acting from self-interested preferences, and tries instead to work out a rational course of action that will best satisfy his or her moral preferences. Now the crucial point in this connection is that in the environmental dilemmas that concern us here, the self-interest to be repudiated by the morally commited person is open to various specifications.

To explain the significance of this point, we return to the environmental ethos, as analysed in sections 2.4, 10.2 and 10.4. In its first stage, the ethos aims to persuade the actors of civil society to take a positive attitude towards the solution of environmental problems through voluntary collective action. In terms of the motives in our survey, they are being persuaded to adopt an attitude of positive Valuation. Passing to the second stage, the ethos tries to impress on every single actor a duty of doing his or her bit in the available schemes of collective action. The actors are here being persuaded to adopt an attitude of positive Willingness as well. Laying out the structure of the ethos in two stages shows that self-regulation policy takes as its analytical point of reference *an actor who is self-interested in the specific sense of wanting to defect unconditionally from negative Valuation*. It is someone, firstly, who does not identify with the project of environmental collective action by citizens. This person resists the suggestion that improving qualities such as a clean atmosphere, biodiversity, and the like, are matters that require people in general to regard such qualities as goods to be promoted through voluntary collective action. It is a person, secondly, who, having no motivation to adjust his or her behaviour voluntarily to protect the environment in the particular case at hand, wants to avoid the cost of cooperating, in his or her own interest. In the context of the two-stage environmental ethos, then, the relevantly basic notion of self-interest is captured by motives of negative Valuation (which the first stage of the ethos tries to overcome) and negative Willingness (which the second stage attempts to rectify).

It follows that the environmental meta-ranking will be one that puts the two orderings QSPR and QPSR at the top. These correspond to the motive structure (V1, W1) of 'full agreement' with the ethos. The environmental meta-ranking will place the orderings RPSQ and RSPQ in last place. These correspond to the motive structure (V3, W3) 'rejection of the ethos'. In between, the environmental meta-ranking distinguishes a number of intermediate motive structures, which correspond to various stances that we have discussed in section 10.4 (see figure 10.1). Ranked by increasing order of distance to the 'most moral' motive (V1, W1), these intermediate motive structures are: 'partial agreement with the ethos' (V1, W2), with consistent orderings QPRS and PQSR; 'rejection of norm' (V1, W3), with consistent orderings PQRS and PRQS; and finally, unwillingness to cooperate from intermediate Valuation (V2, W3), with consistent orderings PRSQ and RPQS.

So conceived, the environmental meta-ranking is constructed lexicographically, to include the five cells in the top row and the right-hand column of the matrix (Vi, Wj) (i, j = 1, 2, 3), as shown in figure 10.1. The cells in the top row of the matrix include motive structures of positive Valuation. These are the ones which are compatible with the individual's affirmation of the first stage of the environmental ethos. They are graded on the Willingness dimension, from W1 to W3. The cells in the right-hand column show motive structures that have negative Willingness in common. They are graded on the Valuation dimension, from V1 to V3, according to the extent to which they are compatible with the first stage of the environmental ethos.

This specification of the environmental meta-ranking has some interesting implications for the design of self-regulation policies. In chapter 13, we shall examine the locations of respondents on the meta-ranking in a comparison of the polar cases of the dilemma: Chemical Waste and Holiday Destination.

To sum up our argument so far, we have been concerned to point out the analytical similarities between our notion of consistent preferences and the meta-ranking framework developed by Sen. We have just shown that this framework is perfectly suitable for application in empirical work with large-scale survey data, as presented in part II. Now it is time to turn to some of the other substantive results of part II. We intend to discuss some theoretical issues raised by the widespread occurrence of unconditionally cooperative motives and preferences in the three environmental cases of the dilemma.

12

Reciprocity and cooperation
in environmental dilemmas

12.1 The puzzle of unconditional cooperation

Rational cooperation from unconditionally cooperative motives and preferences is a fairly common response of the people whom we have interviewed. While Sen might perhaps not be overly surprised about these results, given his belief in the efficacy of unconditional norms of cooperation, the results are likely to be viewed with some suspicion by many others in the field of rational choice theory. In this chapter, we shall not be restating our position in the debate with those who support the thick-theory of self-interested rationality. Rather, we want to comment on a more sophisticated thesis concerning the role of morality in collective action. This thesis is supported by a lot of empirical work. It says that in so far as morality has real force in overcoming social dilemmas, it will tend to be a morality of *conditional reciprocity*, rather than a morality of unconditional cooperation. The preference orderings that correspond to norms of reciprocity are ones like the 'Assurance Game'-ordering QPRS. Such orderings, which are not associated with a dominant strategy, were discussed in the two previous chapters.

As we shall first argue, the empirical plausibility of the reciprocity thesis depends on circumstances in which rational actors are able to monitor each other's behaviour closely, unlike in the large-scale environmental dilemmas we have been studying. Secondly, we defend our view that many of the motives and preferences that we have observed in these dilemmas actually reflect the social force of an unconditional morality. However, it is possible to claim that observed attitudes of unconditional cooperation depend on certain 'hidden conditionalities', which come to the surface once variations in the perceived costs of cooperation of the different cases are taken into account. It may be, in other words, that unconditional moral norms flourish under conditions where people generally expect each other to be able to bear the cost of complying with those norms. If this is indeed true, then the contrast between conditionally and unconditionally cooperative preferences in environmental dilemmas is less stark than is suggested by the dominance rule of rational choice. In the final section, we comment on this suggestion.

12.2 The reciprocity thesis

The failure of the standard model of self-interested rational action to explain frequently observed instances of cooperation in social dilemmas has been well-documented, over large areas of inquiry. It has led to a blossoming of new theoretical and empirical work in evolutionary biology, experimental game theory, social psychology, political science, institutional political economy, and other fields. Elinor Ostrom has provided a comprehensive review of these developments in her 1997 presidential address to the American Political Science Association.[1] We here discuss some of her main theoretical conclusions. As mentioned above, we wish to focus on Ostrom's – widely shared – thesis concerning the important role of reciprocity norms in generating cooperative ways of dealing with social dilemma situations. Our purpose is to show that this thesis, though correct and fruitful in many of the ways suggested by Ostrom, needs to be clarified with respect both to its conceptual basis and its scope of application. In particular, we want to suggest that the thesis is incapable of explaining what is perhaps the main result of our survey, that the responses in three distinctly different environmental dilemmas seem to give evidence of widespread unconditionally cooperative motives, preferences, and rational choice intentions.

The reason why we have selected Ostrom's presidential address for our discussion is not merely its clear and inclusive summary of the literature. Its relevance for the present purpose lies in the avowedly programmatic character of her contribution. For, on the basis of massive evidence of cooperative behaviour that cannot be well-accounted for by the standard theory of rational action, Ostrom proposes to develop 'second-generation models of rationality'. These models would place 'reciprocity, trust and reputation at the core of an empirically tested, behavioral theory of collective action'.[2] The reciprocity thesis, as we shall call it for brevity's sake, is an essential part of this theoretical research programme. It consists of the following four claims. First, the norm of reciprocity in one form or another, is a cultural universal: 'Reciprocity is a basic norm taught in all societies.' Secondly, 'humans inherit a strong capacity to learn reciprocity norms and social rules that enhance

---

[1] See Ostrom, 1998.   [2] See Ostrom, 1998: 3.

the opportunities to gain benefits from coping with a multitude of social dilemmas'.[3]

Thirdly, and more in particular, norms of reciprocity translate into a number of strategic decisions in social dilemmas. These strategic decisions serve to enhance the opportunities of mutual benefit by means of conditionally cooperative action. Ostrom lists five such strategic decisions.

> (1) an effort to identify who else is involved, (2) an assessment of the likelihood that the others are conditional cooperators, (3) a decision to cooperate initially with others if others are trusted to be conditional cooperators, (4) a refusal to cooperate with those who do not reciprocate, and (5) punishment of those who betray trust.
>
> (Ostrom, 1998: 10)

Fourthly and finally, within populations involved in social dilemmas of one kind or another, one can distinguish several other types of normative orientations on how to play the game. As alternatives to the conditionally cooperative one deriving from reciprocity, Ostrom mentions unconditional non-cooperation, artful deceit (occasional cooperation in order to make free riding pay off later on), and finally, unconditional cooperation. This, she claims, is 'an extremely rare norm in all cultures'.[4]

It is not difficult to see the central place of the reciprocity thesis in 'second generation models of rationality'. Anchored firmly in human social evolution by the first two claims, the inherited tendency to cooperate if others do so too is strengthened by its practice. By the third claim, norms of reciprocity are reinforced through the strategic decisions they generate. There is thus a 'virtuous triangle', which increases levels of cooperation and net benefits: 'When more individuals use reciprocity norms, gaining a reputation for being trustworthy is a better investment. Thus, levels of trust, reciprocity, and reputations for being trustworthy are positively reinforcing.'[5] It would be wrong, however, to conclude that Ostrom has not noticed the other side of the coin, the subversion of the virtuous triangle by a mutual assurance crisis, leading to a downward spiral of trust, reciprocity, and reputation. On the contrary, a major part of her proposed research programme is precisely devoted to the question of identifying the 'structural variables' that affect the dynamics of the triangle. Going on from there, Ostrom seeks to formulate the conditions under which individuals can successfully develop robust institutions and practices that may deal with such crises of confidence.[6]

What about the final claim, that the norm of unconditional cooperation is 'extremely rare in all cultures'? Ostrom is not very forthcoming in supplying the arguments and empirical evidence that would support this claim. Its statement comes at the end of a short section, which is mainly devoted to a general

---

[3] See Ostrom, 1998: 10.   [4] See Ostrom, 1998: 11.   [5] See Ostrom, 1998: 13, figure 2.
[6] See Ostrom, 1998: 14–16.

description of the learning processes by which reciprocity norms are internalized, and the role that the five strategic decisions play in these processes. The claim is thus a general one, as is evidenced by her assertion that the different types of normative orientation enumerated above are ones that one finds, in different proportions, 'in any population of individuals'. And, as Ostrom adds in a footnote: 'The proportion of individuals who follow the sixth norm – cooperate always – will be minuscule or nonexistent.'[7]

In discussing the reciprocity thesis, we shall start by simply taking the first of its claims for granted. We accept that reciprocity norms are in some sense basic to all cultures. Neither shall we contest that the usefulness of these norms in enhancing cooperation may account for the inherited capacity of humans to transmit reciprocity over the ages, as the second claim suggests. Our aim here is to question the validity of the fourth claim concerning the rarity of unconditional cooperation norms. This we shall do by examining the suggested *scope* of the second claim, taking due account of Ostrom's third claim concerning the five strategies for enhancing the effectiveness of conditional cooperation.

As was shown above, the second claim says that humans inherit a strong capacity to learn reciprocity norms, so as to be able to cope with '*a multitude of social dilemmas*'. Now it is not entirely clear what Ostrom wants this italicized expression to convey, as part of her second claim. However, if the wide generality of her fourth claim is to be argued on the basis of the preceding three, then surely the second claim must be just as widely general. Thus, 'a multitude of social dilemmas' must here be taken to refer to a whole lot of different types of social dilemma, rather than a whole lot of instances of just one type, or a small selection of types.

Now the problem is that the general scope of the second claim is contradicted by the third claim of the reciprocity thesis. For if the mechanisms by which reciprocity norms are reinforced between individuals in social dilemmas are given by the five strategic decisions, as the third claim has it, then the 'multitude' of social dilemmas must be obviously restricted to certain types of dilemma. These are the types in which the five strategic decisions can be usefully applied. But there may well be important types of social dilemma, in which these five decisions cannot be applied at all, or only to a very limited extent. There are two ways to resolve this contradiction. One is that these other types of dilemma must be excluded from the scope of the second claim. The other possibility is that other behavioural mechanisms exist, which specifically apply to the other types of dilemma, and which ensure in other ways that the reciprocal attitude of conditional cooperation gets selected as the most common way of enhancing opportunities for reaching collectively optimal outcomes.

[7] See Ostrom, 1998: 11, note 26.

Since Ostrom does not mention any such other behavioural mechanisms, we conclude that the first way to resolve the contradiction is the relevant one. The scope of the second claim is thus limited to types of dilemma which allow the five strategies to be usefully applied. As we have argued in section 11.5, social dilemmas can be placed on a continuum of inclusiveness, with two-person interactions at one end, and society-wide interactions at the other. These latter ones are modelled by the Potential Contributor's Dilemma, in which Individual is assumed to be playing against the homogeneous collective of the Others. Ostrom is well aware of this. In fact, she uses a slightly more generalized form of this last-mentioned decision structure to set the stage for her arguments for including reciprocity in the analysis of rational choice.[8] Now the point to be noted is that in a really large-scale Potential Contributor's Dilemma, the five strategic decisions for enhancing the success of conditional cooperation can hardly operate at all. It will not be possible to identify accurately 'who else is involved', at the individual level. And it will rarely be possible to assess the likelihood that specific other individuals are conditional cooperators. All that can be done is to make guesses from past experience about whether or not the anonymous mass of Others, which is decisive for the production of a given common good, will cooperate or defect. The information on which such guesses are based is, of course, far less specific than the information needed to monitor the behaviour of all individuals who are separately involved.

In turn, this implies that the other three strategic decisions that Ostrom mentions, and which are of crucial importance in her account, cannot be implemented with any success. If one cannot really identify and monitor other individuals' behaviour, then neither can one separate the trustworthy from the untrustworthy. Moreover, the very possibility of deciding to go along with nice individuals, while refusing to cooperate with nasty ones, as well as the very possibility of punishing the culprits who betray one's trust, presupposes cases where one can act in a highly selective fashion. In a Potential Contributor's Dilemma, however, it is impossible to act selectively against individual defectors, even if one could identify some of them by careful observation. The only thing that the player can do in any given sequence of rounds of the game is to cooperate or defect, in response to what the anonymous collective of Others does.

Of course, all this by no means rules out the fact that individuals in these larger social dilemmas may be moved by reciprocity norms, and may thus act on moral notions of 'fairness in sharing responsibility'. Such individuals would want to act on Assurance Game-orderings, for example. Nor do we want to rule out the idea that individuals who are in fact moved by reciprocity norms would not withdraw their cooperation when they observe glaring instances

---

[8] See Ostrom, 1998: 3, figure 1.

of free-ridership, and tend to resume cooperation when 'all seems clear'. We are only pointing out that these reciprocity-minded individuals are not in a position to do much, at ground level, to develop the kind of practices that would enable a fine-grained network of trust and reputation to get going. Hence, if one wants to maintain that reciprocity norms will tend to get reinforced in the circumstances of the Potential Contributor's Dilemma, as Ostrom's thesis commits one to maintaining, then one must identify behavioural mechanisms other than the ones listed under the third claim of the reciprocity thesis. Failing this, the reciprocity thesis cannot be accepted in the general form in which it is put forward.

Indeed, we have reasons for thinking that the reciprocity thesis is empirically implausible in specified circumstances of environmental dilemmas. But before these circumstances are identified in the next section, we first examine the evidence that Ostrom has assembled in favour of the reciprocity thesis. In fact, most of the empirical work cited in support of the widespread nature of conditional cooperation is of three kinds. The first is laboratory experiments in two-person situations (such as Prisoner's Dilemmas, ultimatum games, or dictator games). The second is experiments in small groups, in which conditions can be endlessly varied with respect to opportunities for face-to-face communication, individual entry and exit to games, devising punishment rules, and sharing costs of contribution to a collective good. The third kind of evidence in favour of conditional cooperation by rational agents who are sensitive to reciprocity norms, is the experimental work undertaken by Ostrom and others in the management of common-pool resources through non-enforceable agreements. All of these situations are located at the other end of the inclusiveness spectrum from the Potential Contributor's Dilemma. And indeed, when one takes account of the 'structural variables' identified in Ostrom's 'simple scenario' of reciprocal trust-building on the basis of the cited evidence, the two key factors that contribute to its success are seen to be small group size and symmetry of the participants' interests and resources.[9]

There is one other factor of importance in assessing circumstances that contribute to the salience of reciprocity in social dilemmas, which to some extent cuts across the size of the group, or the symmetry of the interests and resources that the participants bring along. This factor bears on the kind of collective good to be produced through cooperation.

Ostrom's review of the literature is largely limited to types of goods that can be regarded as 'common-pool resources', where 'resources' may be broadly taken as referring to either natural ones, such as the fish in a 'tragedy of the

---

[9] See Ostrom, 1998: 15, figure 3. Ostrom rightly lists two additional factors enhancing the chances of success: a 'long time horizon' and low cost of producing the collective good. However, these factors are truly general to all social dilemmas. Hence they are not the key ones in the context of the present issue.

commons', or produced ones, such as an irrigation ditch produced in common by the owners of ten equally large farms (see the example used by Ostrom's illustrative scenario of stable reciprocal agreement).[10]

What makes reciprocity especially salient in these cases is the fact that the benefits of common-pool resources are individually appropriable, and that failure to produce the common-pool resources primarily impacts on the members of the group. However, in the environmental dilemmas we have been considering, these features are far less prevalent. The collective goods that are at issue in all of our cases – assuming for the moment that they are being valued as such by all participants – are better characterized as 'common-sink' resources, by contrast to (natural) common-pool resources.[11] The problem of controlling the spread of toxic household waste over large areas, reducing smog, and, more speculatively perhaps, preventing climate changes resulting from global emissions of carbon dioxide, is a problem of controlling the disposal of different kinds of polluting waste products. It is not primarily a problem of combining the inputs of work for digging irrigation ditches fairly, or of getting agreement on non-enforceable rules for the sustainable exploitation of a jointly used tract of land. Moreover, in the laboratory experiments cited by Ostrom, the gains and losses associated with reciprocal or self-interested action are also common-pool resources, since they are usually confined to the division of variable sums of money under certain structures of incentive, as in ultimatum games. With common-sink goods, however, the possibilities for getting collective action underway by means of reciprocity-enhancing decision strategies are less marked, because the benefits of the goods cannot usually be limited to the group of producers (short of voluntary collective action across large transnational areas), whereas the failure to produce the goods locally will often affect large numbers of non-participants elsewhere.

For this reason too, one may expect that reciprocity norms will be less easy to reinforce in the environmental dilemmas that we have been dealing with. Again, of course, this does not mean that the participants in our three cases could not possibly have been moved by reciprocity norms, given that these norms are 'cultural universals' and have been 'transmitted over the ages', as Ostrom points out. All we are claiming at present is that there is little reason to think it likely that such norms would be selectively promoted in environmental dilemmas through the kinds of mechanism that are central to the argument of the reciprocity thesis.

As will be clear from the discussion of the reciprocity thesis so far, Ostrom quite strongly emphasizes the conduciveness of the morality of reciprocal cooperation to 'levels of cooperation' and the 'net benefits' thereof. In other words, much of her argument in favour of developing more sophisticated models of

---

[10] See Ostrom, 1998: 14.   [11] See Weale, 1992: 192–5.

rationality in which attention is centrally focused on reciprocity norms, is aimed at harnessing this type of morality in the service of collective optimality. Looking at her research programme from this angle, it looks as if Ostrom is siding with Sen's viewpoint regarding morality as a handmaiden of enlightened self-interest (see section 11.3). There would seem to be a substantive disagreement with Sen, however. For, putting it in terms of the latter's analytical framework, Sen ranks unconditional other-regarding morality above conditional Assurance Game-morality in his instrumental meta-ranking, while Ostrom would seem to have it the other way round.

As we shall now argue, however, it is misleading to put the contrast in this way. Given her fourth claim about unconditional morality's rare occurrence, it is tempting to think that Ostrom, like Sen, is engaging in an instrumental comparison between conditional and unconditional morality, but that she is arguing, unlike Sen, that conditional morality wins hands down in securing collective optimality. On a first reading of her review, it might seem that the reason for this is simply that conditional morality gets reinforced by cultural evolution, while the more demanding unconditional morality gets weeded out over the millennia, so that it ultimately becomes 'extremely rare in all cultures'. Yet on closer inspection, this is not what Ostrom actually argues. Her evolutionary line of support for reciprocity norms is based instead on a comparison with narrow self-interest. It may be instructive to quote her at some length on this.

> Human beings do not inherit particular reciprocity norms via a biological process. The argument is more subtle. Individuals inherit an acute sensitivity for learning norms that increase their long-term benefits when confronting social dilemmas with others who have learned and value similar norms. The process of growing up in any culture provides thousands of incidents (learning trials) whereby parents, siblings, friends and teachers provide the specific content of the mutual expectations prevalent in that culture. Parents reward and punish them until cooperation is a learned response. In a contemporary setting, corporate managers strive for a trustworthy corporate reputation by continuously reiterating and rewarding the use of key principles of norms by corporate employees.   (Ostrom, 1998: 11)

This particular argument is located at the other end of Sen's instrumental meta-ranking, so to speak. Reciprocity norms are here said to be winning the evolutionary contest with narrow self-interest: as a result of learning processes, *AG*-orderings do better than *PD*-orderings. Sen would not disagree with this, of course. But what about unconditional morality? Unlike reciprocity norms, norms of unconditional cooperation are not mentioned in the first sentence of the quoted passage from Ostrom, the one that is followed by her cultural evolution account. However, nothing in that account itself suggests that unconditional morality could not be transmitted from one generation to the other by similar kinds of learning processes. For example, as most parents know, to raise a child into someone who can become a trustworthy friend, citizen or business associate, it is neither logically necessary, nor particularly effective, to concentrate on turning the child into a *conditional cooperator.* What counts is making the child capable of acting on reasonable terms of cooperation, which are appropriate for a variety of widely differing contexts. Some of these contexts are specifically moral ones, others less so, or not at all. It would be strange to claim that there is no room whatsoever for promoting attitudes of unconditional cooperation in a complex cultural 'learning process'.

We need not assume, of course, that Ostrom is really committed to that extreme claim. But if she is not so committed, then it would seem to be desirable that 'second-generation models of rationality' would include questions about the role that unconditional compliance to social norms has to play in social dilemmas. Moreover, it should not be assumed that the only valid viewpoint from which to assess unconditionally cooperative behaviour in response to social norms, or public policies, is the one of enlightened self-interest. The reason for rejecting this kind of approach is that it runs the risk of becoming self-defeating, as we have argued in section 11.3. Thus, among the empirical 'models of rationality' to be developed in Ostrom's programme, some at least should be able to accommodate the information needed to study the phenomenon of moral commitment more closely. Our interpretation of reported motives and preferences in terms of the environmental ethos may be taken as one example of how to go about doing this.

12.3 Cost of cooperation and conditionalities in environmental dilemmas

From what has been said so far, one could expect that conditionally cooperative attitudes need not figure largely in the three dilemmas that we have studied, in contrast to what the reciprocity thesis would lead one to think.[12] This expectation is indeed borne out by the motive and preference response in section 10.5, where we concentrated on the responses that are fully (unconditionally) or partially (conditionally) in agreement with the environmental ethos. But in the present context, a more general look at reported preference orderings may be more appropriate, abstracting for the moment from our specific concerns with the ethos underlying the policies of self-regulation. In table 4.2 of chapter 4, one can see that while the percentages of conditionally cooperative orderings vary across cases, they are small in comparison to the percentages of unconditionally cooperative ones in all cases. The conditionally cooperative orderings QPRS, QRPS, QRSP, RQSP, RSQP and RQPS amount to around 5 per cent in Chemical Waste and Energy Saving, and to 10 per cent in Holiday

---

[12] For a theoretical argument to the effect that the reciprocity thesis is plausible even in large-scale dilemmas, see Lewinsohn-Zamir, 1998.

Destination.[13] The unconditionally cooperative orderings are the six with a dominant strategy to cooperate. They amount to 91 per cent in Chemical Waste, 86 per cent in Energy Saving, and 51 per cent in Holiday Destination. In all cases of the dilemma, then, unconditionally cooperative preferences predominate, but far more so in Chemical Waste and Energy Saving than in Holiday Destination. To give a rough indication, one can take the ratios of unconditionally cooperative preferences to conditionally cooperative ones. These ratios are 16.5, 15.8 and 5.3 to 1 respectively. Thus in Holiday Destination, the ratio is roughly a third of that of the two other cases.

We are not able, at this stage of our research, to provide what might amount to a full explanation of these observations. But there is one suggestion that may be worth pursuing. As mentioned in section 7.4, the three cases of the dilemma may be said to differ with respect to the perceived individual cost of participating in collective action. Chemical Waste and Energy Saving can be seen as low-cost cases, relative to Holiday Destination, and hence one may expect that it will be easier to adopt a cooperative attitude in the former than in the latter. Specific reasons for these differentials in perceived cost among cases will be explored more fully in the next chapter. However, the suggestion we have in mind here for explaining the predominance of unconditional over conditional cooperation makes use of the same general point about cost. It is this: differential cost does not merely affect the incidence of cooperative attitudes that can be observed in different cases of the dilemma, as opposed to non-cooperative attitudes. It also affects the ratio of unconditional to conditional attitudes. This is because a low cost of giving up non-cooperative behaviour also makes it much easier to decide to cooperate whatever the others do, if the person is already favourably disposed towards cooperation.

The tendency to display cooperative preferences *in unconditional form* may be related to the personal cost of cooperation in two distinct ways. One is that a cooperatively disposed person may find it far less onerous to adopt the kind of automatic response to choice exemplified by the 'dominant cooperate' strategy, than to adopt the stance of a conditional cooperator. This would seem to be an especially relevant consideration in a large-scale Potential Contributor's Dilemma. For as we have seen in discussing Ostrom's thesis, taking the determined stance of a conditional cooperator in such dilemmas involves taking on genuine worries about what the others are going to do, without being able to do very much about it. So if the cost involved in cooperating is relatively insignificant anyway, then it may be more efficient to cooperate unconditionally than conditionally. One can always shift to another set of preferences later on, if it turns out that one's 'trust on credit' gets wasted repeatedly. Related to the

---

[13] These are the orderings that satisfy the pairwise ranking constraints of a conditionally cooperative ordering, namely Q > P and R > S. These constraints belong to the constraints of the motive structure of intermediate Willingness (W2), as defined in 6.3.

relative ease of the unconditional stance for a cooperatively disposed person, there is a second point about low cost. If someone is willing to cooperate, and finds it efficient not to worry too much about the behaviour of others, then he or she may worry even less, once it becomes clear that the cost of cooperation is low for others too. This consideration will lead to the expectation that the others will also usually do their bit for the environment, and that they too will not continually be on the lookout for signs of defection. Taken together, these two points may start to explain why it is that in the relatively low-cost cases of our survey, the ratio of unconditional to conditional cooperators is overwhelmingly high, as shown above, while it is much lower in the high-cost case of Holiday Destination.

The two points just discussed are consistent with Philip Pettit's analysis of rational cooperation. Against the standard view of theorists like Olson, Pettit argues that rational actors may genuinely cooperate from moral, or otherwise non-self-interested, preferences. But he does insist that, nevertheless, such actors always keep in the back of their minds a narrowly self-interested way of looking at social interaction. As a consequence, so Pettit argues, in cases where cooperation repeatedly leads to bad results, as judged from the self-interested point of view, self-interested motivations will tend to be activated at some point – as it were by a 'red light' – and cooperation will cease. Pettit calls this mechanism 'the virtual reality of *homo economicus*'.[14]

Duly refined, Pettit's mechanism applies to the present problem. Someone who would standardly cooperate in a low-cost case such as Chemical Waste, might become non-cooperative, once faced by the higher cost in the dilemma of Holiday Destination. However, there is another possibility. Unconditional cooperators, who find out that continued cooperation threatens to get them into the sucker position too often in the high-cost case, may be warned by Pettit's 'red light'. But they could still remain disposed to cooperate, at least for the time being. Instead of switching all the way to the viewpoint of narrow self-interest, the perception of a higher cost of cooperation in a case like Holiday Destination may have the effect of switching their ordering of preferences from the unconditional ordering QPSR to the conditional ordering QPRS, for example.

Thus in higher-cost cases, people would become more alert to past experience of being suckered by the Others, and hence more disposed to give up cooperation

---

[14] See Pettit, 1996: 69, note 8. Pettit does not claim that the 'virtual reality of *homo economicus*' is necessarily a unique mechanism, only that it is a common one. One can envisage an analogous mechanism working in situations in which people, who have generally been educated into moral codes of cooperative behaviour, act self-interestedly in a routine way, not caring much about their morality. But only up to a certain point. When the costs that self-interested routines inflict on others become too apparent, then the moral downside of these routines becomes too obvious to ignore, and a 'warning light' could start activating corrective behaviour in line with the internalized moral code. As Pettit admits, this would amount to the presence of a 'virtual morality'.

Table 12.1 *Expectation of the choices of the others*

	Chemical Waste		Energy Saving		Holiday Destination	
	N	%	N	%	N	%
Cooperative	648	65	681	69	58	6
Non-cooperative	220	22	186	19	757	76
No opinion	125	13	126	13	178	18
Total	993	100	993	100	993	100

on grounds of reciprocity failures. In a lower-cost case, on the other hand, they would be less alert to signs of defection, simply because the prospect of being suckered there is taken less seriously. If this is correct, then in high-cost cases, reciprocity norms would tend to replace the routine adherence to unconditional norms of cooperation which is efficient in low cost cases.

There is one piece of survey evidence that speaks in favour of this explanatory guess. If expectations about the cost of cooperation to others are indeed a factor in deciding whether one can safely afford to be an unconditional cooperator, rather than a conditional one, then it would have to be true that respondents in Holiday Destination will not expect as much cooperation from the others as they do in Chemical Waste and Energy Saving. Directly following the Willingness question of the survey, the respondents were asked a question about their expectations concerning others' behaviour. The wording of the question is given here for Holiday Destination:

What do you expect other persons to do about their holiday? We are not asking here what you hope they will do. Do you expect that they will spend their holiday close to home, in view of the consequences for the environment, or do you expect that they will spend their holiday far away from home?

The answers in the response categories 'They will spend their holiday close to home' and 'They will spend their holiday far from home' are labelled as a cooperative and non-cooperative expectation, respectively. The response is given in table 12.1.

Since the ratio of unconditionally to conditionally cooperative preferences is roughly three times as high in the low-cost cases of Chemical Waste and Energy Saving as it is in the high-cost case of Holiday Destination, table 12.1 seems to bear out our explanatory guess. The expectation response across the three cases is quite in line with the notion that the stance of unconditional cooperation for a cooperatively disposed person will be made easier, relative to the conditional stance, when that person expects the others to cooperate, because of common perceptions concerning the low cost of cooperation in the case at hand. Note that we are not here claiming that expectations concerning others' behaviour are crucial in explaining the variations between cases in *cooperative attitude as such*, at the level of preference orderings. The expectation factor is here said to operate on the ratio of unconditional to conditional cooperation, with respect to the preferences that an already cooperatively disposed person would be likely to adopt.

After having addressed the relations between our research method and some of its main findings to wider debates in the literature in the last two chapters, we shall now go on to analyse the responses of the core part of the survey, bearing in mind the environmental meta-ranking developed in chapters 10 and 11. Even though it cannot be said with full confidence that all of our respondents with motives of positive Valuation and Willingness were actually motivated by the environmental ethos, it is reasonable to think that the widespread occurrence of unconditionally cooperative attitudes in the environmental dilemmas could be due to a climate of public opinion which was favourable to the public morality of environmental self-regulation at the time of the survey. As we have argued, the policies of self-regulation have been (and still are, at present) very much concerned with morally influencing the attitudes of Dutch citizens to environmental problems. Thus, in the face of these results, it will be of interest to ask whether the respondents who reported the two 'most moral' preference orderings QSPR and QPSR of our environmental meta-ranking have also reported the 'most moral' motives of positive Valuation and positive Willingness. And in addition, it will be important to know whether the respondents who did so actually reported the corresponding cooperative choice intentions as well. This will be examined in the next chapter.

13

Assessing self-regulation policies

13.1 The context of environmental dilemmas

The strategy of internalizing environmental responsibility commits the government to promote the voluntary cooperation of citizens in environmental dilemmas. Do our data show that this strategy has worked? To the extent that it has, is it a wise and viable policy for the future? And what are the limitations on what the strategy can accomplish in various cases of the dilemma? These are questions addressed in the final three sections of this chapter. But first we must follow up on the groundwork laid in the four previous chapters of this part. Chapters 9 and 10 presented the data concerning the acceptance of self-regulation policies, as well as evidence on the extent to which the respondents agree or disagree with the environmental ethos, at the level of motives and preferences.

To get to the point where the effectiveness of self-regulation policy can be assessed, we shall first track the choice intentions of cooperatively disposed respondents. Thus, our question is not only whether reported motives and preferences are congruent with the environmental ethos, but also whether respondents who display the right kind of motives actually intend to cooperate rationally and consistently with those motives. It is by focusing on *consistent ethical cooperation*, from unconditionally cooperative motives, that we finally capture the degree to which respondents are in full agreement with the content of environmental self-regulation in each case of the dilemma. In section 13.2 we define consistent ethical cooperation, and show that the reponses form a uni-dimensional scale, with Holiday Destination as the hardest case, and Chemical Waste as the easiest one.

In sections 13.3 to 13.5, the location of the cases on the scale of consistent ethical cooperation is explained. Chapter 7 suggested that unidimensional scales with respect to the variables of Willingness, Valuation, and Rational Choice to Cooperate are related to contextual background features of the corresponding environmental decision problems in the real world (figure 7.3). We take up this suggestion here, and identify three features, each of which provides policy-relevant reasons why an individual respondent is likely to score lower on consistent ethical cooperation in Holiday Destination than in Energy Saving or Chemical Waste.

First, respondents have more difficulty in relating their actual decisions about holiday travel to the choice between the cooperative or non-cooperative strategies C and D in the corresponding dilemma. As discussed in section 13.4, such 'mapping problems' show that considerations of the environmental ethos are less salient in Holiday Destination than they are in the other cases. As a result, even respondents who display motives in full agreement with the ethos will be less likely to report the preferences and choices that consistently match their ethical motives.

Secondly, respondents in Holiday Destination are far less likely to report ethical motives than they are in the two other cases. There are two reasons for this, which are discussed in section 13.5. One is that the individual cost of complying with the ethos is much higher for holiday decisions. Another reason is that in Holiday Destination, the gains of universal voluntary cooperation are perceived to be less significant. This is revealed by the data, which show that respondents' belief in the effectiveness of collective action is much lower in Holiday Destination than in either Energy Saving or Chemical Waste. In our treatment of both of these features, we make use of the theoretical findings of chapters 11 and 12. This is done in section 13.6, where we analyse the extent to which the motive response of those who score positively on consistent ethical cooperation in the easiest case of Chemical Waste is distributed along the environmental meta-ranking for the hardest case of Holiday Destination.

Taking account of all three features, our explanation of the unidimensional scale of consistent ethical cooperation may be summed up by a threefold *dimension of private significance*. It is stated in section 13.7. A given area of behaviour in the real world is said to be of 'private' (as opposed to 'public') significance in three respects. For the area in question, the environmental ethos has (1) a low salience, (2) a high individual cost of compliance, and (3) a low perceived gain of collective action. The dimension of private significance is utilized in the final three sections of this concluding chapter, in which we comment on the strengths and weaknesses of the Dutch self-regulation approach.

13.2 Consistent ethical cooperation

When does a respondent's attitude fully conform to the ethos of environmental responsibility? To begin with, such a respondent must display an intention to

Table 13.1 *Cooperation and consistent ethical cooperation in the three cases*

	Chemical Waste		Energy Saving		Holiday Destination	
	N	%	N	%	N	%
Cooperators	921	93	888	89	357	36
Consistent ethical cooperators	593	60	519	52	102	10
All respondents	993	100	993	100	993	100

cooperate. The first row of table 13.1 shows how many respondents have actually chosen the cooperative strategy in the three cases. Call these the *cooperators*. To be a cooperator is a necessary condition for the attitude that fully corresponds to the environmental ethos, but not a sufficient one. The neccesary and sufficient conditions are that the respondent cooperates rationally from a preference ordering, which in turn is consistent with the motives that signify *full agreement* with the ethos. Respondents who satisfy these conditions are called *consistent ethical cooperators*. The observed frequencies in the three cases are listed in the second row of table 13.1.

To see how one gets from the first row to the more selective second row in the table, consider the case of Chemical Waste. Of the 921 respondents reporting a cooperative choice, some cooperate on the basis of a reported preference ordering with a dominant strategy to cooperate, whereas others have reported other preference orderings. Only the former group of respondents satisfies the test of rational choice, as it was defined in chapter 3. Of this group, the subgroup of respondents who cooperate rationally in full agreement with the environmental ethos must have reported either of the two (dominant cooperative) preference orderings QSPR and QPSR, which characterize full agreement, according to figure 10.1. We reproduce that figure here as figure 13.1.

Next, consider the test of consistent preferences, as defined in chapter 6. Not all members of the subgroup of rational cooperators with orderings QSPR or QPSR will actually satisfy this test. Those who do satisfy it must also have reported the unique motive structure that characterizes full agreement with the environmental ethos. According to figure 13.1, this is (V_1, W_1). The final subgroup of cooperators we are looking for has thus reported the cooperative strategy C, and either ordering QSPR or QPSR, and finally, motive structure (V_1, W_1) as well. We have now arrived at the figure for Chemical Waste in the second row of table 13.1. Only 593 of the 921 cooperators are ones that start from ethical motives (V_1, W_1), and satisfy the two tests of consistent preferences and rational choice. These are the consistent ethical cooperators.

Valuation scale	Willingness scale W1		W2		W3	
V1	*full agreement*		*partial agreement*		*rejection of norm*	
	QSPR	**QPSR**	**QPRS**	**PQSR**	**PRQS**	**PQRS**
			QRPS	QRSP	*rejection of ethos*	
V2	QSRP	SQPR	PSQR	PSRQ	**PRSQ**	**RPQS**
			SPQR	SPRQ		
			RQSP	RQPS		
					rejection of ethos	
V3	SRQP	SQRP	SRPQ	RSQP	**RPSQ**	**RSPQ**

Figure 13.1 Preference orderings and motive structures of the environmental ethos.

As a convenient summary of the case-specific differences in table 13.1, between 50 and 60 per cent of the respondents in Chemical Waste and Energy Saving are consistent ethical cooperators, against only 10 per cent in Holiday Destination. The data confirm the proposition that Holiday Destination is the hardest case. With respect to the dichotomous variable of consistent ethical co-operation, the three cases form a scale. The hardest case proposition is borne out more strongly: consistent ethical cooperation in Holiday Destination predicts consistent ethical cooperation in the two other cases.[1] The scalability of the cases with respect to consistent ethical cooperation is of special relevance for policy analysis. As we will argue in the next section, the observed variations across cases can be explained in terms of case-specific background features. These explanations will cast light on the final question we pursue below: what can be said about the effectiveness of pursuing self-regulation policies in different cases of environmental collective action?

13.3 Background features of hard and easy cases

Variations in the cooperative reported behaviour of individual respondents are not adequately explained in terms of their individual characteristics. This was one of the main conclusions of chapter 8. As the analyses showed, co-operative stances in environmental dilemmas are not very responsive to so-ciocultural traits. Nor do they depend much on the broad value orientations of respondents, or even on their general attitudes towards the environment

---

[1] The scale homogeneity coefficient is .49 (a medium scale), and the item homogeneity coefficient of Holiday Destination is .58 (strong scalability).

Table 13.2 *Consistent ethical cooperation, degree of ethical consistency, and share of ethical motives*

	Chemical Waste	Energy Saving	Holiday Destination
	%	%	%
Consistent ethical cooperators	60	52	10
Degree of ethical consistency	65	63	52
Share of ethical motives	92	89	25

('interest', or 'involvement'). What seems to be crucial for the question of how likely a respondent will be to report cooperative behaviour, or display a cooperative attitude – as measured by our questions on the environmental dilemma – is the social context of the case in which the dilemma occurs.

In this section, we introduce our strategy for explaining the contextual background features of the three cases Chemical Waste, Energy Saving, and Holiday Destination. The question is: what makes Holiday Destination the hardest case, and Chemical Waste the easiest one, with respect to consistent ethical cooperation? As was shown in section 13.2, consistent ethical cooperation is a composite variable. It reflects two components: *motives of environmental responsibility* (V_1, W_1), and *internal consistency* between these motives, the matching preferences (QSPR or QPSR), and the cooperative choices that correspond to those preferences. In explaining the differences between the cases, therefore, one should pay attention to both components. Our overall strategy will be to split up the percentage of consistent ethical cooperators of table 13.1 into two ratios. These are shown in table 13.2. The first ratio is called the *degree of ethical consistency*. It is defined as the number of consistent ethical cooperators, divided by the number of respondents with motives of positive Valuation and Willingness (V_1, W_1). This ratio expresses the proportion of respondents with these ethical motives who actually manage to satisfy the two consistency tests. The second ratio is called the *share of ethical motives*. It is defined as the number of respondents with positive Valuation and positive Willingness, divided by the total of 993 respondents. The product of these two ratios is the percentage of consistent ethical cooperation in that total.

The difference between Holiday Destination and the two other cases in the degree of ethical consistency is 52 per cent as against (around) 64 per cent. It will be explained in the next section. Briefly, our argument is that it is harder to display consistency in Holiday Destination, because it is especially difficult for a respondent to map the possible holiday decisions in the real world to the binary choice between cooperative and non-cooperative strategies of the environmental dilemma, as presented in the survey questions. Such 'mapping problems' may differentially affect the consistency results of the three cases.

Next, we focus on the comparatively low share of ethical motives in Holiday Destination. As table 13.2 shows, Holiday Destination's share of ethical motives is only 25 per cent, against shares of around 90 per cent in the other two cases. This important finding was mentioned in section 10.5.[2] In section 13.5, we shall try to explain it by two background features of cases. One of these is the *individual cost of cooperation*. We argue that there are good reasons for thinking that the motives of Willingness and Valuation are relatively scarce in Holiday Desination, because it is significantly more costly for an individual to cooperate in this case than it is in the two others. It must be noted here that we have not included any direct questions about the cost of cooperation in the survey. Yet it is possible to identify two main aspects of cost: *opportunity cost* and *commitment cost*. Each of these affects a respondent's motivation in a way that can explain why Holiday Destination stands out sharply from the other two cases.

However, the share of ethical motives in an environmental dilemma is also bound to be affected by another background feature, which bears on *the perceived gain of universal collective action*, rather than on the individual cost of cooperating. Judging from common sense, this feature would certainly seem to be important. If cases differ in respect of the subjective gain associated with collective action, then – other things being equal – one would expect a low-gain case to display a lower share in the motives of positive Valuation and positive Willingness. Our cases differ in this background feature, because of the scale of the environmental common-sink problems which they address (see section 12.2). This issue will be discussed in the context of a survey question dealing with the respondents' belief in the *effectiveness* of collective action. It is found that respondents in Holiday Destination are far more sceptical about the effectiveness of collective action than they are in the other two cases.

To summarize, our strategy of explaining the variation in consistent ethical cooperation between cases is a two-step affair. The background features of individual cost and collective gain account for the observed shares of motives in full agreement with the ethos (V1, W1), while mapping problems account for the observed degrees of consistency between those motives, the corresponding

---

[2] The shares of ethical motives (V1, W1) are somewhat less than those recorded in table 10.1. This is because the denominator of the share of ethical motives is the total of all 993 respondents, rather than the total of respondents who reported a valid motive, as in table 10.1. It is instructive to compare the shares of ethical motives in table 13.2 to the shares of the matching ethical preferences QSPR and QPSR in the total of all respondents. These shares, as calculated from table 10.2, are 65%, 59% and 31% for Chemical Waste, Energy Saving, and Holiday Destination, respectively. This shows that the difference between the three cases is roughly the same, whether we look at the ethical attitude of respondents at the level of motives, or at the level of preferences.

preferences (QSPR, QPSR) and cooperative choice intentions. Both sets of factors, so we will argue, contribute towards the relatively high percentages of consistent ethical cooperation in Chemical Waste and Energy Saving, and the relatively low one in Holiday Destination.

13.4 Mapping problems and the salience of the environmental ethos

The data on Chemical Waste, Energy Saving, and Holiday Destination are responses to three instances of a common game form, the Potential Contributor's Dilemma. To discover features that affect the degree of ethical consistency across these cases, one is forced to look behind this common form. The form of the dilemma imposes a binary choice of 'cooperation' versus 'defection' on the respondents, which is described in the survey questions of each case. In each case also, this binary choice is meant to represent a specific set of concrete actions that the respondents can imagine themselves performing as actors in the real world. A respondent must be able to classify those real-world actions in terms of their aggregate environmental significance, as being either 'cooperative' or 'noncooperative'.[3]

In some cases it may be difficult to map possible real-world actions onto the binary choice between cooperation and non-cooperation in the matching dilemma, while in other cases this may be quite an easy operation to perform. But there is also another kind of problem to be distinguished. Independently of how difficult it is to classify real-world actions as 'cooperative' or 'non-cooperative', by reference to their aggregate environmental effects, the connection between real-world actions and the *environmental reasons* one may have for performing one of them rather than another, may be perceived as being rather tenuous in some cases, whereas in other cases that connection is an immediate one, which is simple to perceive. Both of these factors affect the degree of ethical consistency, from motives down to choice intentions. They will be henceforth called 'mapping problems'.

Of the three cases studied, Chemical Waste is certainly the easiest case with respect to both kinds of mapping problem. This is because in the real world, the binary choice of Chemical Waste has explicitly been structured by official recycling policies. When someone considers bringing officially listed items of toxic household waste to the designated public collection point, then such actions are easily classified as instances of the cooperative strategy in the survey case. They are readily distinguished from environmentally unfriendly ones, such as dumping batteries in the dustbin, or pouring used paint thinner in the kitchen sink. Thus, in Chemical Waste it is not hard to appreciate that the latter kinds of acts are 'non-cooperative' in the sense intended by the survey, namely harmful

---

[3] The procedure of the interview was described in section 4.2 of chapter 4.

to the environment when performed in the aggregate, and in conflict with official reasons for protecting the environment against the poisoning of soil and water.

In the case of Energy Saving, the real-world equivalents of 'cooperation' and 'defection' are much less straightforward. As we noted in section 4.1, the respondents were instructed to think about economizing on their daily use of warm water and electricity for the sake of the environment, taking as given the existing state of affairs in their household. Given this choice setting, two households with the same use habits might look differently at the environmental significance of their behaviour, depending on whether or not they have previously decided to economize on energy-using durables. In view of such previous decisions, it may become difficult for a respondent to judge to what extent his *current pattern of daily use* is to be classified as 'cooperative' or 'non-cooperative'. For the same reason, it may also be difficult to separate one's own environmental concerns from those of cost and lifestyle, in judging one's own performance with respect to responsible energy management in the household. To some extent, self-regulation policies seek to facilitate precisely this kind of separation, for example by specifying the environmental impact of different items in the household energy bill. But unlike in Chemical Waste, many such policies also tend to run cost and lifestyle reasons for action together with reasons of environmental responsibility. Nevertheless, even though the nature of the binary choice poses larger issues of judgement in Energy Saving than it does in Chemical Waste, the distinction between 'cooperation' and 'defection' is still relatively clear-cut in comparison to Holiday Destination, the case to which we now turn.

While the contrast between spending one's holiday either far away from, or close to, one's home is fairly straightforward, the link with environmental concerns is far less obvious. This is so for several reasons. To start, people are generally less familiar with placing their holiday decisions in the context of an environmental dilemma, and therefore they have more difficulty in relating their own behavioural options to aggregate effects on pollution. Moreover, the environmental effects of holiday decisions – as presented in the survey questions – are due only to differences in the distance travelled to a given place for spending the holiday. Our reason for focusing on travel was that it is the most important factor in terms of environmental effects. But this may not be obvious to all respondents. In any case, the focus on the aspect of travel forces them to look at their holiday decision problem in a far more abstract and synoptic way than is true for the other two cases. More abstract, since they are being asked to concentrate on the causal link between travel distance and pollution, in isolation from the environmental effects of being in place at the resort, summer house, caravan park or camp, at the chosen holiday destination itself. More synoptic, because respondents are required to understand the causal links between 'close to (far from) home' and 'less (more) pollution' in rather general terms, taking into account such things as the likelihood that many people who travel to faraway places will often do so by plane or private car, rather than by rail, bus or bicycle, for reasons of comfort, and because of the limited time available for spending a holiday.

Finally, the planning of holidays involves many other private considerations, most notably financial ones, and ones related to the size and age composition of the household. For all these reasons, the mental operations involved in 'recalculating' one's holiday business in terms that fit into the 'cooperate or defect' choice of the dilemma place far higher demands on household members in this area than when they are faced with similar problems in the areas of energy consumption or toxic waste disposal.

This is likely to be reflected in the survey answers. For example, the response 'far from home' need not always indicate that a mother responding to our interview would really want to 'defect', in the sense of consciously accepting the pollution effect of travelling to Greece in the summer with her family, since she may have hardly thought about the decision in this way before she sat down to answer the questions of Holiday Destination. If, on the other hand, she were reporting her refusal to bring batteries to the collection point, then it would be far more likely that she would be well aware of 'not bothering about the environment'. Likewise, the response 'close to home' in Holiday Destination need not be a 'cooperative' one in the intended sense of the choice question, as 'bringing toxic waste to the collection point' would almost surely be, in the case of Chemical Waste.

In the open questions which we attached to the preference items of the three cases, some respondents in fact commented on Holiday Destination. They said they had different reasons not to travel abroad: for instance, 'we stay at home anyway, because of small children', or simply 'we never go abroad'. Thus, in comparison to the other two cases, it is more difficult to tell how many respondents who reported the cooperative choice in Holiday Destination chose to ignore the environmental reasons of the dilemma, and just cited their usual practices instead.

Now in our research design, mapping problems are indirectly catered for, by measuring the respondent's attitude to the dilemma independently, at the levels of motives, preferences, and choices. As we argued above, observed intentions to cooperate in environmental dilemmas are bound to be more reliable whenever they are consistently related to motives and preferences that are bound up with a sense of environmental responsibility. Nevertheless, the differences in mapping real-world actions onto the binary choice of 'cooperate' or 'defect' may well have some bearing on how difficult it is for respondents to pass the test of consistent preferences and the test of rational choice or, indeed, to form a valid preference ordering in the first place.

To take the last example from Holiday Destination again, someone who decides to make a cooperative choice for reasons that are unrelated to the environmental issue of voluntary collective action will be more likely to show inconsistencies with respect to preference formation and/or rational choice than someone who is aware of the dilemma, and whose attitude (in the real world) is also affected by moral considerations of environmental responsibility. Thus, if extraneous reasons for adopting 'cooperative' or 'non-cooperative' behaviour occur more often in the area of holiday choices than they do, say, in the area of household waste disposal, then this is likely to be reflected by the consistency of the responses to the respective survey items in Holiday Destination and Chemical Waste. In particular, the degree of ethical consistency is affected adversely the more fuzzy is the choice situation of the dilemma. And the fuzzier it is, the less salient the environmental ethos is in the corresponding area of behaviour.

We admit that all of this is difficult to verify directly. As pointed out in chapters 4 and 6, it is not possible to observe directly the 'individual values' of the respondents. One therefore remains ignorant of their final personal reasons for cooperating or defecting. Yet, we think that mapping problems do play an important role in explaining differences which one can observe, albeit indirectly, with respect to the difficulty of cooperating *consistently from environmentally favourable motives*. These differences were expressed in table 13.2 by the degree of ethical consistency, as defined by the ratio of consistent ethical cooperation to motive structure (V1, W1): 65 per cent in Chemical Waste, 63 per cent in Energy Saving, and 52 per cent in Holiday Destination.

13.5 Individual cost and collective gain

In this section we seek to explain the share of ethical motives, as defined by the ratio of positive Valuation and positive Willingness to total respondents: 92 per cent in Chemical Waste, 89 per cent in Energy Saving, and 25 per cent in Holiday Destination (table 13.2). First, we focus on the background features affecting compliance cost. Then we look at features affecting the respondents' perceptions of the gains to be had from voluntary collective action.

At the level of motives, the personal cost of ethical cooperation depends on two strongly related (but independent) features of cases. First, there are features bearing on the *opportunity cost* of cooperative actions. These affect the expected well-being that would be forgone if the household were to rule out non-cooperative actions. Secondly, there are factors affecting *commitment cost*. This is the cost associated with accepting that the ethos of environmental responsibility is morally relevant, and thus imposes a constraint on the freedom to act as one pleases in the relevant area of behaviour.

Let us first compare the opportunity cost of forgoing the non-cooperative alternative in the two polar cases of Chemical Waste and Holiday Destination. In objective terms, there are resource costs to be reckoned in acting cooperatively: the money, available time, skill, and effort which could have been deployed for other purposes, had the environmental constraints on choice not been accepted. Such resources have to be spent in searching for a pattern of environmentally acceptable behaviour, agreeing on that pattern between household members of different ages, lifestyles, and bargaining power, and finally in actually performing the agreed-on actions. In all of these respects, it is not difficult to see that cooperative behaviour in Chemical Waste is not costly in terms of forgone resources, at least in the standard instances where collection points for toxic waste are in close proximity to houses in a normal state of maintenance (i.e. ones not being reconstructed or repainted).

In Holiday Destination, on the other hand, resource costs will usually be far higher. Even in cases where money could be saved by spending the holiday in the Netherlands (and this is by no means certain), the transaction costs of seeking an acceptable alternative to a holiday abroad are considerable. Holidays are discrete events, less susceptible to being treated as a matter of routine than dealing with waste disposal or energy consumption. To settle on a holiday plan in a family is often a time-consuming business, and much more so when environmental constraints have to be debated among the members of the household.

The personal cost of ethical cooperation is not adequately captured by tallying up forgone resources. Resource cost may not even be overridingly important. The reason is that the gains in subjective well-being that households expect from carrying out a non-cooperative course of action differ across cases quite sharply. Again, compare Chemical Waste to its polar opposite, Holiday Destination. For most people, the subjective instrumental value of throwing away toxic waste with the rest of the rubbish will be nil, or even negative, apart from the time and effort that it would save. In comparison, the expected well-being from spending time on holiday is massive. Going on holiday is a highly valued social practice. It consists in taking time off from concerns of work, school, or public affairs. So if the household thinks that its holiday is best spent far from home, then the subjective loss of accepting environmental constraints on recreative travel will be high indeed, whatever the resource implications. Now for most households, the net instrumental value of non-cooperative options is increased because of large social pressures, in particular commercial ones, to travel a long way out. This can be seen, for example, from the steady increases in the number and average distance of recreative trips by air. To put it in the jargon of Dutch policymaking, the private sectors of the economy, both at home and abroad (tour operators, airlines, banks, food, sports equipment, and clothing industries), have invested massively in the 'social instruments' for schooling households in a norm of worldwide mobility when the holiday issue comes up.

The case of Energy Saving is in between the two polar ones in terms of opportunity cost. On the one hand, to save on energy is to save money, but on the other hand, as self-regulation policy recognizes, it takes considerable effort and discipline to organize household behaviour in cooperative patterns. In economizing on the daily use of electricity and warm water (on which our questions of Energy Saving concentrate), members of households have to settle on several different changes of behaviour. And some of these, say cutting off six minutes of one's daily hot shower, may involve losses of instrumental value that are much higher than the cooperative actions involved in Chemical Waste.

Let us now consider commitment cost. Holiday Destination and Chemical Waste are opposite cases in another way as well. According to Sen's account of moral commitment, accepting the constraints of morality often drives a wedge between self-interested preferences and the choice of actions (see section 11.4). And, as we now argue, it will be more difficult to get to the point of actually accepting those constraints in some areas of household behaviour than it is in others. This issue typically arises at an early stage in the decision process, when a person must decide whether or not there is a choice problem of environmental 'cooperation versus defection' to be assessed. Before the issue of giving up non-cooperative options can arise, the person must open up to the environmental choice problem of a particular case and reflect on why it would be appropriate to take demands of environmental morality seriously in the first place.

It might seem strange to look upon this issue as a matter of cost. Often, the notion of cost is restricted to factors that affect personal well-being. But when issues of moral commitment arise, then gains and losses in well-being are not the only relevant considerations. In the present context, the cost of commitment is best seen as the cost involved in losing the freedom to choose as one pleases, for the sake of a putative duty of responsibility to protect the environment. The size of this cost is, of course, not unrelated to the opportunity cost of cooperation, which is measured in losses of personal well-being. But the cost of commitment still needs to be distinguished separately.

This can be clarified by the bathroom example of Energy Saving, which was mentioned above. In considering the loss in well-being of cutting down on long hot showers, someone might admit on reflection that turning off the warm water tap after six minutes, instead of the usual twelve, is not a major sacrifice compared to the beneficial effects that reducing warm water consumption would have, were everyone to act likewise. But this person could go on to reflect that it is asking too much to let the environment invade his own bathroom, as it were. On that further thought, he might think it was entirely justified to reject the ethical injunction to recalculate his own behaviour. He would back this up by saying that committing himself to the environmental ethos is simply out of place in this area of decision, because it is one in which he has a reason to insist on retaining his freedom of choice. As a consequence of such reasoning, the personal cost versus aggregate benefit calculations that policymakers want people to engage in, according to the National Environmental Plans, would be undercut.

To be sure, the bathroom example is not typically a case involving commitment cost for everyone. The point can be put more dramatically, however. Most people would tend to reject environmental constraints on procreation as being morally relevant. They would not be prepared to 'let the environment invade' their decision to have children, even if they were convinced that a new child would add a lifetime of pollution, however frugal the child's future habits. This case of wanting to preserve one's freedom of procreative choice in the face of environmental constraints may seem extreme. But it is likely that the real-world decisions of Holiday Destination come much closer to it than cases of showering habits, or turning down the heating at night. The reason for this is not merely one of high opportunity cost, of thinking that what one can expect to get from a family holiday to Spain or Morocco, instead of staying in one's own country, is instrumentally more valuable than it is to spend six more minutes under the hot shower each day. The main reason, rather, is that holiday decisions are seen as ones in which it is simply more reasonable to want to have freedom of choice. The thought of not being able to go wherever one *might* want to go in summer, for reasons of environmental morality, may well be one that few people will gladly entertain.

As the extreme case of procreation shows, people will insist on freedom of choice in areas of behaviour where free choice has significant expressive value.[4] One generally values having a free hand in these matters, whatever instrumental values are ultimately served by one's choosing among the available options. The choice of having children includes highly significant things that shape one's personal life in the long term: emotional commitment to a partner, the desire to perpetuate a family line, the transformative experience of being a parent, and so on.[5] Undoubtedly, holiday choices are not in the same league as procreative decisions. But in comparison with the other cases, the expressive value of the holiday choice surely must be rated very high. As we remarked above, holidays signify breaking out of normal life for a stated period of time. This is understood, moreover, to be a practice essentially located in the private domain. However restrictive the conventions that govern the holiday behaviour of different social groups may sometimes seem, they have in common the fact that the activities are set apart from public concerns in the widest of senses. The recurring questions as to whether there will be a holiday, rather than just an idle period during vacation time, how long the holiday will last, where it will take place, who will be included; all such things are understood to depend

---

4 The significance of the distinction between instrumental and expressive value for moral reasoning are explained in Scanlon, 1998: chapter 6. Our treatment here is compatible with Scanlon's 'Value of Choice' account.
5 See Dasgupta, 1995.

on considerations that should ideally be raised in isolation from such issues as work, politics, or indeed, environmental morality.

The point about holidays is that they are dispensations from such things. This is why the expressive value of choice in Holiday Destination makes it a case in which people may easily feel justified in resisting environmental prescriptions that they could well accept in other areas of personal decision-making. Compare this to the polar case of Chemical Waste again. Here it appears to be the other way round. The very point of explicitly posing a choice between throwing away paint leftovers in the sink, or getting rid of them at an officially designated recycling facility, consists in acknowledging the desirability, at least in principle, of ruling the former option out of court for environmental reasons. Of course it still remains possible to insist that one's 'integrity as a free person' would require the liberty to remain exempt from moral constraints in this domain as well. But there are no general social reasons readily at hand which would convincingly back up such a judgement. The bathroom example may again serve to show that Energy Saving is an intermediate case, in respect of commitment cost. To the extent that particular uses of energy sources in the household are linked directly to lifestyle habits that people regard as expressing their own personality, the freedom from public constraints on choice will be rated more important. It does seem, however, that most people can be more easily persuaded to reconsider the expressive value of such choices, at least compared to the holiday issue.

Having discussed the background features of individual cost, we now turn to the other major respect in which environmental dilemmas may differ, the perceived benefits from voluntary collective action. Other things being equal, the claims of the environmental ethos will have firmer purchase where it is perceived that there is more at stake in acting on them in the case at hand. One is usually more prepared to take part in collective action at some personal cost, the more one believes that such action, if it succeeds, will be really effective in reducing pollution, or in producing other significant environmental benefits. Here again, Chemical Waste and Holiday Destination would also seem to be polar cases, at least in a small country such as the Netherlands. The main reason for this was mentioned in section 12.2, in connection with our discussion of Ostrom's work on common-pool resources. The benefits of cooperation in Chemical Waste are ones that contribute to the solution of a well-defined local common-sink problem. They consist in helping to prevent soil and water poisoning in one's own area, or at least in the national territory. Also, clean water and unpolluted soil are perceived to be scarce environmental resources in a densely populated country. On the other hand, the cooperation of Dutch households in issues of air pollution and global warming in the case of Holiday Destination involves only a relatively small contribution to a massive global common-sink problem. There would appear to be a 'nested environmental dilemma' here. Dutch people may be inclined to wonder whether the behaviour of millions of households outside

Table 13.3 *Belief in the effectiveness of collective action*

	Chemical Waste		Energy Saving		Holiday Destination	
	N	%	N	%	N	%
Effective	956	96	934	94	567	57
Not effective	37	4	59	6	426	43
Total	993	100	993	100	993	100

the Netherlands will be affected at all by the environmental ethos with which they are asked to comply by their own government.

Our data offer indirect support for this line of reasoning. If respondents think that collective action makes no significant difference in Holiday Destination (for whatever reason), while it does make a difference in Chemical Waste, then this ought to show up in the responses to the following question on the effectiveness of collective action, tabulated above. The question was included in the survey, and it preceded the two questions about Valuation and Willingness. The respondents were asked whether they 'fully agree', 'agree', 'neither agree nor disagree', 'disagree', or 'fully disagree' with the following statements, for each of the cases:

Chemical Waste: 'Separate collection of toxic household waste contributes to a cleaner environment.'

Energy Saving: 'Saving energy in the household contributes to a cleaner environment.'

Holiday Destination: 'Spending the holiday close to home contributes to a cleaner environment.'

Table 13.3 presents the answers to the effectiveness question in dichotomized form, distinguishing between '(full) agreement' and all other response categories, including missing cases. What matters for the present purpose is whether or not the respondent thinks that collective action has a significant positive effect in a particular case. Thus, (full) agreement with the Effectiveness statement is taken to reveal the belief that the designated collective action has a significant positive effect on the environment, and other responses as the belief that it does not. As the table shows, the majority of the respondents fall in the 'Effective' category. In Chemical Waste and Energy Saving there is near-unanimity, whereas in Holiday Destination, the majority is a relatively bare one: 43 per cent either has doubts, or thinks that collective action does not have a significant effect, against at most 6 per cent in the other two cases.

Table 13.4 *Motive response in Holiday Destination of respondents with ethical motives in Chemical Waste*

Holiday Destination

Valuation scale	Willingness scale			Row total
	W1	W2	W3	
V1	**232**	**122**	**130**	484
V2	41	58	**102**	201
V3	19	15	**152**	186
Column total	292	195	384	871

13.6 Comparing motives in the polar cases

The significance of contextual background factors affecting the share of ethical motives can be shown more precisely. We now select the respondents with ethical motives (V1, W1) in the easiest case of Chemical Waste, and then look at the motives they report in the hardest case of Holiday Destination. Table 13.4 gives the result of this exercise.

Consider first cell (V1, W1). It shows that of the 871 respondents who have reported ethical motives in Chemical Waste, and have also reported a valid motive in Holiday Destination, only 232 or 27 per cent retain their ethical motives in the hard case, while 73 per cent switch to another motive structure.[6] As we suggested, this change in motivation is due to the higher costs of individual cooperation, as well as to the lower belief in effectiveness of collective action in Holiday Destination, as compared to Chemical Waste. Next, it can be seen that the motive structures in the top and right-hand cells of table 13.4 (printed boldface) are quite predominant in the total motive response. These motive structures are the ones that we identified earlier as the ones included in the *environmental meta-ranking of motives*. This ranking, as we argued in section 11.5, reflects the judgements that can be made about motive responses (Vi, Wj), from the point of view of the environmental ethos which underlies self-regulation policy. The environmental meta-ranking identifies (V1, W1) as the 'most moral' motive structure, and (V3, W3) as the 'least moral' one.[7]

---

[6] In all, as table 10.1 shows, 909 respondents reported the ethical motive (V1, W1) in Chemical Waste, as against 244 in Holiday Destination. However, only 871 of the 909 respondents with ethical motives in Chemical Waste also reported a valid motive in Holiday Destination. This explains the lower total in table 13.4.

[7] The four cells in the bottom-left part of table 13.4 are not included in the environmental meta-ranking, for reasons that were explained in 10.4. The observed frequencies in these cells are small, relative to the expected frequency of $871/9 = 96.8$. In fact, if one assumes that the 871 respondents with ethical motives in Chemical Waste would exclusively respond to the case

Table 13.5 *Motive response in Holiday Destination of respondents with ethical motives in Chemical Waste, controlled for belief in effectiveness*

Holiday Destination	Group 1: Effective (523 out of 871, or 60%)			
	Willingness scale			
Valuation scale	W1	W2	W3	Row total
V1	204	95	107	406
V2	18	27	42	87
V3	1	1	28	30
Column total	223	123	177	523
Holiday Destination	Group 2: Not Effective (348 out of 871, or 40%)			
	Willingness scale			
Valuation scale	W1	W2	W3	Row total
V1	28	27	23	78
V2	23	31	60	114
V3	18	14	124	156
Column total	69	72	207	348

Looking at table 13.4 once again, it appears that the motives of the respondents who fully agree with the ethos in the easy case of the environmental dilemma are pushed downwards along the environmental meta-ranking once they come to report on the hard case. From table 13.4, one can infer that 44 per cent of the 871 respondents are unwilling to cooperate in Holiday Destination (384 of them report W3). Moreover, 17 per cent of the 871 respondents reject the ethos outright, since 152 of them report the 'least moral' motives in the meta-ranking (V3, W3). It is not clear to what extent these shifts are due to differentials in individual cost or disbelief in the effectiveness of collective action.

However, the data allow one to control the motive response of table 13.4 for the dichotomous variable of Effectiveness, which was displayed in table 13.3 above. This exercise is shown in table 13.5, which partitions the 871 respondents with ethical motives in Chemical Waste into two groups. The members of Group 1 believe that collective action in Holiday Destination is effective, while those in Group 2 do not hold this belief.

of Holiday Destination according to the logic of the environmental ethos, as captured by the meta-ranking, then the whole response would have to be located in the five (boldface) cells of the meta-ranking, and the remaining four cells would have to be empty. To evaluate the observed response statistically, one can regard the block of four cells outside the meta-ranking as an 'error area', and calculate its homogeneity coefficent as $1 - fo/fe = .39$, where $fo = 41 + 58 + 19 + 15 = 133$, and $fe = 387 \times 487 : 871 = 216.4$. The assumption is acceptable only if this coefficient is above .30, which it clearly is.

Quite clearly, the motives of the 523 respondents in Group 1 are more oriented to the 'moral' end of the environmental meta-ranking than the motives of the 348 members of Group 2 are. Respondents whose motives are in line with the ethos in the easy case thus reject the demands of the ethos more readily in the hard case, if they do not believe that voluntary collective action is effective in the latter case. As table 13.5 shows, the downward shift along the meta-ranking, relative to the ethical motive (V_1, W_1) in Chemical Waste that serves as the benchmark here, is radically different between the two groups. Of the 523 respondents who believe in the effectiveness of collective action (Group 1), 39 per cent retain their ethical motives in Holiday Destination, 34 per cent become unwilling to cooperate (W_3) and, moreover, 8 per cent come to reject the ethos outright (V_3, W_3). Of the 348 respondents who do not believe in the effectiveness of collective action (Group 2), the corresponding percentages are 8, 59 and 36 per cent.

The results of table 13.5 should be treated with some caution. They do not show that the variable of Effectiveness is fully independent of cost factors. One might think that there is some causal link between the two, perhaps one reflecting cognitive dissonance.

For instance, the members of Group 2, who are inclined to disbelieve the effectiveness of collective action in Holiday Destination, could also be ones for whom the individual costs of cooperating are particularly high, in comparison to the members of Group 1, who do hold such beliefs. Further research will have to show to what extent the individual cost of cooperating may influence beliefs about the significance of voluntary collective action. What the results of tables 13.4 and 13.5 do show quite clearly, we think, is that efforts to intensify moral persuasion in Holiday Destination could easily become counterproductive. In particular, when people's motives shift downwards along the moral meta-ranking, to positions of negative Willlingness as well as negative Valuation, a point may be reached where they become deaf to the very notion that collective action for the sake of environmental qualities would be a good thing, *even in principle*. We shall comment on this further below.

13.7 The dimension of private significance

The ethos underlying the strategy of internalizing environmental responsibility is truly a public one, backed by official policy efforts in the Netherlands. In the last three sections, contextual conditions were identified under which individuals are more, or less, likely to respond positively to this public ethos in environmental dilemmas. These conditions are here summarized by placing the cases on *a dimension of private significance*. The point of presenting our findings in this way is to suggest that the more 'private' a case is, the more one will observe it to be a hard case, on the scale of consistent ethical cooperation.

A case of the environmental dilemma may be of private significance in the following three respects, depending on the kind of behaviour that is involved in it. First of all, the behaviour may largely escape the demands of the ethos. It is 'private' in the sense that the public ethos is seldom perceived as a salient consideration. As discussed in section 13.4, this means that individuals do not normally consider the environmental impact of alternative actions, and their reasons for performing one action rather than another are often not motivated by normative environmental concern. We have measured this aspect of salience by the degree to which the choices of people who do display ethical motives are in fact consistent with these motives. As table 13.2 shows, the degree of ethical consistency is significantly less in Holiday Destination than in the two other cases.

A case of the dilemma may also be 'private' in another sense, which has to do with reasons for resisting the demands of the ethos, once individuals are made aware of those demands. In this sense, the more private a case is, the smaller its share of ethical motives will be. Table 13.2 reveals that Holiday Destination has a particularly low share of ethical motives, compared to Energy Saving and Chemical Waste. The specific behaviour demanded by the public ethos may be resisted both because it is costly in terms of well-being, given the instrumental value of non-cooperative courses of action, and because of the expressive significance of retaining a free hand across the whole area of behaviour. The first feature makes it easy to decide against sacrificing private gain in favour of a public-spirited contribution, while the last feature, if strongly present, effectively rules considerations of environmental responsibility out of court.

As discussed in section 13.5, Holiday Destination fits this description very well, while Chemical Waste can be easily understood as the opposite case, in that its behavioural area is virtually defined in public terms. Finally, and possibly independently of cost factors, a case of the dilemma may be of private significance because the required behaviour is not perceived to involve significant collective gains. Such a belief may serve to justify the decision to ignore environmental constraints, and choose alternatives that provide net private gain instead. As we have seen from the effectiveness data in section 13.5, Holiday Destination seems to fit this description as well. We think this may be explained by a tendency of the respondents to expand the relevant universe of 'everyone' in Holiday Destination, to include millions of foreigners outside the reach of the public ethos, when it comes to judging the possible benefits of the required collective action. Such benefits would then be estimated as being rather small.

13.8 Self-regulation policy: symbolic or real?

The three cases we have presented in this book show conclusively that it is wrong to think that in environmental matters, ordinary people are caught in the 'social dilemma', as interpreted in the standard sense of an actual Contributor's

Dilemma. In our approach of the actor's perspective, an actual Contributor's Dilemma would have to appear as a case in which virtually all respondents report motives (V1, W3), the 'Prisoner's Dilemma'-ordering PQRS, and the non-cooperative choice D. None of the three cases satisfies that response pattern. Yet, the unidimensional placement of the cases on the variable of consistent ethical cooperation does show that the efforts of self-regulation policy have had an uneven impact on areas of environmental behaviour. Moreover, as discussed in section 9.3, these policies are unevenly accepted as well by the respondents. In both respects, the acceptance of the policies and the agreement with the underlying public ethos, Holiday Destination is a hard case indeed.

What general lessons can be learned from this? Can a case like Holiday Destination be cracked at all, by using the various social instruments? (section 2.3). There is also the question of whether the government can legitimately strive to intensify its efforts in such cases, as it is in principle committed to doing (section 2.4). Is it legitimate for the government to invade the domain of private holiday decisions by insisting that people should recalculate their decision to travel abroad? Whatever the answer to that last question may be, the data we adduced in our contextual analysis of private significance suggest that the possiblities of success are strictly limited.

In discussing this further, it is helpful to respond to a general stance with respect to empirical evidence about hard and easy cases. That stance is occasionally taken in the Netherlands. It fully grants what we have been arguing about the context-sensitivity of cooperative behaviour in environmental dilemmas. But it then goes on to assert, rather cynically, that the bottom line of our story just confirms something which was known all along, after the strategy of internalizing environmental responsibility was launched in 1989. It is this: the self-regulation approach is an example of *symbolic policymaking*. The success of the approach in easy cases generates a warm feeling that something grand is being done by government, in enlisting the help of citizens. And its failure in hard cases can be glossed over by saying that, after all, citizens are maximizers of private gain, when it comes to the crunch. Thus, government can hardly be blamed for such failures. It is just a tragic fact of life that the 'social dilemma', in some form or other, actually holds good, once people are asked to cooperate voluntarily where it really hurts.

To discover this last and very basic point, the cynical stance would also claim that one does not even need to study holiday decisions, the more so since that particular area of behaviour has hardly been the object of self-regulation policy anyway. To get the message, it is more relevant to regard the private behaviour of car-owners. This behaviour clearly shows that car-owners are indeed caught in some form or other of the 'social dilemma'. An example of this last claim is provided by a Dutch report on popular support for environmental policy, which discussed research showing that car-owners are not favourably impressed by the hint contained in the official campaign slogan of the mid-nineties: *The car can do without you once in a while.* People seem to regard travelling in their own cars as a 'constitutional' right, the report says. They will insist on exercising that right unrestrictedly, even when the environmental effects are spelled out explicitly to them.[8] The report generally concludes that travel by private car is a classic case of the social dilemma.

Perhaps there is something to be said for the cynical stance. But it is in several respects a superficial one. To start with the way in which it judges easy cases, our data do indeed indicate that self-regulation policies are something of a success in changing basic attitudes in environmental dilemmas, though more so in the case of Chemical Waste than in Energy Saving. However, the cynical stance ignores the fact that voluntary cooperation is probably the only way of obtaining compliance in these areas, given electoral constraints on legal regulation or substantial financial sanctions. The data on the acceptance of regulation showed that both formal and informal forms of self-regulation are largely accepted in all three cases, in comparison to legal regulation (section 9.3). In juxtaposing the achievements of self-regulation policy in easy cases with the dim prospects of success in hard cases, the cynical response forgets to mention that hard cases are resistant not only to the social instruments of self-regulation, but also – and even more – resistant to other policy instruments. This point casts a different light on the matter. To put it crudely, legal regulation of individual behaviour seems to be ruled out politically in all three cases, while self-regulation policy is at least a political possibility in each of them. The fact that self-regulation policy works in easy cases of the dilemma, therefore, should be a reason to congratulate the government, rather than accusing it of symbolic policymaking because it has not managed to crack the hard case.

13.9 A non-moralistic approach to environmental responsibility

The cynical response contains a valid kernel, however. Our findings on the hard case of Holiday Destination suggest a general recommendation to avoid a *moralistic approach*. It will not do to over-extend the morality of environmental responsibility to areas in which behavioural choices are structured in an essentially private context. As mentioned earlier, the results shown in tables 13.4 and 13.5 suggest that putting moral pressure on people who are favourably disposed to the environmental ethos in easy cases may definitely be counterproductive in hard cases of the dilemma.

This point needs to be clarified in two respects. First, we are not suggesting that it would be *illegitimate* to try and bring the public ethos of environmental responsibility into fields of private decision-making where one may expect high

---

[8] See Raad voor het Milieubeheer, 1995, chapters 4 and 5.

opportunity costs of cooperation, and high costs of commitment. Our point is, rather, that there seems to be a problem of presenting the ethos as a viable position in such domains of action, that is to say, a position which links 'ought' to 'can' in a reasonable way. In chapter 2 it was emphasized that the strategy of internalizing environmental responsibility is not meant to be understood as a project of *virtue-based* moral reform. It is a moral reform project, to be sure, but we have argued that its purpose is strictly compliance-oriented (section 2.5). Understood in that way, issues of counterproductiveness do not tell against the legitimacy of social intervention. They may of course tell against its wisdom, once the issues are properly understood. The fact, if it is one, that polluting holiday travel, or habits like driving one's car one block away to the supermarket to fetch a bottle of wine, are usually seen as private behaviours lying outside the reach of environmental concerns, is no reason for accepting this fact as morally legitimate, or even as 'just a fact of life'.

But, secondly, if the public ethos is indeed regarded by citizens as too demanding in these areas, then self-regulation efforts of persuasion can easily undermine its moral cutting power, and hence deprive it of its instrumental value for changing behaviour in the right direction. This thesis of counterproductiveness can be further clarified as follows, in response to the claim of the cynical stance, that car-owners are caught in a social dilemma of one form or another.

As table 13.4 shows, people who are well-disposed to the ethos in an easy case can come to reject it in a hard case, for reasons related to the cost of cooperation, as well as to the perceived gains of collective action. It would be of interest to know whether respondents would react in a similar way if we had been comparing Chemical Waste to a properly specified environmental dilemma involving private car travel, in the contexts of work, domestic duties, or recreational activities. But suppose for the moment that the configuration of table 13.4 would roughly appear in that kind of comparison as well. (That is to say, suppose that the motives of the car-owners would be like the motives of the respondents in Holiday Destination.) We would then suggest that the claim of the cynical stance is quite inaccurate. The response would show that people react quite diversely. Some take the stance of the confirmed environmentalist (but these people might not be dependent on a car), others are disposed to take the bicycle if only their neighbours would do so as well (the 'reciprocal' environmentalist), and yet others take the free-riding stance typical of the 'social dilemma' (they want others to clear the roads for the environment and give them the space to park their own car, after an unimpeded ride). Finally, there are those who are truly beyond the social dilemma, having decided that it would be a bad thing for *anyone* to start cooperating (they think using the car as one pleases is a 'constitutional right'). In the case of Holiday Destination, this last group is the one with motives (V2, W3) or (V3, W3). For car-owners like these last ones, then, policies of self-regulation may be met with active resentment, rather than just simply being ignored.

We do not want to make any empirical claims about the attitudes and behaviour of car-owners here. The case is obviously important. It was not studied by us for reasons connected with the conditions of our original data collection. But looking at some of the research findings published in the Netherlands, we think that one should be wary of interpreting this case as reflecting the attitudes of the standard social dilemma. For example, an experimental study finds that many car-owners will play down the effectiveness of environmental action when they are confronted with self-regulation messages ('cognitive dissonance'). The study also finds that car-owners start to react adversely when they are confronted with compelling facts about the inefficiency of car travel, in comparison to alternative methods of transport ('reactance').[9] Such mechanisms support our view that some car-owners are likely to respond much as our diehard respondents do in Holiday Destination, for the cost and effectiveness reasons analysed above. This study also supports the finding that letting a public ethos bite too close to the bone in hard cases is to invite outright rejection, as a method of defending oneself against the 'unreasonable' incursions into private life by an ethos which is nevertheless accepted as reasonable in other cases of the dilemma. In this respect, then, self-regulation policy runs the real risk of becoming counterproductive in hard cases.

Yet not everyone reacts adversely, and the ratio of diehards to conditional or unconditional cooperators is not fixed in perpetuity. So hard cases are not ones that government should necessarily stay away from, if it really is prepared to back up the environmental ethos. We have shown above that Holiday Destination is not a case devoid of cooperative motives (tables 13.2 and 13.4). Nor are self-regulation policies rejected unanimously even there (table 9.1). So in this case, one should consider focusing on social instruments that aim to increase the salience of the issue, without trying to bring about ethical motives where they do not exist. This is basically a question of two things: disseminating the relevant information on how different patterns of holiday behaviour are actually developing, and what aggregate environmental effects those developments have, and then seeking to engage the groups in the population whose habits are most amenable to change in the right direction, by means of lifestyle examples. This 'lifestyle compatible' approach is in fact what the government thinks should be a feature of its new policies of 'sustainable consumer behaviour', in particular with respect to recreation.[10] However, the success of such modest policies will be limited as long as the environmental salience of holiday travel, especially by air, is at the same time constantly being undermined by commercial developments (Air Miles savings) and by major political decisions, such

---

[9] See Tertoolen 1994.
[10] See the environmental programme *Milieuprogramma 2000–2003*, 1999: 41.

as the recent one allowing Schiphol Airport to expand considerably, despite the acknowledged environmental downsides and the noise nuisance which this decision involves. It would seem that the limits of self-regulation here coincide with the social ambivalences engendered by a truly elastic application of the discourse of sustainability (see section 2.2).

13.10 Self-regulation in proportion to facilitation

Thus, another way of thinking about non-moralistic policies of self-regulation is to request the government to put its money where its mouth is. If environmental 'oughts' are to be reasonably aligned to what citizens 'can do', then moral pressures to obey the ethos should be proportional to concrete and politically visible efforts of the government to facilitate cooperative behaviour. This is of course a very rough rule of thumb. But it surely helps to identify comparative limitations to self-regulation policy, and to judge the effectiveness of the persuasive approach which is central to this kind of policy.

Take our comparison of the polar cases, Chemical Waste and Holiday Destination, on the dimension of private significance. The success of the former is mainly due to the fact that public intervention could easily succeed in facilitating cooperative behaviour, thus increasing the salience of environmental issues, lowering the personal cost of cooperation, and short-circuiting the considerations that lead to a high cost of commitment to the ethos. In a way, as we have said, Chemical Waste, and other voluntary waste recycling programmes for organic waste, paper, and glass, create bits of social infrastucture in the public domain. These act to permanently deprive the behaviour of its private significance, and make it conform to clearly articulated and relatively simple norms. In Holiday Destination, on the other hand, the prospects of physically facilitating cooperative behaviour are, of course, extremely limited. The government can hardly requisition the islands in the north of the Netherlands to serve as ecological summer camps for people who would otherwise take a package tour to Benidorm or Miami. So Holiday Destination is a case in which self-regulation policy should be limited to increasing the salience of the issue, as described briefly above. Specific efforts of persuasion to pull holiday behaviour into the public domain should thus be avoided.

The environmental dilemmas of car-owners that we distinguished above are intermediate cases, like Energy Saving, and like the case of buying environmentally sound products at higher prices. Here, one can at least try to align persuasive effort in proportion to the possibilities of physical facilitation. However, the rule of proportionality – to apply moral pressure commensurately with concrete efforts of facilitating desired kinds of action – can go either way. Especially in car travel cases, there clearly seems to be a political choice. Only a government that follows a rather activist approach in opening up new infrastructural choices can afford to promote its environmental ethos more aggressively, without adverse effects. As we noted in section 2.3, environmental policy has tended to regard physical facilitation as an appendage of the social instruments, generalizing from facilitation provisions in the successful waste disposal cases. This kind of generalization, of course, underestimates the extent to which infrastructural conditions would need to be changed in order to facilitate meaningful changes in mobility behaviour.

For many car-owners, the notion of the social dilemma may simply be irrelevant. It suggests options of acting cooperatively that have often been closed for them. Previous choices in respect of career and partnership, place of work and domicile, or choice of school for the children, have constrained the typical car-owner's current menu of choices in respect of time use and mobility. So if environmentally responsible behaviour of the kind that would have to be listed as 'cooperative', in a car-owner's dilemma, runs up against such constraints, then insisting on obedience to the public ethos will be viewed as the imposition of an alien set of dictates, precisely because the unique point of appeal of that ethos – the *voluntariness* of collective action – is shown to be an illusion.

In such cases, to put it crudely, one would want to say that the government must 'pay up or shut up'. It must be prepared to go quite a long way to reconstitute urban traffic, build more underground car parks, encourage zoning regulations with parking-free streets, and subsidize low pricing and high availability of cab services and public transport. It should negotiate with firms about flexible working times and possibilities to carry out tasks at home, discourage offers of lease cars for private use as perks in wage contracts, search for better ways of sharing cars in an effort to reintroduce car-pooling, and so on.[11] Given sufficient time, such measures could affect mobility choices in a way that would indeed open real chances for 'self-regulation between citizens' and 'self-regulation by government'. But just as obviously, perhaps, the policy measures just listed transcend the domain of self-regulation policy. Failing the political space to pursue them, however, the nifty campaign slogan cited above will at best remain irritatingly beside the point for many dependent car-owners. For after all, the fact that 'the car can do without you once in a while', does not imply that 'you can do without the car'.

[11] See P. Smit, R. Stallen and H. van Gunsteren 1999: chapters 2 and 3. The authors characterize these measures as ones aiming for change in the 'demand conditions of mobility', within an 'egalitarian' policy orientation of 'quality of life, sustainability and justice'. They show that actual policy thinking in respect of car mobility is oriented instead to technical solutions that aim to influence supply conditions (such as road use pricing), within an orientation of 'orderliness and control'.

References

Aarts, Kees and Huib Pellikaan. 1993. Sociale dilemmas. In Bert Pijnenburg and Paul Pennings (eds.) *Student en Politiek '92*. Enschede: University Twente, 87–103.

Aarts, Kees, Huib Pellikaan, and Robert J. van der Veen. 1995. *Sociale Dilemmas in het Milieubeleid*. Amsterdam: Het Spinhuis.

Anker, Hans and Erik V. Oppenhuis. 1995. *Dutch Parliamentary Election Panel-Study 1989–1994*. Amsterdam: Steinmetz Archive / Swidoc.

Arrow, Kenneth J. 1963. *Social Choice and Individual Values*. New Haven: Yale University Press.

Axelrod, Robert. 1984. *The Evolution of Cooperation*. New York: Basic Books.
   1997. *The Complexity of Cooperation: Agent-Based Models of Competition and Collaboration*. Princeton: Princeton University Press.

Bartels, Gerard C. 1994. *Saillante Resultaten uit het Milieu-Communicatieonderzoek*. The Hague: VROM.

Carson, Rachel. 1962. *Silent Spring (with an introduction by Vice President Al Gore)* Boston: Houghton Mifflin Company.

Cohen, Gerald A. 1997. The Site of Distributive Justice: Where the Action Is. *Philosophy and Public Affairs*, 26: 3–30.

Dasgupta, Partha. 1997. Population Growth: The Evidence. *Journal of Economic Literature*, 33: 1879–1902.

Elster, Jon. 1989. *The Cement of Society: A Study of Social Order*. Cambridge: Cambridge University Press.

Frank, Robert. 1988. *Passions Within Reason: The Strategic Role of the Emotions*. New York: Norton.

Friedman, Jeffry. 1995. Special Issue: Rational Choice Theory and Politics. *Critical Review*.

Goodin, Robert E. 1992. *Green Political Theory*. Cambridge: Polity Press.
   (ed.). 1996. *The Theory of Institutional Design*. Cambridge: Cambridge University Press.

Green, Donald P. and Ian Shapiro. 1994. *Pathologies of Rational Choice Theory; A Critique of Applications in Political Science.* New Haven: Yale University Press.

Hardin, Garrett. 1968. The Tragedy of the Commons. *Science,* 162: 1243–8.

1993. *Living Within Limits: Ecology, Economics, and Population Taboos.* Oxford: Oxford University Press.

Hardin, Russell. 1971. Collective Action as an Agreeable n-Prisoner's Dilemma. *Behavioral Science,* 16: 472–81.

1982. *Collective Action.* Baltimore: Johns Hopkins University Press.

Knoke, David and George W. Bohrnstedt. 1994. *Statistics for Social Data Analysis.* Itasca: Peacock Publishers.

Koutsoyiannis, A. 1985. *Modern Microeconomics.* London: Macmillan.

Kreps, David M. 1989. Nash Equilibrium. In John Eatwell, Murray Milgate, and Peter Newman (eds.) *Game Theory.* London: Macmillan, 167–77.

LeGrand, Julian. 1997. Knights, Knaves or Pawns? Human Behaviour and Social Policy. *Journal of Social Policy,* 26: 149–69.

Lewinsohn-Zamir, Daphna. 1998. Consumer Preferences, Citizen Preferences and the Provision of Public Goods. *Yale Law Review,* 108: 377–406.

Milieuprogramma 2000–2003. 1999. Second Chamber no. 27404/1–2. The Hague: Government Printing Office.

Miller, David. 1999. Social Justice and Environmental Goods. In A. Dobson (ed.) *Fairness and Futurity.* Oxford: Oxford University Press, 151–72.

Mokken, Robert J. 1971. *A Theory and Procedure of Scale Analysis.* The Hague: Mouton.

Morrow, J. D. 1994. *Game Theory for Political Science.* Princeton: Princeton University Press.

Musgrave, Richard A. and Peggy B. Musgrave. 1984. *Public Finance in Theory and Practice.* New York: McGraw-Hill Book Company.

Myerson, Roger B. 1991. *Game Theory: Analysis of Conflict.* Cambridge, MA: Harvard University Press.

Neumann. John von and Oskar Morgenstern. [1944] 1971. *Theory of Games and Economic Behavior.* Princeton: Princeton University Press.

NMP1. *Nationaal milieubeleidsplan.* 1988. Second Chamber 1988–9, 21137. The Hague: Government Printing Office.

NMP2. *Nationaal milieubeleidsplan 2.* 1993. Second Chamber 1993–4, 23560, 1–2. The Hague: Government Printing Office.

NMP3. *Nationaal milieubeleidsplan 3.* 1998. Ministry of the Environment (VROM). The Hague: VROM (97591/b/2-98).

North, Douglass C. 1990. *Institutions, Institutional Change and Economic Performance.* Cambridge: Cambridge University Press.

Nota Produkt en Milieu. 1993. Second Chamber 1993–4, 23562, 1. The Hague: Government Printing Office.

Olson, Mancur. 1971. *The Logic of Collective Action: Public Goods and the Theory of Groups.* Cambridge, MA: Harvard University Press.

Ostrom, Elinor. 1990. *Governing the Commons: The Evolution of Institutions for Collective Action.* Cambridge: Cambridge University Press.

1998. A Behavioral Approach to the Rational Choice Theory of Collective Action. *American Political Science Review*, 92: 1–23.

Ostrom, Elinor, Roy Gardner, and James Walker. 1994. *Rules, Games and Common-Pool Resources*. Ann Arbor: University of Michigan Press.

Parfit, Derek. 1987. *Reasons and Persons*. Oxford: Clarendon Press.

Pellikaan, Huib. 1991. Collectieve Actie en het Student's Dilemma: een Empirisch Onderzoek. *Acta Politica*, 26: 303–26.

1994. *Anarchie, Staat en het Prisoner's Dilemma*. Delft: Eburon.

Pettit, Philip. 1996. Institutional Design and Rational Choice. In Robert E. Goodin (ed.) *The Theory of Institutional Design*. Cambridge: Cambridge University Press, 54–89.

Raad voor het Milieubeheer. 1995. *Draagvlak voor het Milieubeleid* (RMB 95-05). The Hague: Raad voor het Milieubeheer.

Rapoport, Anatol. 1964. *Strategy and Conscience*. New York: Schocken Books.

Rapoport, Anatol and Melvin J. Guyer. 1966. A Taxonomy of 2x2 Games. In L. von Bertalanffy and Anatol Rapoport (eds.) *General Systems Yearbook*, 11: 203–14.

Rasmusen, Erik. 1991. *Games and Information: An Introduction to Game Theory*. Oxford: Blackwell.

Riker, William H. 1990. Political Science and Rational Choice. In: James E. Alt and Kenneth A. Shepsle (eds.) *Perspectives on Positive Political Economy*. Cambridge: Cambridge University Press, 163–81.

RIVM (Rijksinstituut voor Volksgezondheid en Milieuhygiene). 1988. *Zorgen voor Morgen. Nationale Milieuverkenning 1985–2010*. Alphen aan den Rijn: Samson H. D. Tjeenk Willink.

Scanlon, Timothy C. 1998. *What We Owe to One Another*. Cambridge, MA: Harvard University Press.

Sen, Amartya K. 1967. Isolation, Assurance and the Social Rate of Discount. *Quarterly Journal of Economics*: 112.

1974. Choice, Orderings and Morality. In S. Körner (ed.) *Practical Reason*. Oxford: Blackwell, 54–67.

1977. Rational Fools: A Critique of the Behavioral Foundations of Economic Theory. *Philosophy and Public Affairs*, 6: 317–44.

Smit, P., P. J. Stallen, and H. van Gunsteren. 1999. *Nieuwe Gronden*. Publicatiereeks milieustrategie 1998-9. The Hague: VROM.

SCP 127, Ruud Hoevenagel, Umberto van Rijn, Linda Steg, and Hans de Wit. 1996. *Milieurelevant Consumentengedrag; Ontwikkeling Conceptueel Model*. The Hague: Sociaal en Cultureel Planbureau.

SCP 156, Linda Steg. 1999. *Verspilde Energie? Wat Doen en Laten Nederlanders voor het Milieu*. The Hague: Sociaal en Cultureel Planbureau.

Taylor, Michael. 1976. *Anarchy and Cooperation*. London: John Wiley.

1982. *Community, Anarchy and Liberty*. Cambridge: Cambridge University Press.

1987. *The Possibility of Cooperation*. Cambridge: Cambridge University Press.

Tertoolen, Gerard. 1994. Uit eigen beweging . . . ?! Doctoral Thesis, University of Utrecht, Utrecht: Faculty of Social Sciences.

Ullmann-Margalit, Edna. 1977. *The Emergence of Norms*. Oxford: Clarendon Press.

Veen, Robert J. van der. 1981. Meta-rankings and Collective Optimality. *Social Science Information*, 20: 345–74.

1996. How Motives Speak to Preferences (unpublished paper). Seminar for Political Theory, Nuffield College Oxford.

Veen, Robert J. van der and Huib Pellikaan. 1994. Motives, Preferences and Choices: A Framework for Testing their Consistency in Survey Research. *Acta Politica*, 29: 411–51.

Veldkamp, Marktonderzoek. 1994. *De draaggolfcampagne*. n.p: Veldkamp Marktonderzoek.

VROM. 1993. Brainstormsessie Sociale Regulering 5 November. Bijlage 4. The Hague: VROM.

Weale, Albert. 1992. *The New Politics of Pollution*. Manchester and New York: Manchester University Press.

Wildavsky, Aaron. 1995. *But Is It True? A Citizen's Guide to Environmental Health and Safety Issues*. Cambridge, MA: Harvard University Press.

World Commission on Environment and Development (WCED) 1987. Gro Harlem Brundtland, chair. *Our Common Future*. Oxford: Oxford University Press.

WRR (Wetenschappelijke Raad voor het Regeringsbeleid). 1992. *Milieubeleid, Strategie, Instrumenten en Handhaafbaarheid*. The Hague: SdU Publishers.

Index

Aarts, Kees, xiv
acceptance
    compared with agreement, 152, 153–5,
        229–30
    and rejection, 158 table 9.1
    scale analysis, 158–60
actors
    assumption of homogeneous, 55
    as knaves, pawns or knights, 167–9
    pessimistic or optimistic, 90
    subjectivity, in rational choice theory, 47–9
    see also citizens
actor's perspective, 10, 59–63, 67, 84, 122,
        124, 195
    on collective action, 47–63, 86
    on environmental dilemmas, 10–14, 80,
        98–100, 133, 229
    model, 147 fig. 8.2
    in Potential Contributor's Dilemma, 62–3
    and sociocultural model, 146–7
age
    and environmental behaviour, 140–1
    and valid orderings, 79–80 table 4.3
agreement
    compared with acceptance, 152, 153–5
    with environmental ethos, 161–77
    full or partial, 174–6 tables 10.1 & 10.2
    measuring, 154, 158–60
air travel
    impact on atmosphere, 4, 39–40
    see also Holiday Destination example
Arrow, Kenneth, 10, 58, 59, 60, 61, 84, 101,
        102, 122
    as if morality, 184–6

assessment
    of self-regulation policies, 27, 153, 210–34
    see also policy assessment
Assurance Game ordering, 22–3, 24, 181–2,
        197, 201–2
attitudes
    and environmental ethos, 22–3, 154,
        211–13, 230
    intensity of cooperative, 124–5, 133–5
    to environmental issues, 123
    to governmental self-regulation policies,
        19–20, 154
    test of consistent preferences, 108–16
    to voluntary collective action, 5–6, 9
authoritarian regimes, 55–6
awareness, 19, 38, 40, 41

behaviour
    determinants of, 136–8, 141 table 8.2
    from motives to, 20, 146–8
behavioural assumptions, 124
bias
    political corrrectness, 98
    social desirability, 14, 15n83
Brundtland Report (1987), 28–9, 31–2, 43
But Is It True? (Wildavsky), 3–4

car-owners, 229–30, 231–2, 233–4
Carson, Rachel, Silent Spring, 3
cases
    background features of hard and easy,
        213–16
    comparison of motives in hard and easy,
        225–7

cases (*cont.*)
  non-equivalence of, 124–35
  see also hardest case
causal model, macro-sociological
    characteristics, 18
Chemical Waste example, 10, 68–9
  belief in effectiveness, 224
  choice of strategy, 91–5
  choices and reported behaviour, 142–3
  consistent ethical cooperation and, 212
  individual cost and collective gain, 219–20,
    223
  individual values and, 104
  information on, 72–4
  official structuring in, 216–17
  vs. Energy Saving, 130 table 7.2
  vs. Holiday Destination, 129 table 7.1
Chicken Game orderings, 192
Chinese communes, 185, 193
'Choice', 145 table 8.3
  connecting motives and reported behaviour,
    146–8, 148
  to cooperate or defect, 138, 142–6
choice, *see also* freedom of choice
choice of strategy, 91–5
  and dominance rule, 96–9 table 5.3, 103,
    118–19
  reflection in decision situations, 179–80
  reliability, 103
  and revealed preference, 85–6
citizens
  choices, 44–5
  as environmentally responsible consumers,
    19–20
  level of acceptance of self-regulation policy,
    151–60
  level of agreement with environmental
    ethos, 161–77
  moral resources, 6
  as rational actors, 6
  self-regulation by, 155, 234
  as sources of pollution, and agents of
    change, 34, 37–8
  see also actors
citizenship, virtue-based concept of,
    42–6
class struggle, 50
Club of Rome, *Limits to Growth*, 3, 69
coercion, 6, 9, 48, 49, 56
  vs. persuasion, 156
cognitive dissonance, 232
cognitive process, and intensity structures,
    133–5 fig. 7.3
cognitive-motivational strategies, and
    preferences, 142–6

collective action
  actor's perspective on, 47–63
  environmental pollution as a problem of,
    3–27
  Hardin on, 52–5
  potentiality vs. actuality, 7
  problems of, 41, 49–55, 60–3
  role of morality in, 197–209
  theories of, 47–59
  see also logic of collective action; voluntary
    collective action
Collective Action (R. Hardin), 52–5
collective gain
  individual cost and, 211, 215–16, 219–25
  see also perceived gain
collective goods, 8, 43, 47, 49, 202–3
'common environmental objectives', 6, 7–9,
    15–16, 20, 43
common good *see* collective goods
'common-pool' problems, 153, 202–3, 223
'commons, tragedy of the', 55, 56
'common-sink' problems, 153, 203, 215, 223
community, environmentally self-regulating,
    28
compliance
  active, 34, 151, 168
  basis of self-regulation, 42–6, 186, 230, 231
  conditional or unconditional, 166–7
  costs of, 156, 165, 219–25
conditionality, 20–4, 49, 113, 153, 170–3, 204
conformity, 14, 233
consistency, of motives and preferences, 16,
    27, 101–23, 178, 187–92
'consistency ratio', 116
consistency test
  failure of, 92–3
  of rational choice, 90–5, 102
  re preference orderings, 83, 108–16
'consistent ethical cooperation', 25–6, 27, 153,
    210, 211–13, 219, 227–8, 229
  cooperation and, 212 table 13.1
consultation, 41
consumption behaviour
  adjustment of patterns, 33
  Dutch studies, 136–8
  rationality of, 48–9
  regulation of, 19, 39
context, 124, 137–8, 210–11, 211, 214, 227–8
Contributor's Dilemma
  actual, 63, 151, 172–3, 179–80, 228–9
  see also Potential Contributor's Dilemma
cooperation, 19, 49
  conditional, 205–7
  conditional and unconditional, 22–3, 153,
    166–7, 170–3, 179, 204–5

costs of conditionalities, 205–9
determinants of, 24–7
intensity of attitudes, 124–5, 133–5
intention of, 211–12
norms of, 165–6, 170–3
prevalence of motives, 14, 152
the puzzle of unconditional, 197–8
rarity of unconditional, 199–205
and reciprocity, in environmental dilemmas, 197–209
as routine, 24
see also 'consistent ethical cooperation'; mutual cooperation; rational cooperation from moral commitment; reciprocity
corporate actors
legal constraints on, 38–9
as target groups, 36–7
costs
collective, 8
commitment, 215, 219, 221–3
of cooperation and conditionalities, 153, 205–9
of cooperation in hardest case, 153, 160, 167
individual, 24, 27, 211, 215, 219–25
opportunity, 164–5, 215, 219–21
counterproductiveness, 227, 231–2
countervailing powers, liberal theory of, 50
covenants, by firms, 36–7

decision structures, 7–9, 11, 178
democratic regimes, 9, 56–7, 156
dominance rule, 10–11, 84, 87–91, 103, 122, 178
and choice of strategy, 96–9 table 5.3, 103, 118–19
the robustness of the, 95–8

ecology, 55–6
economic actors, 98–100
see also entrepreneurs; firms
economic growth *see* growth
economics, 85
education, and plurality of norms, 57
effectiveness, 51–2, 54, 98, 148, 210
belief in collective action, 153, 215, 224–7
efficiency, 51–2, 54, 98
empirical approaches, 5, 59–60, 100
Energy Saving example, 10, 69–70, 217
belief in effectiveness, 224
choice of strategy, 91, 92, 94–5
choices and reported behaviour, 143–4, 144–5
individual costs and collective gain, 220–2

individual values and, 104
vs. Chemical Waste, 130 table 7.2
vs. Holiday Destination, 130 table 7.3
entrepreneurs, 52, 98–9
'environmental crisis industry', 4
environmental dilemmas, 7–9
assumptions in, 48–9
determinants of cooperation in, 24–7
hard and easy cases, 124–5
and the logic of collective action, 5–10
'nested', 223–4
rational choice theory and, 10–14
reciprocity and cooperation in, 197–209
environmental ethos, 19, 29, 46
agreement response, 174–6
analysis of, 20
conditional or unconditional moral commitment, 20–4, 49
and individual values, 152
level of agreement with, 161–77
motive structures in, 169–73
salience of, 26–7, 153, 211, 216–19, 228, 232–3
and the social dilemma, 40–2
two stages of, 161, 162–7, 195–6
environmental impact assessments, 21, 38
environmental management, 43, 56
'environmental meta-ranking', of motives, 153, 193–6, 209, 225–7
environmental policy campaigns, 21, 35–40, 154
environmental policy plans, 19, 21
Dutch and the idea of self-regulation, 29–35
environmental problems
affective condition, 71
cognitive condition, 71, 78
evaluative condition, 71
three different, 78–82
environmental qualities, 8, 49
attachment of positive values to, 41–2, 162–7
Netherlands, the, 30
and quantitative objectives, 33–4, 45
environmental responsibility, 40–1
attitudes to, 211–13
internalization of, 20, 29, 34–5, 41–2, 44, 152, 161, 164–6, 186, 210–11, 227–8
a non-moralistic approach to, 230–3
resistance to, 227–8
environmental values, internalization of, 19–20, 161, 163–4, 169–70
expectations, about choices of others, 204, 208–9 table 12.1
expressive value, 222–3, 228

facilitation, physical
  as a social instrument, 39, 40, 217, 233–4
  self-regulation in proportion to, 233–4
firms
  covenants, 36–7
  legal constraints, 38–9
  and oligopoly, 50–1
  self-regulation policies, 21
forests, acidification of Dutch, 30
freedom of choice, 222–3
free-ridership, 23, 47, 49, 169, 172–3, 231

'game against nature', 87–9
'game form', 11n
game theory, 85–9, 100, 122
  equilibrium in, 87
generations
  transmission of unconditional morality
    across, 204–5
  well-being of present and future see
    intergenerational equity
global environmental issues, 4
good life, 43
Gore, Al, 3
government
  legitimacy of social intervention, 136, 157,
    229, 231
  opposition to regulation by, 8–9
  policy instruments, 34–5, 36
  self-regulation by, 19, 155, 158–60, 234
  and target groups, 31
  see also state neutrality
Green, Donald P., Pathologies of Rational
    Choice Theory, 59, 103, 121
Grim-strategy, 56
gross domestic product (GDP), and
    environmental pollution, 32–3
growth
  economic–environmental trade-offs, 31–2,
    34
  limits to, 3–4
  and observed pollution, 19
  see also sustainable growth

hardest case
  background features, 213–16
  counterproductiveness in, 227, 231–2
  deterministic model, 128
  model of, 125–31 figs. 7.1 & 7.2, table 7.4,
    138–9
  probabilistic model, 128–31
  see also Holiday Destination example
Hardin, Garrett, Living within Limits, 55–6
Hardin, Russell, Collective Action, 52–5, 56,
    147

Holiday Destination example, 10, 20, 23,
    70–1, 147
  belief in effectiveness, 224
  campaigns and, 154–5
  choice of strategy, 93, 95, 121
  choices and reported behaviour, 144
  costs of cooperation, 207–8
  and the environmental ethos, 211, 213,
    217–19
  ethical consistency and, 214–15
  as hardest case, 24–7, 81–2, 125, 174–6,
    213, 229, 232–3
  individual cost and collective gain, 219–20,
    228
  individual values and, 104
  and market competition, 39–40
  motive responses, 225–7
  resistance to regulation, 159–60
  vs. Chemical Waste, 129 table 7.1
  vs. Energy Saving, 130 table 7.3
homo economicus, 179, 207

incentives, moral, 185, 193
income, and environmental behaviour, 140–2
individual action, 42, 51–2
  condition of ineffectiveness, 54
individual values, 59, 60, 100, 101
  and environmental ethos, 152
  and preferences, 103–8, 122
individuals
  or firms, 48, 99
  vs. Others, 53 fig. 3.1
inferences, validity of, 9–10
information
  campaigns, 38–9, 232–3
  in survey interview, 72–4
institutional approaches, 56, 124
instrumental approaches, 34–7, 183–7
instruments see policy instruments
intensity structures, and cognitive process,
    133–5 fig. 7.3
interests, 9–10
  individual vs. collective, 42, 50–1, 82–3
  'true', 187–8
  see also self-interest
intergenerational equity, 42, 43–4, 163
Intergovernmental Panel on Climate Change
    (IPCC), 'Aviation and the Global
    Atmosphere', 4
internalization
  of environmental responsibility, 20, 29,
    34–5, 41–2, 44, 152, 161, 164–6, 169–73,
    176–7, 186, 210–11, 227–8
  of environmental values, 161, 163–4,
    169–70

item homogeneity (Mokken), 126, 128
iterated games, 56

learning process, and transmission of
    unconditional morality, 204–5
legal regulation, 19, 36, 230
    acceptance of, 154, 155–60
    monitoring and compliance cost, 160
LeGrand, Julian, 168, 186
lifestyle choices, 21, 38, 232–3
Limits to Growth (Club of Rome), 3, 69
Living within Limits (G. Hardin), 55–6
local government, self-regulation policies, 21
logic of collective action, 4–5, 6, 49–55, 56,
    108
    environmental dilemmas and, 5–10
Logic of Collective Action, The (Olson),
    49–55

macro-sociological characteristics, 18, 123
Malthus, Thomas, 3
mapping problems, 211, 214–19
market competition, self and group interest,
    50–1
marketing, as a social instrument, 21, 38
Marxism, 50
meta-ranking, 178–83, 190–2
    see also environmental meta-ranking; moral
    meta-ranking
Mokken, Robert
    item homogeneity, 126
    scale analysis, 17, 24–5, 125–6, 131–3
monitoring, 23
monopoly, 51
moral commitment, 6, 56, 152, 164, 179,
    221
    conditional or unconditional, 20–4
    and enlightened self-interest, 183–7
    and rational cooperation, 152, 178–96
    rationality of, 21, 187–92
'moral meta-ranking' (Sen), 21–2, 152–3,
    178, 180–3, 204
moral persuasion, 28, 41, 157, 227
moral reform, 19, 20, 28, 35
    as historically contingent, 42–6
morality, 23, 179, 189
    role in collective action, 197–209
motivation, 'thick' description of, 168–9
motive structures, in environmental ethos,
    169–73 fig. 10.1, 213 fig. 13.1
'motive-preference' response, 116–17 table 6.4
    significance of consistency, 118–21
motives
    comparison in hard and easy cases, 225–7
    compromise, 189–92

consistency between preferences and, 16,
    101–23 fig. 6.5, 187–92
cooperative see conditionality; cooperation;
    unconditionality
diversity and plurality of, 59–60
environmental meta-ranking of, 153
ethical, 214–19
ethical interpretation of, 169–73
physical facilitation and, 39, 40, 233–4
in relation to preferences, 14–17, 60–3,
    100, 118–21
translation into behaviour, 146–8
on the Valuation and Willingness scales,
    103–8 table 6.3
mutual cooperation, solutions for, 56–7

Nash equilibrium, 87
national environmental issues, 4
natural resources
    as 'commons', 55
    voluntary management, 56
negotiation, 36, 37, 41
Netherlands, the
    air traffic pollution, 98, 232–3
    environmental policies, 5, 6
    Law on Chemical Waste Products (1976), 68
    National Environmental Policy Plans,
        28–46, 151; (NMP1: 1989), 32, 35–6, 43,
        152; (NMP2: 1993), 43; (NMP3: 1998),
        32–3, 37, 39–40
    National Sustainability Debates, 39–40
    self-regulation policies in, xiii, 18–20
    self-regulation as a policy concept, 28–46
    Social and Cultural Planning Office (SCP),
        136–8, 140
New Politics of Pollution, The (Weale), 42, 44
non-equivalence, 26–7, 62, 82, 124–35
    and reported behaviour, 17–18, 123
    of social dilemmas, 133–5
normalizing effect, 26, 154–5, 160, 176
norms
    content of public vs. private discretion,
        26–7
    education and, 57
North, Douglass, 124

observer's perspective, 52, 55, 57–8, 67,
    80, 84
    compared with actor's perspective, 86
oligopoly, 50–1
Olson, Mancur, 4, 7, 9, 47, 53, 56, 61, 108,
    122, 147
    The Logic of Collective Action, 49–55
optimality, collective, 183–7, 203–4
Ostrom, Elinor, 24, 153, 198–205

Others, 193
    expectations about choices of, 204, 208–9
        table 12.1
    individuals vs. 53 fig. 3.1
    'other-regarding' preference ordering,
        181–3

Pathologies of Rational Choice Theory (Green
    and Shapiro), 59
peer group pressure, 19, 157
perceived gain, 27, 211, 215, 223–5, 228
perspectives *see* actor's perspective; observer's
    perspective
persuasion
    by communication, 38
    by negotiation, 36, 37
    or coercion, 156, 233
    see also moral persuasion
pesticides, effect on agricultural production, 3
Pettit, Philip, 207
planning, indicative objectives, 30–1
pluralism, 57
policy, and theory, 149–234
policy assessment, 5, 25–7, 153, 210–34
policy design
    determinants of cooperation in, 24–7, 151
    implications of environmental meta-ranking
        for, 196
policy goals, scale levels, 30
policy instruments, 34–7, 230
    command, 36
    communicative, indirect use of, 39–40
    persuasion, 36
    structurating, 38–9
    transaction, 36, 37
    see also social instruments
policymaking
    ambitions of, 45
    cooperative notion of, 34
    symbolic, 229
political corrrectness, bias, 98
political theory, normative, 42–6
pollution, environmental
    and gross domestic product (GDP), 32–3
    as a problem of collective action, 3–27
population growth, 3, 55
potential collective action *see* environmental
    dilemmas
Potential Contributor's Dilemma, 48, 60–3
    fig. 3.3, 68, 109 fig. 6.2, 133, 188, 193,
        216
    in the actor's perspective, 62–3 fig. 3.4
    or actual dilemma, 86–7, 100, 168–9
    elements of an environmental, 71–2
    large-scale, 201, 206–7

and narrow self-interest, 194–5
re Chemical Waste, 91–5
revealed preference and, 85–6
and test of consistent preferences, 108–16
universally cooperative or noncooperative
    outcome, 194
practical reasoning, model of, 101–3 fig. 6.1,
    133
predatory behaviour, 23
preference orderings
    age variable, 79–80
    completeness, 84
    diversity of, 100, 122, 189
    identical, 81 fig. 4.3
    and measurement, 12–13, 67–83
    measuring, 71–8 table 4.2
    meta-ranking, 179–96
    and motive structures, 108–16, 171–3, 213
        fig. 13.1
    in Potential Contributor's Dilemma, 60–3
    ranking, 74 table 4.1, 178–9
    for reciprocity, 197, 205–9
    transitive, 58, 84, 126
    valid, 78–9 fig. 4.2
    see also Assurance Game; Chicken Game;
        Potential Contributor's Dilemma;
        Prisoner's Dilemma
preferences
    changing people's, 40
    and cognitive-motivational strategies, 142–6
    consistent
        as control variable, 119–21 table 6.5; in the
            meta-ranking, 187–92; in the three cases,
            116–18
    ethical interpretation of, 169–73
    and individual values, 103–8, 122–3
    and levels of agreement, 174–6
    measuring individual, 48–9
    'moral meta-ranking' (Sen), 21–2, 152–3,
        178, 180–3, 204
    and motives, consistency of, 101–23,
        187–92
    motives in relation to, 14–17, 60–3, 100,
        118–21
    Sunday Preferences, 14
    test of consistent, 102–3, 108–16
    see also revealed preference, theory of
price
    in competitive market, 50
    signals in social self-regulation, 40
Prisoner's Dilemma, 54 fig. 3.2
    game form, 181 fig. 11.1, 187
    n-person, 52–5, 56, 57–8, 193, 195
    preference ordering (PD-ordering), 54–5,
        57–8, 108, 169, 172

reconstructed meta-ranking in, 192
  fig. 11.3
Sen's meta-ranking in, 183 fig. 11.2
two-person, 21–2, 195
private
  'dimension of private significance', 26–7,
    211, 222–3, 227–8, 229, 233–4
  vs. public norms, 26–7, 230–3
problem-themes, 29, 31
procreation, freedom of choice in, 222
product certification, 38
proportionality, rule of, 233–4
public goods
  economic theory of, 50
  see also collective goods
  public opinion, 3, 209
  public, vs. private norms, 26–7
  publicity, 185–6

Rapoport, Anatol, 90
rational choice, 10–14, 84–100
  and agreement with environmental ethos,
    177, 178–96
  conditions of, 84–7
  consistency test, 90–5 table 5.2, 102–3
  to cooperate, 125
  dominance rule, 10–11, 84, 87–91, 95–8,
    103, 122, 178
  economist's understanding of, 179, 207
  models of, 56
rational choice theory, 5
  actor's subjectivity in, 47–9
  assumption of self-interest, 49–50, 59
  failures of, 121–3
  and moral cooperation, 152–3
  pathologies of, 59–60, 121
rational cooperation
  from moral commitment, 152, 178–96
  Pettit on, 207
Rational Fools (Sen), 179
rationality
  'second-generation' models, 198–9,
    205
  thick-theory of, 52–5, 57–8, 59, 60–3,
    168–9
  thin-theory, 10, 58–9, 59–63, 84–5,
    102–3
reactance, 232
'reasonableness' conditions, 164–7
reasoned choice, model of, 101–3
reciprocity, 6, 23–4, 56, 182
  claims about, 198–9
  conditional, 197
  and cooperation, in environmental
    dilemmas, 153, 192, 197–209

thesis, 198–205
  trust and reputation, 153, 198–9
recycling of toxic waste see Chemical Waste
  example
regulation
  financial, 34, 36
  measuring resistance to, 159–60
  multilevel, 31–2
  physical, 34, 36
  scale analysis of types, 158–60
  see also legal regulation; self-regulation
religion, and environmental behaviour, 139,
    140–1
reported behaviour, 17–18, 136–48
  alternative model, 142–6
  and non-equivalence, 17–18
  six cases of, 139 table 8.1
  sociocultural model, 137, 138–42,
    146
  vs. actual, 17–18, 123
reputation, trust and reciprocity, 153,
    198–9
research design, xiii, 18
resistance, to environmental responsibility,
    227–8
response effects, avoiding, 82–3, 98
responses, 11–14, 49
  aggregate differences in cooperative, 17
  composite, 25–6
  individual, 17
  socially biased, 14, 15n83
responsibility
  collective, 31–3, 155
  network of obligation, 44–5
  personal, 164–6, 169–73
  see also environmental responsibility
revealed preference, theory of, 85–6
Riker, William, 10, 58–9, 60, 61, 84,
    122

salience, 26–7, 153, 211, 216–19, 228,
    232–3
sanctions, 23
scalability
  of the cases, 131–3
  coefficients of, 132–3 table 7.5
scale analysis (Mokken), 17, 24–5, 125,
    131–3
self-interest, 6, 84, 168–9
  enlightened, and moral commitment,
    183–7, 204 narrow, 48, 179, 183, 187,
    189, 204, 207–8; and Potential
    Contributor's Dilemma, 194–5
  in rational choice theory, 49–50
  sacrifice of, 180–3

self-regulation
    acceptance of, 155–60, 176–7
    assumptions of, 35, 41, 46
    capabilities, 34, 35, 41, 46, 168
    by citizens, 155, 157–60, 234
    compliance-based or virtue-based, 42–6,
        186, 230, 231
    Dutch environmental policy plans and the
        idea of, 29–35
    ecological, 29
    economic, 29
    by government, 155, 157–60, 234
    medium and message, 154, 176–7
    as a policy concept, 28–46
    in proportion to facilitation, 233–4
    social, 19, 29–35, 36
self-regulation policies
    assessment of, 27, 210–34
    level of acceptance, 151–60
    in the Netherlands, xiii, 18–20
    symbolic or real, 228–30
Sen, Amartya, 21, 22, 152–3, 164, 178,
        180–3, 197, 204, 221
    Rational Fools, 179
Shapiro, Ian, Pathologies of Rational Choice
        Theory, 59, 103, 121
Silent Spring (Carson), 3
social choice theory, 126
social control, 38, 40
social dilemmas, 55–9, 60, 228–9, 231
    continuum of inclusiveness, 193–4,
        201–3
    and environmental ethos, 38, 40–2, 167,
        179
    non-equivalence of, 133–5
    and reciprocity norms, 200–1
    size and conditionality of response,
        153
    size continuum, 24, 153
    three potential, 67–71
    use of term as model, 56
social engineering, usefulness of moral
        codes in, 183–7
social instruments, 19, 25, 35, 220, 232
    acceptance of, 153–5, 176–7
    direct or indirect, 39–40, 157
    Dutch, 28, 35–40
    facilitating, 39, 40, 217, 233–4
    marketing as, 21
social learning, 38
socially biased responses, 14, 15n, 83
sociocultural model
    extended, 143 fig. 8.1
    of reported behaviour, 137, 138–42, 146,
        213

'spaceship ecology', 55–6
state neutrality, 43–4
strategies, 11–14
    choice of, 91–5
    cooperative, 11, 85, 89, 125, 148
    defect see non-cooperative
    'game form', 11
    maximin, 90
    non-cooperative, 11, 85, 88–9, 148
    and reciprocity norms, 199
subjectivity, of the actor in rational choice
        theory, 47–9, 60–3
survey (1994), 5, 65–140
    core components, 125
survey research
    empirical methods, xiii
    wording of questions, 82–3
sustainability, 19, 33, 39–40, 176,
        232–3
sustainable growth, 29, 32–3, 42, 43,
        163, 164–5
systems theory, 29–30

target groups, 29, 31, 34
    corporate actors and citizens, 36–7
    task assignments, 31
taxation, 40, 156
theory, and policy, 149–234
Tit For Tat, 56
trade-offs, 31–4
'tragedy of the commons', 55, 56
transitivity, 58, 84, 126
travel, foreign holiday see Holiday Destination
        example
trust, 23, 36–7, 56, 153
    'on credit', 206–7
    reciprocity and reputation, 153, 198–9

unconditionality, 20–4, 49, 153, 170–3,
        179, 197–8, 204–5, 210
    and hidden conditionalities, 197–8
USA, environmental dilemmas, 3–4
utility, subjective, 48

Valuation dimension, 15–16, 20, 101, 148,
        163–4
    constraints and consistent sets, 112
        fig. 6.3
    and environmental ethos, 169–73, 195–6
    motives, 103–8 table 6.1
values, 8, 15–16, 59–60, 213
    see also environmental values; individual
        values
virtue, basis of self-regulation, 42–6,
        186, 231

voluntary associations, self-regulation
    policies, 21, 56
voluntary collective action, 5, 20, 44–5, 125,
    151
  and environmental ethos, 163–5, 167–9,
    176–7, 186, 234
  opposition to, 8–9
voting habits, and reported behaviour,
    139

waste, toxic *see* Chemical Waste example
Weale, Albert, 28, 34, 44–5
  The New Politics of Pollution, 42, 44
Wildavsky, Aaron, *But Is It True?*, 3–4
Willingness dimension, 15–16, 20, 23, 101,
    125, 148, 164, 166–7
  constraints and consistent sets, 113 fig. 6.4
  and environmental ethos, 169–73, 195–6
  motives, 103, 105–8 table 6.2